BREAKING CONVENTION: ESSAYS ON PSYCHEDELIC CONSCIOUSNESS

BREAKING CONVENTION: ESSAYS ON PSYCHEDELIC CONSCIOUSNESS

EDITED BY CAMERON ADAMS, DAVID LUKE, ANNA WALDSTEIN, BEN SESSA AND DAVID KING

Published by
North Atlantic Books
P.O. Box 12327
Berkeley, California 94712

Cover design by Jasmine Hromjak
Cover art by Blue Firth
Book design by Emerald Mosley
Printed in the United States of America

Breaking Convention: Essays on Psychedelic Consciousness is sponsored by the Society for the Study of Native Arts and Sciences, a nonprofit educational corporation whose goals are to develop an educational and cross-cultural perspective linking various scientific, social, and artistic fields; to nurture a holistic view of arts, sciences, humanities, and healing; and to publish and distribute literature on the relationship of mind, body, and nature.

North Atlantic Books' publications are available through most bookstores. For further information, visit our website at www.northatlanticbooks.com or call 800–733–3000.

Library of Congress Cataloging-in-Publication Data
Breaking convention : essays on psychedelic consciousness / edited by Cameron Adams, Anna Waldstein, Ben Sessa, David Luke And David King.
    pages cm
  Selected essays presented at Breaking Convention: A Multidisciplinary Conference on Psychedelic Consciousness held April 1–3, 2011 at Canterbury, UK.
  Summary: "Presents essays and articles exploring the history, use, and benefits of psychedelics from the international conference of the same name"-- Provided by publisher.
  ISBN 978-1-58394-771-5
  1. Altered states of consciousness. 2. Hallucinogenic drugs—History. I. Adams, Cameron Littleton, 1971- II. Breaking Convention: A Multidisciplinary Conference on Psychedelic Consciousness (2011 Canterbury, England)
  BF1045.A48B74 2014
  154.4—dc23
                    2013044273

1 2 3 4 5 6 7 8 Sheridan 18 17 16 15 14

Printed on recycled paper

DEDICATION

Blow Orange

CONTENTS

INTRODUCTION TO THE MDMA DEBATE

POLY AND MONO: REFLECTIONS ON THE VALIDITY OF "POLY DRUG USE"

FROM META-SIN TO MEDICINE: A PROGRAMME FOR FUTURE RESEARCH INTO THE HEALING POWER OF PSYCHEDELICS

A DECLARATION OF PSYCHEDELIC STUDIES

BIOPHENOMENOLOGY OF ALTERED STATES

COGNITIVE PHENOMENOLOGY OF MIND MANIFESTATION

INTRODUCTION

CONSCIOUSNESS AND PSYCHEDELIC THINKING

Consciousness is defined in numerous ways, with little agreement among philosophers or other scholars about its most basic features. Is the brain (or another organ) a receiver or generator of consciousness? What is the range of conscious states experienced by human beings? How do we determine which, if any, states of consciousness are 'normal' and which are best classified as *'altered'*? What else, in the world around us, is capable of experiencing consciousness? While we are likely to find agreement that our senses provide only partial information about the objective world we are a part of, attempts to understand the relationship between human consciousness and extramental reality (i.e., the parameters of conscious experience) have led to much controversy in Western philosophy.[1]

Likewise, among the world's general populace, local theoretical explanations of experience as well as popular/everyday ways of experiencing consciousness may or may not be informed by elite theories of mind-body dualism and/or embodiment. For example, ethnographic research conducted among people suffering psychopathology and possession in Kerala, India shows that these patients experience a continuum of states of being that includes the body, mind, consciousness, and self/soul but that do not replicate Western mind-body dualism.[3] Tantric scholars give primacy to the body and assert that consciousness must be embodied and may be generated by touching the skin. While other senses are known to hinder the achievement of the 'highest' states of consciousness, touch may be an aid to liberation and increased awareness of the intertwining of self and other.[2] On the other hand, empirical observations of brain structure (observed through hunting and warfare) among the Desana lead to the shamanic philosophy that the mind, as seat of consciousness, is also bilateral: the left side is abstract/intuitive and the right side is practical in making manifest the thoughts of the left. Desana shamans manipulate brain function by altering sensory awareness and inducing specific states of consciousness.[4]

To the contemporary, cosmopolitan insider, the understanding of psychedelic consciousness consists of personally meaningful experiences that can bring us into contact with the unknowable, help repair fragmented minds and increase wellbeing. It has been argued that solutions to current and future global ecological crises may be informed by an improved awareness of psychedelic consciousness (see[5]). That is, the creative inner spaces of the mind connect us with the rest of humanity, life, ecological processes and universal laws. However, most substances classified as psychedelic (e.g. LSD, MDMA, psilocybin, ayahuasca, peyote and many others) have been globally prohibited for over half a century, with some localised protections for religious use. This includes the prohibition of many species of plants, fungi and animal excretions that have been used spiritually, therapeutically and recreationally for the length of human history. Sadly, the prohibition of psychedelic 'drugs' has limited the exploration of consciousness, advances in neuroscience and neurobiology and the healing potential, both psychological and physical, of psychedelics. This has occurred concurrently with a gradual suppression of cognitive freedom through a pervasive media system that keeps our minds focused on shopping, eating, banking and warring.

Alan Watts[6] and others have maintained that true psychedelic experiences share the characteristics of other mystical experiences and that their key elements include focusing on the present moment, understanding how we are all connected to the universe and being aware that all forms of life are variations on a theme and are of a single energy. The psychedelic experience breaks down our cultural constructions of reality and changes our perspectives. Psychedelic thinking is the integration of the insights gained from psychedelic experiences with our everyday life. Though prohibited through both overt and subtle means, the states of consciousness that are reached through the psychedelic experience and that inspire psychedelic thinking are vital aspects of the human condition and quite possibly our very survival.

Economic development, based on systems of production, exchange and consumption that disengage humans from the rest of nature, is often hailed as the hallmark of human progress. Advances in biomedical practice, democratic social organisation and labour-saving technology are some of the means that proponents of human progress pursue in order to achieve states of progressive modernisation. Unfortunately, it is becoming difficult to deny that such ideas of progress lead humans toward overconsumption, uniformity, enslavement, violent conflict and uncontrolled population growth. Humanity needs alternative models of organising large societies if we are to avoid such catastrophes as Malthusian collapse or nuclear annihilation. Though marginalised or even prohibited, we propose that psychedelic thinking can inspire multiple alternatives to progress as we know it.

Psychedelic thinking includes critical and creative processes that involve questioning assumptions about daily life, human society and reality itself, as well as connecting diverse ideas in novel ways to address the shortcomings of our experienced world. To engage in psychedelic thinking one must explore phenomena with perspectives derived from a variety of worldviews, conscious states and subjective experiences. Humans achieve psychedelic thinking

in a number of ways that often involve intimate spiritual relationships with animals, plants and places, as well as supernatural
entities. We may also become conditioned to think in psychedelic
ways without such relationships through sustained engagement with
different ways of life.

In today's fast-paced world where documentary film or week-
long holidays pass for engagement with nature or other cultures,
the prohibition of psychedelic substances has blocked access to
the most reliable and culturally compatible means to the perspective required for psychedelic thinking. Likewise, research into the
use of these therapeutically proven agents has ground to a halt.
Yet, a surprisingly large number of thinkers from a multitude of
approaches have maintained an interest in these substances. Like
Galileo, these intrepid individuals are looking towards a hopeful
future where reason will trump superstition driven by misguided
morality. Many of them, in 2011, came together in Canterbury,
UK to share their findings, experiences and insights.

BREAKING CONVENTIONS: A CONFERENCE ON THE CUTTING EDGE OF CONSCIOUSNESS

There are many ways to initiate altered states of consciousness
which help us understand our connection to everything else in the
world (see Reynolds, this volume and[7-8]). Of these, the most widespread method of inducing psychedelic experiences is the ingestion
of 'mind-manifesting' substances. Although the roles psychedelic
species play in human evolution are not well understood, growing
evidence suggests that we have lived in environments that are rich
in psychoactive substances for as long as we have been human.[9]
Thus, it is likely that psychedelic experiences helped humans living
in small, dispersed populations to sustain themselves by inspiring
diverse ways of life. It is also probable that shamanism, which is at
once the oldest form of religion and a method of healing dysfunc-
tional bodily, social, environmental and cosmological relationships,

developed from human encounters with psychedelic plants. Yet currently, we are living in a prodigal progressive era that would benefit from a re-engagement with psychedelic approaches to our world.

Though still generally a taboo even in academia, psychedelics have remained an interest of many thinkers who have silently studied this topic, often underground with great personal sacrifice. In the last two decades, a door has opened allowing legal medical and therapeutic research on psychedelics to resume. This opening has allowed other scholars to become increasingly bold in stating their interest in psychedelic substances. On 1–3 April 2011, Breaking Convention: A Multidisciplinary Conference on Psychedelic Consciousness brought over 80 speakers and 600 delegates from 30 countries to Canterbury, UK to discuss states of consciousness induced by psychedelics, and their broader scientific, social, spiritual and artistic implications. This conference was the first of its kind in the UK, and was successful beyond our wildest expectations; when we began the planning for this conference we expected around 12 speakers and for it to take place over an afternoon.

On that April Fool's weekend many excellent talks were presented. And, indeed, we were fools, in the best of senses. First, we are saying something that has been controversial and is often thought to be better left alone. Yet, these ideas are leaking into the mainstream, little by little. Newspapers, magazines and even the exceedingly conservative Fox News have run positive stories about psychedelic medicines recently. There are global initiatives to rethink the War on Drugs. Still, many influential world leaders appear to have their heads in the sand on this issue. The fool's role is to speak frankly to those in power, presenting what is ignored or downplayed in the high risk game of political manoeuvring.

Also, we were fools in the sense of the Green Man (or April Fool), as described by Crowley.[10] The Green Man holds the mysterious power to bring on Spring, whose return awakens the fool in all of us. It was palpable that we all felt this onrush of a spring following a preternaturally long winter of psychedelic prohibition.

That weekend, an artistic and intellectual experiment was conducted that allowed a collective definition of consciousness to emerge. The Consciousness Field is a travelling interactive installation through which visual anthropologist Maria Lopes collects ideas about what consciousness is. The piece is made up of hundreds of pompoms of different colours and sizes, and brain shaped cards on which viewers are asked to write their own definitions of consciousness. After each exhibit, Lopes conducts a frequency analysis on all the definitions to find word patterns. During Breaking Convention she collected 69 definitions and the word that appeared the most was 'awareness'; the same outcome has emerged everywhere else the piece has been displayed. With the awareness of the importance of speaking openly and honestly about psychedelia, we present this anthology of essays on psychedelic consciousness.

ESSAYS ON PSYCHEDELIC CONSCIOUSNESS

Unfortunately, we cannot present the whole breadth and depth of the conference here given the multitude of presenters but instead offer a small representative sample from such wide ranging approaches as archaeology, history, literature, philosophy, medicine, psychology, parapsychology, anthropology, law and politics.

We begin this collection with three essays exploring the archaeological and ethnographic evidence for psychedelic consciousness. Froese starts us off with the earliest evidence of the modern human mind, a time when we as a species graduated from simply making tools to marking them. This transition to the aesthetic, it is argued, is related to the rise of initiation as a means of enculturation, which, by analogy with modern evidence is intimately related to the use of altered states of consciousness. Reynolds then shows how shamanic and initiatory practices are evidenced in Irish tombs dating from 5,000 years ago. It is argued that shamanic worldviews are world-wide and at their core is psychedelic consciousness. Finally Luna presents the nature and experience of the shamanism of the

Americas which was nearly destroyed by European colonialism. It is shown that this is a sophisticated approach to understanding the world and that we have much to learn from it.

The next four essays take modern psychedelic history as their focus. Jay explores early psychedelic research where self-experimentation was not only the norm, but of prime importance. Self-experiment shows the complexity of the psychedelic experience and leads to an increased subtlety of understanding which cannot be reached through the current objective methodologies. Dickins then presents a review of literary morsels from 1954–1964 presenting the powerful therapeutic experiences of psychedelics. These works, from shortly before psychedelic prohibition, were an attempt to socially and culturally legitimise the use of hallucinogens beyond the realm of scientific investigation. Public outrage at nuclear and chemical weapons in the post-World War II era coupled with the widespread acknowledgement of the safety of psychedelics led to, as Hobbs reports, the British military researching LSD. However, in 1966, LSD was vilified, deemed dangerous and made illegal. Roberts presents the media flurry and political discourse around this event and posits an 'Establishment' that felt endangered by psychedelic consciousness as the explanation for the unprecedented rapidity of this legislation. Legal use of psychedelics for recreation, spiritual exploration, medicine and research ended and we entered a 40-year dark age for psychedelic consciousness.

Feilding opens the rest of the book to the current climate of psychedelic research by presenting the Beckley Foundation's work in supporting psychedelic research and policy change. Feeney and Labate then review the recent use of religious freedom arguments in Europe for protecting the use of ayahuasca in ceremonial contexts. The results have been variable and this essay can be seen as a key document for preparing future legal strategies for psychedelic legitimisation.

The succeeding three articles explore medical research into psychedelics. We begin with a warts-and-all transcript of the lively debate on MDMA held at Breaking Convention. Klein then looks at the phenomenon of poly drug use. Though it has been paraded out as a new scourge, poly drug use is shown to be the normal state of affairs. Instead, the new rhetoric around poly drug use appears to be a feeble effort of legitimisation in the failing War on Drugs. Looking forward, Adams poses avenues open to future research that could illuminate the complex nature of psychedelic healing.

We leave medical research with Devenot who notes that the psychedelic renaissance is heavily biased towards scientific research and argues for the foundation of a critical psychedelic studies in philosophy and the humanities. The balance of this volume addresses these aspects beginning with philosophical approaches by Pokorný and Bicknell who both provide phenomenological readings of psychedelic consciousness. Pokorný explores the nature of consciousness itself by exploring its multi-state nature and the fallacious belief that only one state, alert wakefulness, is the measure of all states. Bicknell then illuminates the concept of 'mind manifesting' in psychedelic consciousness as a state that presents the nature of mind as an object of consideration, an experience with the potential to undermine our long held models of reality.

We wrap up this volume with five essays on the bigger picture of psychedelic consciousness. Luke presents the relationship between psychedelics and parapsychological phenomena and argues that current work in this juncture is hindered because both fields are on the fringe, discouraging researchers from taking on two potentially risky topics (in terms of career) at once. Rowlandson then comments upon the debate on the relationship between psychedelics and mysticism, which may be unresolvable due to the shifting sands of meaning and definition of these two ineffable experiences. Letcher follows by looking at how psychedelic experiences become meaningful by comparing them, at the theoretical level, to music. In both cases, the unexpected plays with culturally conditioned expectations thus evoking emotional and meaningful responses. Voss then reminds us that there are multiple levels of knowing and that they give us access to different aspects of reality. Rational discourse is but one mode and may not be commensurate with what psychedelic consciousness can present. Finally, Congo-Nyah, Komaromi, Murray and Waldstein present us with an ethnographic illustration of a way of being at the intersection of psychedelic experience, mysticism, music and 'higher' levels of knowing, Rastafari practices for developing enhanced consciousness through a complex relationship with Herbs.

We close the book with a bold vision of the future where psychedelics and expanded consciousness are incorporated as a respected aspect of modern cosmopolitan society. Doblin presents what he and the Multidisciplinary Association for Psychedelic Studies (MAPS) are working towards.

The various authors of this book represent the vanguard of what is being called the second golden age of psychedelic research. It is our hope that this volume encourages and motivates a future generation of psychedelic thinkers to stand up to the taboo that has been placed on psychedelics. We must bring these occult plants and chemicals into the light of reasoned discussion so that their relative safety and hidden merits can be more widely known.

1. Laughlin CD, Throop CJ. Husserlian meditations and anthropological reflections: toward a cultural neurophenomenology of experience and reality. *Anthropology of Consciousness.* 2009;20(2):130–70.
2. Martin Skora K. The pulsating heart and its divine sense energies: Body and touch in Abhinavagupta's Trika Saivism. *Numen.* 2007;54(4):420–8.
3. Halliburton M. Rethinking anthropological studies of the body: Manas and Bōdham in Kerala. *American Anthropologist.* 2002;104(4):1123–34.
4. Reichel-Dolmatoff G. Brain and mind in Desana shamanism. *Journal of Latin American Lore.* 1981;7(1):73–98.
5. Brown DJ. Special edition: Psychedelics and ecology. *MAPS Bulletin.* 2009;19(1).
6. Watts A. Psychedelics and religious experience. *California Law Review.* 1968;56:74–85.
7. Lewis-Williams JD, Pearce D. *Inside the Neolithic Mind: Consciousness, Cosmos and the Realm of the Gods.* London: Thames and Hudson; 2005.
8. Williams M. Shamanic interpretations: reconstructing a cosmology for the later prehistoric period of north-western Europe. Unpublished Ph.D dissertation, University of Reading; 2001.
9. Sullivan RJ, Hagen EH. Psychotropic substance-seeking: Evolutionary pathology or adaptation? *Addiction.* 2002;97:389–400.
10. Crowley A. *The Book of Thoth: A Short Essay on the Tarot of the Egyptians, Being the Equinox, Volume III.* Weiser Books; 1944.

ALTERED STATES AND THE PREHISTORIC RITUALISATION OF THE MODERN HUMAN MIND

TOM FROESE

Prehistoric art from all over the world is often characterised by similar kinds of abstract geometric patterns. There is an abundance of spirals, zigzag patterns, crosses, grids, and other visual forms. Many of these motifs are repeated across independent cultural contexts, yet they do not appear to be images of natural phenomena. One possibility is that they symbolise some of the essential visual features of altered states of consciousness, which can be induced by shamanic trance.[1] Indeed, there is abundant evidence that the ritualised experience of altered states played a significant role in many prehistoric societies around the world.[2,3] The similarities of the prehistoric patterns could thus be explained in terms of a common mechanism of altered states, for instance the workings of our species-specific brain. This proposal has gained support in the archaeological community with the extensive work of Lewis-Williams and his colleagues, who even extrapolate this idea to explain the art of the Upper Palaeolithic.[4]

In general, it is plausible that some of the content of prehistoric art originated in the experience of altered states. However, it is still an open question of the extent to which non-ordinary states could also have played a role in the origin of art itself, i.e., in the transition from tool-making to tool-marking. Lewis-Williams and colleagues explicitly assume that the modern human mind was already in existence in the Upper Palaeolithic. We share the same neurobiological basis with those 'anatomically modern humans,' and they were situated in a socio-cultural setting infused with symbolism, which marks them as being 'mentally modern humans' as well. But how did these ancestors arrive at this point in the first place? Lewis-Williams[4] assumes that Darwinian biological evolution must have simply caused the right kind of neurological changes, but to what circumstances were they adapting? Could it be that evolution was tracking changes that were taking place in the socio-cultural milieu?

ON THE ORIGINS OF PREHISTORIC ART

Surprisingly, at least from our modern perspective, technological evolution had remained remarkably stereotyped for millions of years.[5] The process started over 3 million years ago (MYA) in Africa when the first hominids, e.g., *Australopithecus afarensis*, began using stone tools to cut flesh from animal bones and to access bone marrow.[6] Currently, the oldest unequivocal evidence for the manufacture of such stone tools (so-called 'Oldowan' technology) dates from about 2.5 MYA. This technology is associated with more recent species of Australopithecus and the first species of the genus Homo that also appear around this time.[7] It then took until about 1.5 MYA until a new set of stone tools developed, including hand axes and cleavers (so-called 'Acheulean' technology). This technology coincided with new species of Homo, namely *H. ergaster* and *H. erectus*.[8] The first sporadic use of fire may date from this period as well, but it took yet another million years, until about 500,000 years ago, before fire was habitually controlled for a variety of purposes.[9] Alongside the mastery of fire there appeared species of archaic *Homo sapiens,* such as *H. neanderthalensis*.[8] Technological change during this Lower Palaeolithic period was proceeding at a remarkably slow rate, roughly the pace of biological evolution itself. This makes sense if we consider these tools as extensions of the functionality of the biological body. They are products of early hominid niche construction, just like some animals construct burrows and nests.

The speed of technological change started to increase in the Middle Palaeolithic, which is dated from about 300,000 to 40,000 years ago. This period is framed by the first appearance of anatomically modern humans, *H. sapiens sapiens*, and the extinction of all other hominid species, including *H. neanderthalensis*.[8] During this much shorter timespan there was a diversification of functionality, design, and materials, including the manufacture of composite tools, such as spears. Most importantly, starting from around 100,000 years ago, there were symbolic practices. At that time there were sites and tools for pigment processing, perhaps for body decoration,[10] and items with abstract geometric engravings.[11] There is also evidence of bodily ornamentation, such as the use of shell beads.[12] These symbolic practices increased in diversity during the Upper Palaeolithic, which is dated from about 40,000 to 10,000 years ago. The first representational images were made, such as the famous cave paintings in France and Spain. There was an increased variety of artistic practices, including more ornamentation, decoration of tools, as well as the first sculptures, such as the famous 'Venus' figurines.[13]

Note that the pace of technological innovation during the Upper Palaeolithic is no longer measured in millions of years, but rather in tens of thousands of years. This acceleration continued through the Neolithic period and the rest of history, right into our present era of information technology.[5] Thus, technological change had started to outpace biological change, which operates at the longer timescales of adaptation and speciation. Of course, the first hominids were already adapting to a niche that was partially of their own creation, but this was no different from other animals. But from the Middle Palaeolithic onwards, a purely biological explanation of technological change is no longer adequate. The accelerated change of technological and symbolic practices must therefore be a reflection of other kinds of changes, most likely taking place in the socio-cultural context.[14] Accordingly, anatomically modern humans arose in a transitional period, during which there was a relatively sudden switch from biologically to socially driven changes in behavioural practices.

In order to get a better idea of what these circumstances might have been like, it is useful to consider the oldest archaeological evidence for the presence of mentally modern humans, artistic creation. It is notable that red ochre is the only artifactual material frequently encountered alongside stone tools of the Middle Palaeolithic in Africa.[15] Given that this roughly coincides with the origin of anatomically modern human beings, it is tempting to interpret the use of ochre in terms of symbolic practices, such as body painting, and therefore as evidence of the origin of mentally modern humans as well. Some of the earliest well-founded evidence for specifically symbolic practices has come from excavations of a coastal cliff in South Africa called Blombos Cave.[11] Beginning about 100,000 years ago, there was a cultural tradition of decorating small pieces of red ochre with incised abstract patterns. The pattern of a particularly striking piece dating from about 73,000 years ago is shown in Figure 1.

It is highly implausible that the markings on this piece, i.e., a horizontal pattern of crosses marked by three horizontal lines (above, in the middle and below), were made accidentally. Accordingly, this finding strongly suggests that the symbolic capacities of mentally modern humans were already in place during the Middle Palaeolithic, perhaps even coinciding with the biological evolution of anatomically modern humans. Previous to this time the making of tools had only been related to satisfying basic biological necessities. However, such needs do not explain the marking of tools with precise geometrical patterns. The artistic intention and its abstract content indicate a capacity for detachment from immediate concerns, and a motivation to reflect and act upon this new space of possibilities.[16]

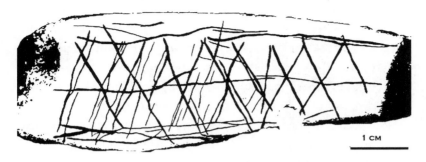

FIGURE 1: Abstract geometric incisions made on one side of a red ochre piece around 73,000 years ago found in Blombos Cave, South Africa. This and similar pieces from the same location are currently the oldest known examples of specifically symbolic practices. (Image adapted from[11] with permission of Christopher Henshilwood)

ON THE ORIGINS OF ENCULTURATION

The facts that technological change had begun to outpace biological change and the practice of decorating pieces of ochre goes beyond satisfying basic biological necessities, suggest that a culture and an appropriate process of enculturation must have been operative by this time. Can we specify this cultural context more precisely? We know that zigzag patterns are a common feature of prehistoric art related to shamanic practices, as well as a typical visual form of altered states of consciousness.[1] Moreover, it is well-documented that altered states constitute an essential part of many tribal rites of puberty, which are also an explicit practice of enculturation.[17,18] This may therefore be a potential interpretation of the findings at Blombos Cave.

In order to get an idea of what such a prehistoric ritual might have looked like we can draw inspiration from ethnographic records. It was the anthropologist van Gennep[18] who first observed that rites of passage feature a central transitional period, in which normal psychic behaviour is suspended. He also realised that this transitional period, which he called 'liminal,' was not some aberrant psychosis, but a universal and essential element of human development and enculturation. Accordingly, the liminal period is a most carefully regulated event, which is preceded by pre-liminal rites ('rites of separation') and followed by post-liminal rites ('rites of incorporation'). Rites of passage are performed for various occasions, but an especially important category are initiation rites, including puberty rites. To further illustrate this idea, let us consider some examples of girls' puberty rites in South Africa:

> *At the onset of the first menstruation a girl, either alone or together with other girls undergoing the same transformation, will be covered with a blanket and* secluded in a special hut. *Venda and Zulu girls stay for approximately one week; Tsonga girls stay up to one month and can only be visited in the evening by the girls of her neighborhood who come to* dance and sing *with her. Subjected to different forms of* hardships, *such as sitting for hours in icy water, eating unpalatable meals, being pinched and teased, she receives considerable* sexual instructions, *such as how to lengthen the labia and avoid being pregnant while indulging in playful familiarities with boys. The rite usually concludes with a* bath *at the river, the* smearing *of the body with* red ochre, *and the receiving of a special funnel-shaped object (*thahu*) which she would henceforth tuck into her girdle at the back. (emphasis added)*[19 p197]

Several aspects of this rite are suggestive of the circumstances found at Blombos Cave. Most straightforwardly, there is the requirement of extended physical and social seclusion at a special place, which is naturally provided by Blombos Cave itself, especially since it is situated on a coastal cliff. There is the idea of a purifying bath in water, which could be provided by the nearby sea. And there is the notion of colouring the girl's body with red ochre. Interestingly, in a Blombos Cave sediment layer dating to about 100,000 years ago, two examples of red ochre-processing 'toolkits' were discovered.[10] The shell receptacles still contained a red mixture. This mixture did not contain any glue-like components, so it is reasonable to suppose that the toolkits were used to process paint. Due to the paucity of other archaeological remains in that particular layer of sediment, the archaeologists argued that the cave was only temporarily used specifically for a paint-related activity, which fits with the idea of social seclusion.

Interestingly, the puberty rite concludes with the reception of a special symbolic item. Could the decorated pieces of red ochre found at Blombos Cave have played a similar role? The red colour would be appropriate, since among recent non-literate cultures red is closely associated with reproduction, blood, mothers, and with rituals related to life and death.[20] This symbolism is especially relevant in the context of female puberty, which involves the onset of menstruation. It is also possible that the activity at Blombos Cave included a liminal period of extended social isolation, alternating with dancing and singing, as well as the endurance of imposed hardships. According to Turner,[17] such non-ordinary circumstances have a profound effect on the initiate's mind, especially given that their altered state is physically, socially and symbolically enacted.

To further support and generalise these ideas, let us consider another example; the girls' puberty rite of the Khoekhoe, a tribe that has lived in the south of Africa for at least two millennia. Following a girl's first menstruation, she is secluded up to several weeks in a special hut. During this liminal period, she and the people around her must adhere to complex social taboos. Eventually, after participating in elaborate purification and social reintegration rites, the girl is finally ready to receive visitors as a young marriageable woman:

All her relatives and friends pour in, each with some present of beads, or earrings, or other finery. [...] The girl shines with clean, well-greased skin, she is scented all over with the buchu she and her friends have ground [Agathosma spp., a fragrant and medicinal herb], her face is painted in various curious patterns with red and white mineral powder mixed with fat, and her body is loaded with the presents.[21 p275]

Again, there are several informative correlations between this rite and the archaeological findings at Blombos Cave. In addition to what we discussed before, there is the notion of body ornamentation with jewellery and with paint. Similarly, excavations have uncovered a large number of shell beads, which were habitually made starting from about 75,000 years ago.[12] Moreover, the mixture in the ochre-processing toolkits is comparable to this account; it had been made by grinding red ochre using large white quartz crystals, and it included animal bone marrow fat.[10] Additionally, since the engravings were found on some of the same pieces that were used to produce red powder, the archaeologists hypothesised that these patterns may reflect designs that were ultimately intended for other media, including skin.[11] It is therefore tempting to speculate that they were intended for a symbolic practice comparable to the "various curious patterns" that are painted on a Khoekhoe girl's face during the conclusion of her puberty rites.

It seems plausible that humans were already performing such rites of passage over 100,000 years ago. But why? Van Gennep[18] conceives the main function of these rites as smoothing over the social instabilities caused by changes in an individual's social condition. However, as Turner[17] notes, the liminal period often involved a considerable amount of socially subversive activity by the participants as well. Incorporation into ordinary social reality was often achieved by a temporary, socially sanctioned detour through non-ordinary individual reality. The communal enaction of non-ordinary states of affairs may thus have played an important positive role in itself. Turner emphasised that the liminal period leads to the temporary formation of a spontaneous 'communitas'; during this time all participants share in an existentially profound experience on equal terms, no matter their normal social status. He therefore saw a valuable pedagogical role in the rites of passage. The rites not only strengthen a sense of group identity, they also play a formative role in the participants' own personal development. Additionally, Turner[17] elaborated the idea that puberty rites are a process of enculturation. He illustrates this idea by giving an example of female puberty rites practiced by the Bemba of Zambia:

> *The wisdom (mana) that is imparted in sacred liminality is not just an aggregation of words and sentences; it has onto-logical value, it refashions the very being of the neophyte. [...] the secluded girl is said to be "grown into a woman" by the female elders—and she is so grown by the verbal and nonverbal instruction she receives in precept and symbol, especially by the revelation to her of tribal sacra in the form of pottery images.*[17 p103]

It is interesting to note the prominence played by sacred symbols during these rites, which provides us with another possible interpretation of the decorated ochre pieces of Blombos Cave. Certainly, puberty rites and symbolic culture are closely intertwined. The meaning of the symbols is conventionally determined and must therefore be socially transmitted in some effective manner. At the same time the initiation into a tribe's sacred symbolism has existential significance; it 'refashions the very being' of the initiate. This mental restructuring is an explicit goal of many puberty rites, for instance the Bemba's idea of 'growing' a child into an adult person.

ON THE ORIGINS OF HUMAN CONSCIOUSNESS

Perhaps the most striking feature that sets the modern human mind apart from non-human minds is a highly developed form of consciousness, including self-awareness. Although we normally take this consciousness for granted, it actually takes many years to become fully formed. This developmental process appears to proceed largely spontaneously, and at least in our culture there is no explicit facilitation in this regard. Nevertheless, normal mental development depends on an appropriate socio-cultural context, and even then success is not guaranteed, as evidenced by the fact that many psychiatric disorders of consciousness are linked to adolescence.[22] Accordingly, it is likely that these circumstances were even more problematic when the biological, social and cultural conditions of the first human beings were only beginning to appear. Could it be that in those times the social practice of puberty rites was used as a means to explicitly bring about the development of an adult form of consciousness?

Let us start with another piece of ethnographic inspiration. It is well known that one of the main traditional uses of shamanic rites all over the world is to retrieve the 'soul' of patients who are severely ill.[3] In some cases this may amount to a ritualised restoration of self-awareness to an unresponsive patient. This practice illustrates how a rite of passage, in this case related to a passage through illness, can be related to the ritualised invocation of consciousness. Furthermore, there are widespread myths about the shaman's role in providing 'souls' for children:

> *The Goldi, the Dolgan, and the Tungus say that, before birth, the souls of children perch like little birds on the branches of the Cosmic Tree and the shamans go there to find them. This mythical motif, which we have already encountered in the initiatory dreams of future shamans, is not confined to Central and North Asia; it is attested, for example, in Africa and Indonesia.*[3 p272-3]

The idea that the shaman is responsible for procuring a child's soul from the branches of the Cosmic Tree may be a hint of ancient times in which human consciousness was something that had to be ritually fashioned. The prevalence of tribal puberty rites further underlines this idea because, as the Bemba would say, the child is like a seed that has to be 'grown' into an adult. What could have made such rituals effective in developing consciousness?

One potent restructuring force is music. Drumming and chanting are universal features of shamanic rituals, and they often accompany rites of passage (like the dancing and singing during South African puberty rites). Furthermore, during altered states there can be powerful synergies between song and the quality of the unfolding experience.[23] Intriguingly, the origin of human language may not have arisen, primarily, from bodily gestures or predator alarm calls, but rather from extended vocalisations similar to animal song.[24] And human language is, of course, closely associated with human consciousness and in particular self-awareness.

A ritualised crisis could also facilitate the origin of consciousness. Heidegger's[25] analysis of a crisis during tool-use helps to illustrate this point. While you are absorbed in an activity of tool-use, there is no well-defined distinction between subject and object. Self and tool are transparent in the flow of activity. But if the tool breaks, you undergo a spontaneous transformation of experience. The tool is now an explicit object of your perception. Simultaneously, your absorption is interrupted; you become a conscious observer faced by a broken tool. It seems plausible that the awkward taboos, physical exclusion, and hardships that are enforced during puberty rites have a similar kind of effect on the minds of the participants. The socially enacted crisis provokes a form of self-awareness, which is then retained by post-liminal rites of social reintegration and symbolic incorporation.

This ethnographically informed interpretation of the archaeological discoveries at Blombos Cave suggests an intriguing hypothesis, a practice of socially enacting a liminal experience in the form of puberty rites may have been closely related to the first emergence of enculturated and conscious, of mentally modern, humans. It is likely that altered states of consciousness not only played an essential role in shaping the content of the first works of art; they also helped to bring about the first symbolic intentions as such.

1. Lewis-Williams D, Dowson TA. *The Signs of All Times: Entoptic Phenomena in Upper Paleolithic Art.* Current Anthropology. 1988;29(2):201–45.
2. Devereux P. *The Long Trip: A Prehistory of Psychedelia.* Brisbane, Australia: Daily Grail Publishing; [1997] 2008.
3. Eliade M. *Shamanism: Archaic Techniques of Ecstasy.* Princeton, NJ: Princeton University Press; [1951] 2004.
4. Lewis-Williams D. *The Mind in the Cave: Consciousness and the Origins of Art.* London, UK: Thames & Hudson; 2002.
5. Ambrose SH. *Paleolithic Technology and Human Evolution.* Science. 2001; 291(5509):1748–53.
6. McPherron SP, Alemseged Z, Marean CW, Wynn JG, Reed D, Geraads D, et al. *Evidence for stone-tool-assisted consumption of animal tissues before 3.39 million years ago at Dikika, Ethiopia.* Nature. 2010;466:857–60.
7. Semaw S. *The World's Oldest Stone Artefacts from Gona, Ethiopia: Their Implications for Understanding Stone Technology and Patterns of Human Evolution Between 2.6–1.5 Million Years Ago.* Journal of Archaeological Science. 2000;27:1197–214.
8. Wood B. *Human Evolution: A Very Short Introduction.* Oxford, UK: Oxford University Press; 2005.
9. Roebroeks W, Villa P. *On the earliest evidence for habitual use of fire in Europe.* Proceedings of the National Academy of Sciences of the USA. 2011;108(13):5209–14.
10. Henshilwood CS, d'Errico F, van Niekerk KL, Coquinot Y, Jacobs Z, Lauritzen S-E, et al. *A 100,00-Year-Old Ochre-Processing Workshop at Blombos Cave, South Africa.* Science. 2011;314:219–22.
11. Henshilwood CS, d'Errico F, Watts I. *Engraved ochres from the Middle Stone Age levels at Blombos Cave, South Africa.* Journal of Human Evolution. 2009;57:27–47.
12. d'Errico F, Henshilwood CS, Vanhaeren M, van Niekerk KL. *Nassarius kraussianus shell beads from Blombos Cave: evidence for symbolic behaviour in the Middle Stone Age.* Journal of Human Evolution. 2005;48:3–24.
13. Balter M. *On the Origin of Art and Symbolism.* Science. 2009;323:709–11.
14. Stiegler B. *Technics and Time, 1: The Fault of Epimetheus.* Stanford, CA: Stanford University Press; 1998.
15. Watts I. *The pigments from Pinnacle Point Cave 13B, Western Cape, South Africa.* Journal of Human Evolution. 2010;59:392–411.
16. Froese T. *From adaptive behavior to human cognition: a review of Enaction.* Adaptive Behavior. Published online 14 February 2012.
17. Turner V. *The Ritual Process: Structure and Anti-Structure.* Piscataway, NJ: Aldine Transaction; 1969.
18. van Gennep A. *The Rites of Passage.* Chicago, IL: The University of Chicago Press; [1908] 1960.
19. Afolayan FS. *Culture and customs of South Africa.* Westport, CT: Greenwood Press; 2004.
20. Wreschner EE. *Red Ochre and Human Evolution: A Case for Discussion.* Current Anthropology. 1980;21(5):631–44.
21. Schapera I. *The Khoisan Peoples of South Africa: Bushmen and Hottentots.* London, UK: Lowe and Brydone; 1930.
22. Paus T, Keshavan M, Giedd JN. *Why do many psychiatric disorders emerge during adolescence?* Nature Reviews Neuroscience. 2008;9:947–57.
23. Shanon B. *The Antipodes of the Mind: Charting the Phenomenology of the Ayahuasca Experience.* Oxford, UK: Oxford University Press; 2002.
24. Merker B, Okanoya K. *The Natural History of Human Language: Bridging the Gaps without Magic.* In: Lyon C, Nehaniv CL, Cangelosi A, editors. Emergence of Communication and Language. London, UK: Springer-Verlag; 2007. p. 403–20.
25. Heidegger M. *Being and Time.* New York, NY: Harper and Row; [1927] 1962.

TRACING NEOLITHIC WORLDVIEWS: SHAMANISM, IRISH PASSAGE TOMB ART AND ALTERED STATES OF CONSCIOUSNESS

FFION REYNOLDS

In the last 20 years or so, new interpretations regarding engraved art have emerged in which some imagery is associated with shamanism. The aim of this article is to argue that shamanism is a near-universal paradigm which can be used successfully to interpret the art of the Boyne Valley passage tombs in Ireland as shamanic representations of entoptic visual experience induced by altered states of consciousness. This research provides a potent tool for reconstructing Irish Neolithic worldview and symbolism, as well as the social organisation of religion and beliefs about death and the supernatural. This article will present a series of diagnostic examples of engraved art found on architectural pieces of stone at two Boyne Valley passage tombs: Newgrange and Knowth, Co. Meath, reinforcing the fact that shamanic worldviews are indeed a world-wide and innate phenomenon.

SHAMANIC ACTS

Before turning to the engraved art itself, I will first briefly outline the main characteristics of 'shamanism.' Interpretations of the 'shaman' have varied considerably over the years, with many early thinkers arguing that shamans were demonic charlatans.[1] From the mid-nineteenth until the mid-twentieth century, many considered the shaman to be afflicted with a psychiatric or epileptic condition. This notion was soon discredited as a misinterpretation of Altered States of Consciousness (ASC) in shamanic rituals.[2,3] This extreme view of shamanism has now been replaced with a more holistic application, with several authors viewing shamanism—or 'neo-shamanism'—as a form of psychotherapeutic healing.[4] Today we witness the revival of shamanic ceremonies in many indigenous populations.[5-7] This seems to be coupled with a popularisation of shamanism in postmodern Western society.[8-10]

'Shamanism' is a modern construct or framework and has been applied to various people and various situations through time. This includes those which see shamanism as innate or as a neuropsychological phenomenon.[11-13] This position has developed to include my own ideas of a possible near-universal application of shamanism.[14] These views have not escaped criticism, however, with many arguing that shamanism is a very specific form of worldview which should not be applied cross-culturally.[15]

Even so, central to the arguments of this article is the vital importance of the shaman in the construction of worldview. In order to demonstrate this, I will draw on the work of several anthropologists and archaeologists. This will include early theories of shamanism like the classic work of Mircea Eliade,[16] but will mostly focus on the most recent theories by writers such as Piers Vitebsky[17] and Lewis-Williams and Pearce.[3]

Following these authors, a shaman can be viewed as a highly skilled individual who 'acts out' or performs particular tasks within the community. The shaman, from this perspective, may be viewed as an important mediator between worlds. Shamans are performers of particular roles, skills and arts that require the participation of others while they alter their consciousness using various techniques, including hallucinogenic substances, hypnotism, trickery, chanting, dance and healing. They are ambiguous individuals.

It has been suggested that Neolithic Irish passage tombs, dating to around 5,000 years ago, were associated with a complex of consciousness-altering traditions, linked to the practice of shamanism.[12,18,19] This article is principally concerned with this important and overriding feature of shamanism—altered states of consciousness.

ALTERED STATES OF CONSCIOUSNESS

Everyone is capable of reaching some form of ASC.[20] Weil goes so far as to suggest that the "desire to alter consciousness periodically is an innate normal drive analogous to hunger or the sexual drive."[21 p17] The shared sensations of ASC are well documented in ethnographic literature.[22,23] These techniques are applicable to all people at all times and can be implemented as easily by Western peoples as by traditional cultures.

The following list shows the various ways a person can enter an ASC. The first two techniques on the list warrant further clarification since they are the most widely used and are the ones most associated with shamanism. The use of drumming to change consciousness depends on the frequency of the beat and when it matches a theta brain wave of four to eight cycles per second, an ASC can be achieved.[24] Psychotropic drugs cover a wide range of substances of which it is the hallucinogens that are most often associated with altering consciousness. Hallucinogens act upon neural stimulations since they effectively contain the same chemicals that are found naturally in the human brain and are released when brain waves slow. Effectively, taking hallucinogens merely serves to speed up the altering of consciousness that could otherwise be achieved through any one of the following methods:[25,26]

A: auditory driving such as drumming and singing

B: hallucinogens

C: fasting and nutritional deficits

D: physical or sensory deprivation including 'hostage situations'

E: increased mental activity

F: meditation

G: strong flickering light

H: excessive movement or dance

I: austerities such as wounds and feats of endurance

J: intensive temperature conditions

K: sleep and dream states

L: staring into a mirror

M: sexual restrictions

N: alcohol

O: migraine and other pathological symptoms

P: posture

Q: pilgrimages to specific locations

(List compiled from Lewis-Williams and Pearce;[3] Williams[27])

Attributes of ASCs include seeing geometric forms, breathlessness, weightlessness, rising up from the body, incapacitation of the body, taking on a new material form, oscillating noise, tingling of the skin, muscular pains and feelings of being stretched.[27] Although mental experiences are more culturally controlled, it is thought that in the early stages of ASCs all people may sense similar swirling luminous geometric forms. These are known as entoptic phenomena deriving from the central nervous system—visual effects whose source is within the eye itself. You can see them by rubbing a finger against the eyelid of a closed eye.

ENTOPTIC VISUAL PHENOMENA

Lewis-Williams and Dowson[12,19] propose that many of the abstract marks found in prehistoric art are entoptic and derive from neuropsychological processes. That these are determined by shamanistic practices has caused an explosion of theoretical discussion.

The entoptic model is based on a huge corpus of work. Even though there are several entoptic shapes, certain forms occur time and time again. Listed below are six of the most common shapes, which were originally derived from work done by neurologists and psychologists.[28–32] These are:

A: a basic grid and its development in a lattice and expanding hexagonal pattern

B: sets of parallel lines

C: dots and short flecks

D: zigzag lines crossing the field of vision (reported by some subjects as angular, by others as undulating)

E: nested catenary curves

F: filigrees or thin meandering lines (see Figure 1 overleaf)

It was Lewis-Williams and Dowson[12] who first introduced the entoptic neuropsychological model to explain the art motifs of the Upper Palaeolithic areas of Southern Africa and the Californian Great Basin. It is a certainty that the human nervous system and its capacity to produce entoptic visual imagery in prehistory is the same as today, and so it is said to be universal. These studies were soon followed by Bradley's,[33] which incorporated motifs from Neolithic Ireland, Brittany and Iberia. The neuropsychological model, however, did not resist opposition. It was soon criticised by many scholars for having some basic methodological flaws and for not sticking to fundamental scientific principles. Dronfield,[18,34] especially, set out to resolve these problems, and added an extra control component to the model: samples of non-entoptic art. He

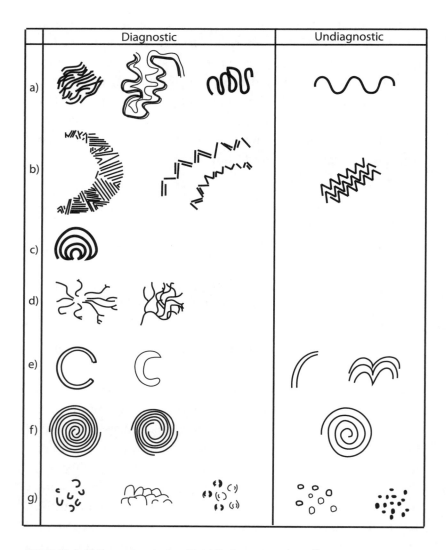

FIGURE 1: (Left) Diagnostic entoptics; (Right) Undiagnostic entoptics.[34]

produced an analytical model, which included studies of art which do *not* occur in an ASC. By using his model in this article, it was found—with approximately 80% confidence—that Irish passage tomb art is fundamentally similar to, as opposed to merely resembling, arts derived from entoptic phenomena.

PASSAGE TOMB ART IN THE BOYNE VALLEY

Some of the most convincing possibilities of engraved entoptic phenomena and shamanic practice in prehistory concern passage tombs. This class of Neolithic monument was constructed across the west and north of the British Isles. Well-known examples include Newgrange and Knowth in Ireland, but there are many others, including for instance Bryn Celli Ddu and Barclodiad-y-Gawres in north Wales. Their layout can be diverse, yet all possess a narrow and restricted passage that leads from the outside world to an internal chamber. In many instances, it was here that the remains of the dead were placed. The tombs themselves may have acted as receptacles for the veneration of ancestral human remains, although they may have been used for more than just burial. Passage tombs may be understood as settings for rituals which involved the living and the dead—perhaps a nexus for shamanic acts—a place where alternative dimensions could be experienced and where *communication* between the living and the dead could take place.

This article will focus on two famous passage tombs from Ireland, Newgrange and Knowth, which overlook the bend of the river Boyne (Figure 2). I will argue that these tombs may have acted as focus for ritual and shamanic performance in the form of ASCs. The main tombs at Newgrange Site 1 and Knowth Site 1 were constructed between 3295 and 2925 BC, and are associated with smaller passage tombs.[35] The main tomb at Newgrange has three smaller satellite tombs, and Knowth has at least 18 smaller satellite tombs. For a full description of the complexities associated

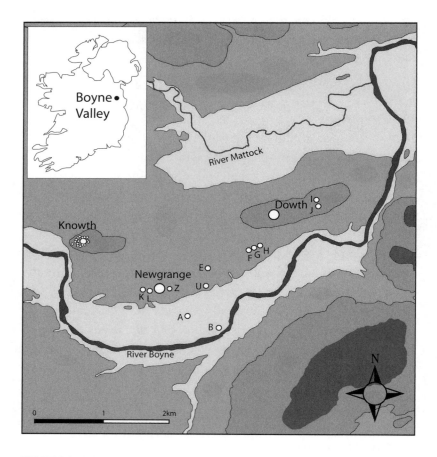

FIGURE 2: Location map of Newgrange and Knowth passage tombs, Co. Meath, Ireland.

with the sequence of building and orientation of the main tombs and their satellites, see Cooney.[36] This article will focus on the main tombs only, and I turn next to discuss these in more detail.

ENTOPTIC SHAPES AT NEWGRANGE

The main tomb at Newgrange Site 1 consists of a massive kerbed ovoid mound, more than 80m diameter, with 97 stones incorporated into the kerb. Within it is a cruciform internal tomb structure with a passage measuring c.19m long (Figure 3).

A distinguishing feature of Newgrange is the roof-box, which is located above the main entrance to the passage. According to O'Kelly[35] the aperture was constructed as an opening through which the midwinter rising sun illuminated the chamber at the end of the passage. The effect of the beam of light in the interior of the Newgrange tomb is well known, but it should be remembered that in the Neolithic, experience of this would have been restricted to the people who interacted with the ancestors and the otherworld. The entoptic shapes depicted on the stones of Newgrange Site 1 are illustrated in Figure 4.

ENTOPTIC SHAPES AT KNOWTH

Knowth Site 1 has the largest concentration of megalithic art in Europe, with more than 300 decorated stones.[37] Within the main mound are two passage tombs, one opening from the east side of the mound and the other from the west (Figure 5).

Knowth Site 1 measures 80m by 95m, with the kerb and interiors containing an abnormally large quantity of engraved abstract art. More than a quarter of Europe's megalithic art and about 45% of Ireland's passage tomb art is found at Knowth, with Site 1 accounting for about 83% of the total.[38] I will only focus on the engraved art at Site 1, which has 197 stones in total. The entoptic shapes occurring on the stones at Knowth Site 1 are illustrated in Figure 6.

FIGURE 3: The passage tomb at Newgrange after restoration. Courtesy of Ken Williams.

DISCUSSION AND CONCLUSIONS

The chief intention of this article is to re-establish the notion that the practice of shamanism is a near-universal phenomenon, going back beyond recorded history. The use of a shamanic worldview as a model with which to approach the past is a useful one, and this article has gone some way to identify precise examples of entoptic phenomena at specific engraved stones at both the main tombs at Newgrange and Knowth, Co. Meath, Ireland. I suggest that these engraved images are derived from entoptic hallucinations experienced during an ASC, a crucial aspect of shamanism.

Many authors working in archaeology and rock art studies, who suggest that shamanism may have existed during the Neolithic and before, also believe strongly that drugs may have been involved.[39–41] Drug taking is often associated with shamanism in Latin America, where the most common drugs are peyote, ayahuasca and datura,

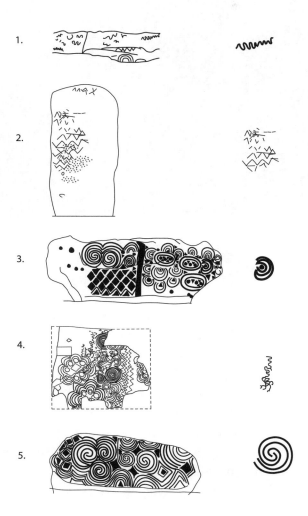

FIGURE 4: Entoptic shapes at Newgrange: (1) meander on kerbstone K52; (2) fortification on orthostat R18; (3) arc-spiral on K52; (4) filigree on East recess roof stone; (5) multiple spiral on kerbstone K1.

FIGURE 5: The passage tomb of Knowth. Courtesy of Ken Williams.

although over 100 hallucinogens are known.[42,43] Elsewhere in Europe, historical studies suggest that cannabis, henbane, mandrake, psilocybin mushrooms and deadly nightshade were all used as hallucinogens.[44–46]

It is probable that drug taking also occurred in prehistory and its antecedents may be traced back to Neanderthals.[47] Andrew Sherratt[40] has pointed out that any prehistoric culture may have used drugs and hallucinated with them. For example, witchcraft is common in mythologies, involving magic potions and brews, and henbane has long been suspected of having some link with European witchcraft, since it can induce hallucinations, delirium and sensations of flying and enhanced night vision. Consequently, there are a number of theories which claim that hallucinogens were part of prehistoric ritual activities, for example in the European Neolithic. Henbane occurs not infrequently in seed assemblages from Europe from the Neolithic onwards, with increasing frequency.

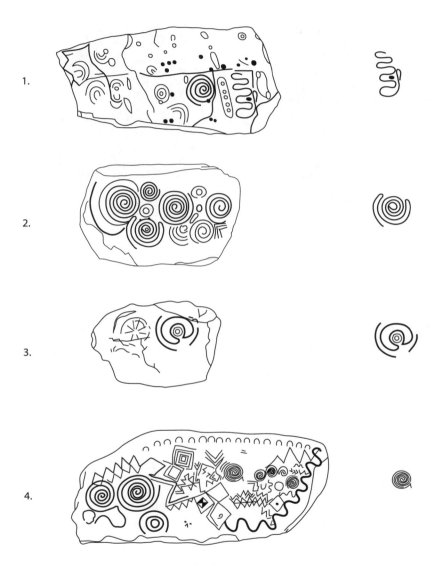

FIGURE 6: Entoptic shapes at Knowth: (1) meander on kerbstone K83; (2) arc-spiral on kerbstone K56; (3) loop arc on kerbstone K68; (4) multiple spiral on kerbstone K13.

FIGURE 7: (Left) Newgrange kerbstones K1, K52 and K67. (Right) Drawing of imagery of early stages of hallucinogen intoxication.

This is particularly significant, since it is neither a staple food plant nor a common weed of cereal crops and its occurrence is in several cases the result of deliberate deposition.[48] Archaeological evidence for henbane in the Neolithic has been recovered following the excavation of a henge monument at Balfarg Riding School in Fife.[46,49] Seeds and pollen of black henbane *(Hyoscyamus niger)* were reported from a deposit encrusted on the outer surface of a Grooved Ware potsherd.

The use of hallucinogenic substances in ritual contexts, like henbane, is arguably fundamental to Neolithic religion. Taking anthropological analogies seriously, and working from what is already known from ethnographic reports, worldview analogies such as shamanism should not be ruled out. The association of such substances with advanced levels of ritual initiation in which small numbers of people are admitted to communion with the spirits of the dead—often in the presence of their bones (a close analogy is found in New Guinea[49])—is coupled with the evidence from entoptic phenomena and engraved art.

It was thought that any effort to retrieve meaning from rock art or to make suggestions about social structure of consciousness-altering would remain entirely hypothetical. Yet, a drawing of what a subject experienced shows a spiral, and curving around the right-hand side, there is a lattice pattern that is intimately associated with the spiral. The likeness between this drawing and motifs at Newgrange is striking and may be highly significant (Figure 7). With the recognition that entoptic phenomena can be pinpointed exactly to certain stones, this article argues that we should not assume that shamanic practices involving altered states of consciousness were alien to our Neolithic predecessors.

1. Jilek WG. *Transforming the Shaman: Changing Western Views of Shamanism and Altered States of Consciousness.* Investigatión en Salud. 2005;3(1):8–15.
2. Bednarik RG. *On Neuropsychology and Shamanism in Rock Art.* Current Anthropology. 1990;31(1):77–84.
3. Lewis-Williams JD, Pearce D. *Inside the Neolithic Mind: Consciousness, Cosmos and the Realm of the Gods.* London: Thames and Hudson; 2005.
4. Wallis RJ. *Shamans/Neo-Shamans: Ecstasy, Alternative Archaeologies and Contemporary Pagans.* London: Routledge; 2003.
5. Bacigalupo AM. *Shamans of the Foye Tree: Gender, Power, and Healing Among Chilean Mapuche.* Austin: University of Texas Press; 2007.
6. Dowson TA. *Re-animating Hunter-gatherer Rock-art Research.* Cambridge Archaeological Journal. 2009;19(3):378–87.
7. Sillar B. *The Social Agency of Things? Animism and Materiality in the Andes.* Cambridge Archaeological Journal. 2009;19(3):367–77.
8. Atkinson JM. *Shamanism Today.* Annual Review of Anthropology 1992;21:307–30.
9. Harvey G. *Animism: Respecting the Living World.* New York: Columbia University Press; 2006.
10. Ingold T. *The Perception of the Environment.* London: Routledge; 2000.
11. Clottes J, Lewis-Williams JD. *The Shamans of Prehistory: Trance and Magic in the Painted Caves.* New York: Routledge; 1998.
12. Lewis-Williams JD, Dowson TA. *The Signs of All Times: Entoptic Phenomena in Upper Palaeolithic Art.* Current Anthropology. 1988;29(2):201–45.
13. Pearson JL. *Shamanism and the Ancient Mind: a Cognitive Approach to Archaeology.* New York: Alta Mira Press; 2002.
14. Reynolds F. *Regenerating Substances: Quartz as an Animistic Agent.* Time and mind: the Journal of Archaeology, Consciousness and Culture. 2009;2(2):153–166.
15. Bahn PG. *Save the Last Trance For Me: an Assessment of the Misuse of Shamanism in Rock Art Studies.* In: Francfort H-P, Hamayon N, editors. *The Concept of Shamanism: Uses and Abuses.* Bibliotheca Shamanistica vol. 10. Budapest: Akadémiai Kiadó; 2001. p.51–93.

16. Eliade M. *Shamanism: Archaic Techniques of Ecstasy* (Task, W, translator). Princetown: University Press; 1964.
17. Vitebsky P. *The Shaman.* London: Macmillan; 1995.
18. Dronfield J. *Subjective Vision and the Source of Megalithic Art.* Antiquity. 1995;69:539–49.
19. Lewis-Williams JD, Dowson TA. *On Vision and Power in the Neolithic: Evidence from the Decorated Monuments.* Current Anthropology. 1993;34(1):55–65.
20. Noll R. *Mental Imagery Cultivation as a Cultural Phenomenon: the Role of Visions in Shamanism.* Current Anthropology. 1985;26(4):443–61.
21. Weil AT. *The Natural Mind.* Boston: Houghton Mifflin; 1972.
22. Lewis IM. *Ecstatic Religion: an Anthropological Study of Spirit Possession and Shamanism.* Harmondsworth: Penguin; 1971.
23. Harner MJ. *The Way of the Shaman: a Guide to Power and Healing.* New York: Harper and Row; 1980.
24. Kristoffersson R. *The Sound Picture of the Saami Shaman Drum.* In: Ahlbäck T, Bergman J, editors. *The Saami shaman drum*: based on papers read at the symposium on the Saami shaman drum held at Åbo, Finland; 1988: Åbo: Donner Institute for Research in Religious and Cultural History; 1991. p.169–82.
25. Furst, PT. *Flesh of the Gods: the Ritual Use of Hallucinogens.* London: George Allen and Unwin; 1972.
26. Devereux P. *The Long Trip: a Prehistory of Psychedelia.* New York: Arkana; 1997.
27. Williams M. *Shamanic Interpretations: Reconstructing a Cosmology for the Later Prehistoric Period of North-Western Europe.* Unpublished Ph.D dissertation, University of Reading; 2001. Klüver H. *Mescal Visions and Eidetic Vision.* American Journal of Psychology. 1926;37(4):502–15.
28. Klüver H. *Mechanisms of Hallucinations.* In: McNemar Q, Merrill MA, editors. Studies in personality. New York: McGraw-Hill; 1942. p.175–207.
29. Knoll M, Kuger J. *Subjective Light Pattern Spectroscopy in the Encephalographic Frequency Range.* Nature. 1959;184(4701):1823–4.
30. Horowitz MJ. *The Imagery of Visual Hallucinations.* Journal of Nervous and Mental Disease. 1964;138(6):513–23.
31. Siegel RK. *Hallucinations.* Scientific American. 1977;237(4):132–40.
32. Bradley R. *Death and Entrances: a Contextual Analysis of Megalithic Art.* Current Anthropology. 1989;30:68–75.
33. Dronfield J. *The Vision Thing: Diagnosis of Endogenous Derivation in Abstract Arts.* Current Anthropology. 1996;37(2):373–91.
34. O'Kelly M. *Newgrange: Archaeology, Art and Legend.* London: Thames and Hudson; 1982.
35. Cooney G. *Landscapes of Neolithic Ireland.* New York: Routledge; 2000.
36. Eogan G. *Megalithic Art and Society.* Proceedings of the Prehistoric Society. 1999;65:415–46.
37. Eogan G. *Knowth and the Passage-tombs of Ireland.* London: Thames and Hudson; 1986.
38. Rudgley R. *The Alchemy of Culture: Intoxicants in Society.* London: British Museum Press; 1993.
39. Sherratt A. *Sacred and Profane Substances: the Ritual Use of Narcotics in Later Neolithic Europe.* In: Garwood P, Jennings D, Skeates R, Toms J, editors. *Sacred and Profane: Proceedings of a Conference on Archaeology, Ritual and Religion.* Oxford: Oxford University Committee for Archaeology Monograph No. 32; 1991. p. 50–64.
40. Sherratt A. *Introduction: Peculiar Substances.* In: Goodman J, Lovejoy PE, Sherratt A, editors. *Consuming Habits: Drugs in History and Anthropology.* London: Routledge; 1995. p. 1–10.
41. Furst PT. *Hallucinogens and Culture.* San Francisco: Chandler and Sharp; 1976.
42. Hultkrantz A. *The Relations Between the Shaman's Experiences and Specific Shamanistic Goals.* In: Bäckman L, Hultkrantz A, editors. *Studies in Lapp shamanism* 16. Stockholm: Stockholm Studies in Comparative Religion; 1978. p.90–109.
43. Emboden W. *Ritual Use of Cannabis Sativa L: a Historical-thnographic Survey.* In: Furst P, editor. *Flesh of the Gods: the Ritual Use of Hallucinogens.* London: George Allen and Unwin; 1972. p.214–36.

44. Harner MJ. *Hallucinogens and Shamanism.* Oxford: Oxford University Press; 1973.
45. Moffatt B. *An Assessment of the Residues on the Grooved Ware.* In: Barclay GJ, Russell-White CJ, editors. *Excavations in the Ceremonial Complex of the Fourth Millennium BC at Bafarg/Balbirnie.* Proceedings of the Society of Antiquaries of Scotland. 1993;123: 108–10.
46. Solecki R. *Shanidar IV, A Neanderthal Flower Burial in Northern Iraq.* Science 1975;190:880–1.
47. Long DJ, Tipping R, Holden TG, Bunting MJ, Milburn P. *The Use of Henbane (Hyoscyamus niger L.) as a Hallucinogen at Neolithic 'Ritual' Sites: a Re-evaluation.* Antiquity. 2000;74:49–53.
48. Barclay GJ, Russell-White CJ, editors. *Excavations in the Ceremonial Complex of the Fourth Millennium BC at Balfarg/Balbirnie.* Proceedings of the Society of Antiquaries of Scotland 1993;123:42–210.
49. Barth F. *Cosmologies in the Making: a Generative Approach to Cultural Variation in Inner New Guinea.* Cambridge: Cambridge University Press; 1987.

TOWARDS AN EXPLORATION OF THE MIND OF A CONQUERED CONTINENT: SHAMANISM, SACRED PLANTS AND AMERINDIAN EPISTEMOLOGY

LUIS EDUARDO LUNA

The conquest of the Americas by the empires of Europe nearly resulted in the total loss of the cultural, technical and intellectual achievements of one third of the population of the world of that time. The Amerindian crops adopted by the European conquerors spread around the world: corn, potatoes, manioc, tomatoes, pepper, calabash, certain beans, as well as stimulants such as cacao, coca and tobacco. Yet the advanced technical capabilities of many Amerindian societies in the fields of astronomy, engineering, medicinal plants, ceramics, weaving, basketry and—as is becoming increasingly evident—the sophisticated and efficient use of the land, did not have any significant global impact.

Apart from the academic work of relatively small circles of historians, ethnologists, anthropologists and the obscure accounts of travellers, there was no European acknowledgment of a single philosophical idea from the people of the Americas prior to the recently awakened interest in Amerindian shamanism.[1] There was no technical or philosophical/theological exchange between the peoples of the two continents. Europeans viewed the Amerindian population only as objects of conversion, assimilation, subjugation or annihilation.

The sacred books of the Maya were burned in 1562. The quipus of the Andes—a work of the Devil according to sixteenth century friars—were destroyed by decree in 1583. The sacred groves, temples and places of worship of the Amerindians were desecrated. Revered works of art were melted down for the price of their gold. The repository of Amerindian traditions, the bearers of wisdom who 'remembered' and knew 'how to speak,' were hunted and killed. Their knowledge was treated as the work of Satan.

Perspectives on the nature of reality of a whole continent were obliterated with the transplantation into the Americas of an Indo-European syndrome that had already destroyed the spiritual manifestations of European Neolithic cultures largely associated with the natural environment.[2] At the time of the arrival of the European conquerors, the 'Old World' for a long time had been engulfed in ideological religious wars in which deviation from pronounced dogmas could be punishable by death.

All of this went hand in hand with deforestation, a development that can be traced to the Mesopotamian myth of Gilgamesh, the first hero in world literature, who embarked on a quest to kill Humbaba, the demon of the forest, who lived in the mountainside cedar groves harvested to the last by the ancient Sumerians.[3] The deforestation of Europe was carried out for agriculture, to create grasslands for the grazing of livestock to satisfy an insatiable appetite for meat and milk, for construction—both domestic and military—and for strategic or religious reasons.

The Americas are still being subjected to the kind of devastating deforestation that already by the time of the conquest of America had decimated the forests of much of Europe, North Africa and the Middle East. Domesticated plants and animals from Eurasia accompanied the conquest of the Americas, destroying much of the original biota, in what has been called 'ecological imperialism.'[4] At the same time the indigenous population was condemned to humiliation, subjugation and poverty, barely surviving history's greatest ethnocide. Almost by a miracle after 500 years of persecution, one aspect of Amerindian cosmology did survive, although in an attenuated form: shamanism.

SHAMANISM IN THE AMERICAS

The term "shamanism" is used here to refer to an innate human capacity, culturally manifested in various ways, which include several universal elements: altered states of consciousness (ASCs), community rituals, spirit world interaction and healing.[5,6] A cognitive and personal transformation is achieved by means of various techniques used to enter into an 'integrative mode of consciousness,'[5,6] which include sensory overload or deprivation, drumming, chanting, fasting, isolation, meditation and hyperventilation. Both in the past as well as in the present numerous examples can be found of the use of psychotropic plants, often in combination with one or more of the other techniques.

The cognitive changes thus achieved may involve journeying to complex, stratified and interconnected worlds perceived as ontologically real, and contacting entities often related to the natural environment, such as animal spirits, or the spirits of the dead. These changes may involve a symbolic death, or transforming into an animal such as a bird or a powerful predator to visit specific realms or to better perform a certain task. Shamanism entails a socially recognised status that includes being able to heal, cause harms, prophesy, mediate social conflict or obtain leadership by means of the knowledge and power acquired by such techniques and supernatural contacts. Shamanism was of central importance in the Americas prior to the arrival of Europeans, and still plays a central role among contemporary indigenous groups as well as among certain segments of the mestizo population.

The archaeological record suggests that shamanism may have often been intimately associated with the use of certain plants, usually considered as sacred, and as proposed by Winkelman,[5,6] now known as psychointegrators. When examined from the perspectives of the shamanic paradigm, much of the art left behind by pre-Columbian societies, as well as specific paraphernalia, point in this direction.

Winkelman[5,6] argues that psychointegrators, and the related concept of integrative modes of consciousness, manifest theta wave synchronisation (3–6 cycles per second). This allows one to access information from the brain stem, or reptilian brain—that regulates vegetative processes such as breathing, heartbeat, and the fight or flight mechanism—as well as the palaeomammalian brain, or limbic system—that supports functions such as emotion, behaviour, long-term memory and olfaction—is accessed. In this way information that is normally habituated or relegated to the subconscious is made available through a reverse inhibitory process.

Additionally, at the physiological level psychointegrators may enhance the way the serotonin system functions; modulating and integrating information within the brain.[5,6] They also release certain dopamine-related capacities of the brain normally repressed by serotonin, and consequently enhance the functioning of the dopaminergic system, which is fundamental to the motivational and learning processes of the brain. Winkelman suggests that the resulting mentation (how you think) and emotion (how you feel) may produce a holistic state of psychological integration and emotional growth.

Psychointegrators contain alkaloids surprisingly similar to human brain neurotransmitters. They are traditionally used across cultures in a religious, spiritual and often therapeutic context, and the similarity may enhance innate capacities of consciousness—such as for spiritual experiences or the presentiment of the spirits embodied in nature—and the integration of various forms of information.

The standard Eurocentric worldview has no place for the powerful cognitive transformation facilitated by psychointegrators. For this reason the typical inhabitant of a Eurocentric worldview is unable to make any sense of examples of Amerindian art. In Europe, prior to the advent of modern art, there were few representations of cognitive changes such as of body perception, of the disintegration of the self, or of the perception of non-natural entities that may be produced by psychointegrators. But once shamanism and integrative states of consciousness are taken into account, a great deal of Amerindian art begins to make sense.

A case in point is the pioneering work of Reichel-Dolmatoff and his study of pre-Columbian gold work.[8] He argues that by recognising the relationship between ritual objects and shamanic ideology a deeper significance is revealed. In fact, the greater part of the figurative representations constitutes a consistent and articulated complex of shamanic art, with transformation as the unifying theme.[8] He contends that much of the known artwork can be explained in terms of the shamanic paradigm; certain iconographic elements may serve to identify particular figures as shamans, such as special headdresses, specific postures, rattles, and more significant representations of animal transformation or journeys by means of animal auxiliaries.

Among the ritual objects investigated are several golden snuff trays from the territory of the Muisca people in the central highlands of present-day Colombia.[8] The snuff trays, decorated with felines and birds commonly associated with shamanism, were once used for the storage of small amounts of the highly psychoactive powder obtained from the crushed roasted seeds of *Anadenanthera peregrina*. The ritual objects also include golden poporos once used for the storage of small amounts of lime as well as poporo sticks topped with tiny and complex heads with apparent shamanic motifs used in the consumption of coca.

Representations of birds or winged objects are also predominant in the gold work. Reichel-Dolmatoff suggests that the winged motif is related to shamanism and is a conscious or unconscious allusion to shamanic flight. In many instances he recognises, in different

FIGURE 1: Pre-Columbian gold work.

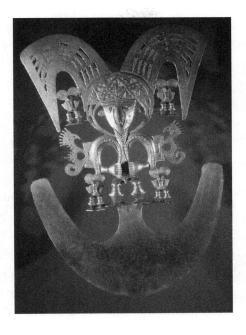

FIGURE 2: Pre-Columbian gold work.

styles and variations, the figures as that of a shaman transformed into a bird, a 'bird-man' (Figures 1–2). There are also highly abstract examples of gold work, which are obviously variations of the bird-man motif, once the basic elements are recognised.

Effigies of various animals, sometimes of a fantastic, non-naturalistic nature, occasionally accompany the central figure, which are interpreted as animal auxiliaries, perhaps representing qualities such as sharpness of sight or hearing, aggressiveness, the ability to undergo metamorphosis, etc. The incorporation of these animal qualities or the transference of them to their patients is a key characteristic of shamans in many cultures.[9]

There are also examples of golden figurines with a toad spread on the head of the central figure.[8] This may be a reference to *Bufo marinus,* whose parotid glands produce bufotenine, a psychoactive alkaloid. Also, figurines with semi-spherical bodies on the head may be a reference to psychoactive mushrooms.[10] In some of these figures both elements appear.

The gold work preserved at the Museo del Oro is thus: "a treasure of shamanic art, a treasure of forms and ideas which for thousands of years have constituted one of the cornerstones of the Indian cultures of this country,"[8] and the bird-man, the ecstatic shaman, is one of its key symbols.

Stone suggests 'shamanic embodiment' as an expression of self along a continuum that may go from predominantly human to creative mixtures embedding animal selves to images almost wholly given over to the ineffable.[11] In order to represent a shaman, a liminal being who is both Here and Not-Here, there is a deliberate engagement with ambiguity, perhaps the essential feature of shamanism, which "productively fires the artistic imagination, catalysing inventive ways to express the ineffable cosmic flux," and using such strategies as:

> *juxtaposition, conflation, substitution of parts, pars pro toto (the part stands for the whole), inversion, double reading through contour rivalry, figure-ground reversal, and three-dimensional versus two-dimensional aspects, mirror-imaging, abstraction, and interiority.*[11 p67]

Among the myriad possible artistic approaches to the paradoxes intrinsic to embodying the shamanic, four general traits emerge: creative ambiguity, authority, cephalocentrism and the trance gaze.[11] Stone's compelling and encompassing argumentation is impossible to encapsulate in a few paragraphs. Here are some ideas I found particularly attractive. How can the artist through colours, shapes, and lines in a static image capture the flux of liminality, of existing somewhere suspended between states of being, of true multiplicity in the Self? Amerindian art gives a plethora of solutions. The artists have no artistic mandate to reproduce terrestrial appearances. They have as their goal the recorporealisation of the shaman, something that entails a decorporalisation, just as does the visionary experience, into a spirit-body as holder for the being in trance. The visionary experience, on the other hand, requires participation in a convincingly non-human-centred gestalt of all nature infused with life and obviates the need to make hard-edged visual distinctions between a person and a bat or a peanut and a divine being. The artist is able to throw aside discrete categories and mimetic attachments to this world and its static constituents by creating combinations that defy description. The Western worldview limits our understanding of such art objects because seemingly neutral terms such as 'image,' 'depiction,' and 'representation' inevitably communicate the opposite of the shamanic approach to the object. Amerindian artists on the other hand embrace creative ambiguity. The object we call an effigy of a shaman served as both a visual rendition of the shaman's many selves and as one of the shaman's subjective selves.[11]

We may infer that seen as a whole, Pre-Columbian art is full of allusions to unseen realms, shamanic transformation, subjective states and alternative modes of cognition, which are generally missed by western observers. One of the most common themes is the jaguar transformation. The human/feline motif is found in the earliest South American cultures, such as the Caral (c. 4600 BP) of Coastal Peru. The idea that shamans are able to transform into jaguars is widespread even today in the Amazon.[12] Transformation into other animals, such as serpents or harpy eagles, to acquire certain qualities or cognitive abilities, is also believed to be possible. Therianthropes, a composite of human and animal, sometimes of several of them, as well as many other motifs expressing various inner states, are thus common in Amerindian iconography. Therianthropes may be either a representation of entities acquiring anthropomorphic features in order to communicate with human counterparts, or an expression of a subjective perceptional mode in which the human acquires animal qualities. These images would instantly evoke in Amerindian people particular cognitive states related to multidimensional, multilayered cosmologies, spaces in the mind (perhaps the perception of alternate realities) nowadays mostly forgotten but once visited by our ancestors, as may be deduced from numerous examples of Palaeolithic rock art.[13–15]

PSYCHOINTEGRATORS

Throughout the Americas in the past, and in some places today, shamanism has gone hand in hand with the use of psychointegrators. The best known are peyote (*Lophophora williamsii*) and psylocybin mushrooms in Mesoamerica; several species of *Brugmansia, Anadenanthera colubrina* and *Anadenanthera peregrina* in South America and the Caribbean; the various San Pedro cactus (*Trichocereus spp.*) in Andean and Coastal areas of Peru; ayahuasca (*Banisteriopsis caapi + Psychotria viridis*) and yajé (*Banisteriopsis caapi + Diplopterys cabrerana*) in the Upper Amazon; and of course tobacco, sacred in the whole of the Americas; and coca, still used ritually among Andean people. In more restrictive areas, many other psychotropic plants were or are still used.

Psychointegrators have been used in the Americas since antiquity[16] with *Anadenanthera colubrina* already being used in Inca Cueva, Puna de Jujuy, Argentina around 2100 BC.[17] It played a central role in the extraordinary Tiwanaku culture, roughly from 300 to 1000 AD, as evidenced in representations of snuff paraphernalia on monoliths, and the ubiquity of snuff kits—including tablets, inhalators, spoons and pouches with powder from seeds of this plant—recovered from the Tiwanaku influenced San Pedro de Atacama, Chile[18] (Figures 3–4).

The oldest evidence of the use of *Trichocereus pachanoi* dates from around 2000 to 1500 BC in Las Aldas on the north-central coast of Peru.[19,20] The San Pedro cactus played a central role in Chavin culture in the northern Andean highlands of Peru, as evidenced in figures from the religious and political centre of Chavin

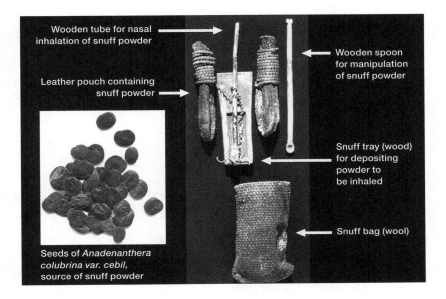

FIGURE 3: Paraphernalia from San Pedro de Atacama. Courtesy of CM Torres.

de Huántar (900 to 200 BC, Figure 5) as well as from Nazca (100 BC to 700 AD).

The oldest known dates for tobacco are from the North Coast of Peru, with dates ranging between 2500 and 1800 BC.[21] Coca chewing in northern Peru began at least 6000 BC.[22] As for the plants involved in the preparation of ayahuasca and yajé there is no clear evidence of their use earlier than the statements by eighteenth century missionaries, who considered the preparations to be agents of the Devil. However, given the antiquity of the use of other psychotropic plants, it seems unlikely that yajé or ayahuasca is a relatively recent innovation. In any case, it is not possible, when dealing with ancient America, to ignore the central role of psychointegrators, nor the weight of history when discussing the current, and in some case growing use of some of these plants in our contemporary world.

FIGURE 4: The Ponce monolith in the Kalasasaya yard
of Tiwanaku. Courtesy of CM Torres.

CONCLUDING WORDS

The techniques for achieving altered states are culture-specific. Like the mastery of any other technique, they require a special form of training. However, the various techniques have a biological dimension that is common to all human beings. Hopefully the development of some of the new theories of human consciousness will take into account tools that traditional societies have used for thousands of years.

Frecska argues for existence of dual complementary methods of knowledge acquisition which reflect the physical universe's duality and complementarity as in particles and waves, mass and energy, local effects and non-local connections.[23] Two sources of knowledge are posited: perceptual-cognitive and direct-intuitive, with the former having fewer problems than the latter with replicability. Perceptual-cognitive knowledge is electrochemical (based on local effects), operates via neuroaxonal networks, is linguistic albeit not necessarily verbal, and relies on modelling a subject-object division. It peaks in Western scientific thinking. Direct-intuitive knowledge is quantum-physical (based on nonlocal connections), operates via sub-neural networks, it is ineffable and relies on direct experience with no subject-object division. It is the source of contemplative traditions.

Clearly, psychointegrators do not simply disrupt normal perception. It seems that through them, by mysterious ways of mind exploration not yet understood, it is indeed possible to access valid information not readily available by ordinary means. Psychointegrators offer complex, often beautiful, coherent and useful experiences, to which some traditional societies assign great value. To dismiss such experiences as aberrations of the mind under the effect of drugs, which is the ordinary accepted discourse, is quite biased. No account of the universe in its totality can be final, which leaves these other forms of consciousness quite disregarded.[24]

FIGURE 5: Therianthrope with feline characteristics holding a stalk of San Pedro cactus. Circular Plaza of the Old Temple, Chavin de Huántar. Courtesy of CM Torres.

Science explores the vast riches of outer space, as well as the minute yet immense realms of subatomic particles. We explore the depths of the oceans and the forests, high mountains and deserts. Yet the exploration of consciousness is still a forbidden realm, vastly explored by shamanic societies yet neglected in contemporary science due to religious preconceptions carried throughout centuries.

Amerindian art, largely inspired by altered states of consciousness, has a message for us. It expresses forms of cognition neglected by most, but still accessible to all humans. The ontological reality of the worlds perceived through psychointegrators in the final analysis depends on the perceiver's worldview. Many traditional societies would not doubt the existence of parallel and multidimensional worlds. With the exception of contemporary theories in physics and cosmology, modern thinking does not admit them. Short of direct experimental verification, orthodox scientific thinking treats talk of parallel and multidimensional universes as fiction if not as the projections of a deranged mind. This is not usually corroborated by those who have immersed themselves deeply in the study or experimentation of integrative states of consciousness.

The fact is that, whether we want it or not, these other dimensions—whatever their ontological reality—constantly emerge in our daily life, either through the stories we tell our children, in the arts, in some of the religions we create, and certainly in our dreams. These other worlds and beings greatly enrich our existence. Without them, as without our remaining forests and their animals, the world would be a duller place.

1. A remarkable exception would be the influence of Iroquois Confederacy ideas on the Constitution and Bill of Rights of the United States (see http://www.senate.gov /reference/resources/pdf/hconres331.pdf).

2. Gimbutas M. *The Language of the Goddess*. San Francisco: HarperSan Francisco; 1989.

3. Harrison RP. *Forests: The Shadow of Civilization*. Chicago and London: The University of Chicago Press; 1992.

4. Crosby A. *Ecological Imperialism: The Biological Expansion of Europe, 900–1900*. Cambridge: Cambridge University Press; 1986.

5. Winkelman M. *Psychointegrator plants: Their role in human culture and health*. In: Winkelman M, Andritzky W, editors. *Yearbook of cross-cultural medicine and psychotherapy: Sacred plants, consciousness and healing*. Vol. 6. Berlin: Verlag und Vertrieb; 1996. p.9–53.

6. Winkelman M. *Shamanism: A Biopsychosocial Paradigm of Consciousness and Healing*. Oxford: Praeger; 2010.

7. Klein D, Cruz Ceballos I. *El Arte Secreto del Ecuador Precolombino*. Milán: 5 Continentes Ediciones; 2007.

8. Reichel-Dolmatoff G. *Goldwork and Shamanism: An Iconographic Study of the Gold Museum*. Medellín: Editorial Colina; 1988.

9. Luna LE, Ameringo P. *Ayahuasca Visions: The Religious Iconography of a Peruvian Shaman*. Berkeley: North Atlantic Books; 1992.

10. Schultes RE, Bright A. *Ancient Gold Pectorals from Colombia: Mushroom Effigies?* Botanical Museum Leaflets, Vol. 27, Nos. 5–6: 113–141. Harvard University, Cambridge, Massachusetts; 1979.

11. Reichel-Dolmatoff G. *The Shaman and The Jaguar: A Study of Narcotic Drugs Among the Indians of Colombia*. Philadelphia: Temple University Press; 1975.

12. Stone, RR. *The Jaguar Within: Shamanic Trance in Ancient Central and South American Art*. Austin: University of Texas Press; 2011.

13. Clottes J, Lewis-Williams D. *The Shamans of Prehistory: Trance and Magic in the Painted Caves*. New York: Harry N. Abrams, Inc. Publishers; 1998.

14. Lewis-Williams D. *The Mind in the Cave: Consciousness and the Origins of Art*. London: Thames and Hudson; 2002.

15. Hancock G. *Supernatural: Meetings with the Ancient Teachers of Mankind*. London: Century; 2005.
16. Torres CM. *Archeological Evidence for the Antiquity of Psychoactive Plant Use in the Central Andes*. Annales del Museo Civico Rovereto 1996;11:291–326.
17. Fernández Distel, AA. *Hallazgo de pipas en complejos precerámicos del borde de la Puna Jujeña (Republica Argentina) y el empleo de alucinógenos por parte de las mismas culturas*. Estudios Arqueológicos 1980;5:55–75.
18. Torres CM, Rebke DB. *Anadenanthera: visionary plant of ancient South America*. New York: The Haworth Press; 2006.
19. Fung R. *Las Aldas: Su ubicación dentro del proceso histórico del Perú antiguo*. Dédalo 9–10, Museu de Arte e Arqueología, Universidade de Saô Paulo, Brazil; 1972.
20. Polia Meconi M. *Despierta, remedio, cuenta…: Adivinos y Médicos del Ande*, 2 vols. Lima: Fondo Editorial, Pontificia Universidad Católica del Perú; 1996.
21. Pearsall DM. *The Origins of Plant Cultivation in South America*. In: Cowan CW, Watson, PJ, editors. *The Origins of Agriculture: An International Perspective*. Washington: Smithsonian Institution Press; 1992. p.173–206.
22. Dillehay TD, Rossen J, Ugent D, Karathanasis A, Vásquez V, Netherly PJ. *Early Holocene coca chewing in northern Peru*. Antiquity 2010; 84(326):939–53.
23. Frecska E. *The Shaman's Journey: Supernatural or Natural? A Neuro-Ontological Interpretation of Spiritual Experiences*. In: Strassman R, Wojtowicz S, Luna LE, Frecska E, editors. *Inner Paths to Outer Space: Journeys to Alien Worlds through Psychedelics and Other Spiritual Techniques*. Rochester, Vermont: Park Street Press; 2008. p.162–206
24. James, W. *Varieties of Religious Experience*. New York: Modern Library; 1929.

"A TRAIN OF DELIGHTFUL VISIONS": EARLY SCIENTIFIC ENCOUNTERS WITH PSYCHEDELICS

MIKE JAY

"NOTHING EXISTS BUT THOUGHTS": NITROUS OXIDE

In a clinical laboratory in Bristol in April 1799, the young chemist Humphry Davy became the first person to inhale a psychoactive dose of nitrous oxide. He was astonished to feel "a highly pleasurable thrilling in the chest and extremities," and to observe that "the objects around me became dazzling and my hearing more acute."[1 p458] The experiment progressed to violent exhilaration and eventually to oblivion; a few days later, after he had recovered his senses and reassembled his memories from scribbled notes, he offered the gas to his friend, the poet Robert Southey. Southey was equally astonished by "a sensation perfectly new and delightful," and declared that "the atmosphere of the highest of all possible heavens must be composed of this gas."[1 p508-9]

The experiments of Davy and his associates, at the dawn of the nineteenth century, mark the beginning of the modern scientific engagement with psychedelics. Nitrous oxide was a new substance, not known in nature, with entirely unpredicted effects on human consciousness; it was the first time that such a substance had been explored systematically by a group of researchers attempting to describe and understand its effects on the mind. Psychedelic plants had been used since time immemorial in cultures across the globe, but the meaning of the experience they generated had always been implicit in the plant itself, and its ritual and cultural context. For the Western scientific mind, any such meaning needed to be discovered, or invented.

Robert Southey's phrase "the atmosphere of heaven" gives an indication of the spirit, playful in form but serious in intent, in which these early psychonauts framed their experience. The language is superficially religious, but the effect is the opposite: to reclaim transcendence from the monopoly of religious dogma. 'Atmosphere,' an exclusively scientific term at this time, signals that the most exalted realms of human experience can now be attained via the laboratory rather than the Holy Spirit. But the lyrical metaphor also points to the limits of materialist explanations: the epiphany can no more be reduced to hard data than it can be bounded by scripture. Such new and extraordinary mental states demand a new language, beyond both faith and reason, to capture their essence.

It was around this search for a "language of feeling,"[1] p494 as Davy called it, that the nitrous oxide experiments came to focus: a parallel quest to that which the young poets of the circle, such as Southey and Samuel Taylor Coleridge, were pursuing in their art. Initially, the trials had been conceived within a medical framework—the search for a novel treatment for consumption, or tuberculosis—but nitrous oxide's startling subjective effects opened up a much wider field of enquiry. How could an artificially created substance have such a profound effect on the human mind? There were deep chemical and medical mysteries here—the nature of respiration, the connection between mind and body, the chemical basis of life—but there were also questions that chemistry could not begin to answer. As the gas took hold, many subjects felt an overwhelming sense of cosmic revelation: but was this an illusion of the senses, or a glimpse into a deeper reality?

Davy investigated these questions in as many ways as he could think of, not least via self-experiment with heroic doses of gas.

He made dozens of trials on tissue samples and live animals; he ran experimental sessions with volunteer subjects including fellow chemists, doctors, poets, playwrights, social reformers and philosophers, and he inhaled the gas himself, often several times a day, filling notebooks with chemical data, poetic fragments and snatches of revelation.[2] On Boxing Day 1799 he made a climactic self-experiment in which he stripped to the waist, placed a thermometer under his arm and enclosed himself in an airtight box into which 20 quarts of nitrous oxide was pumped every five minutes. After an hour and a quarter, when he felt that his system was saturated, he stepped from the box and breathed a further 20 quarts directly from an oiled silk bag. At this dosage, his consciousness was entirely transformed:

> *I lost all connection with external things; trains of vivid visible images passed through my mind and were connected with words in such a manner as to produce perceptions perfectly novel. I existed in a world of newly connected and newly modified ideas [...] with the most intense belief and prophetic manner I exclaimed to Dr. Kinglake, "Nothing exists but thoughts!"*[1] p488-9

In transcending the limits of space and time, Davy claimed, he had also transcended the question of whether the effects of the gas were 'all in the mind.' He had shown, through empirical means, the extent to which reality itself is constructed in the mind, from the information relayed by the senses. A consciousness-altering agent such as nitrous oxide, by radically altering the human sensorium, was able to generate an entirely different reality.

Although the nitrous oxide experiments were regarded as a therapeutic failure and largely ignored by the medical profession, they were influential on nineteenth-century culture in numerous ways. They gained in profile from the subsequent careers of their subjects: in 1813 Robert Southey was made Poet Laureate, and by the 1820s his lyrical endorsements were being used to advertise nitrous oxide demonstrations, or 'laughing gas' shows, which became a staple of popular entertainment. Davy's insight that the imagination has the power not merely to reflect or interpret the world but to create it would be developed, not least through Davy's close friend Samuel Taylor Coleridge, into the philosophical under-pinning of the emerging Romantic movement.[3] Most significantly Davy himself went on to become President of the Royal Society and a sensationally popular science lecturer, the first to engage the non-specialist public with its dramas and discoveries. His fame was intimately entwined with his youthful self-experiments with the gas, which became an emblem of the heroic commitment to the pursuit of knowledge that science demanded of its practition-ers in the new century.

This first scientific encounter with the new mind-altering drugs, as its fame spread, established several bold precedents. It made self-experimentation, and the qualities of subjective experience, central to their investigation. It staked radical claims about the extent to which such experiences could recalibrate the relationship between subjective experience and the material world, insisting that the former constructs the latter. It also invented a novel but enduring format for psychedelic reportage. Davy's published ac-count of the experiments combined organic chemistry with poetic introspection, creating a hybrid of mutually unintelligible lan-guages to bridge the gap between science and sensation. The work of Alexander and Ann Shulgin, whose division of their ground-breaking drug reportage into 'synthesis' followed by 'qualitative comments' or 'extensions' has become the classic contemporary style, illustrates Davy's success in establishing an enduring form at the first attempt.[4,5]

"PERSONAL EXPERIENCE IS THE CRITERION OF TRUTH": HASHISH

Because self-experimentation with psychedelic drugs is so firmly excluded from the mainstream of scientific practice today, it is often assumed that the 'scientific method' is intrinsically unable to accommodate it. But this exclusion is a relatively recent phenomenon: for the majority of the time between Davy's experiments and the present, the scientific investigation of psychoactive drugs was driven by personal experiment. The discovery of both ether and nitrous oxide anaesthesia, for example, were the result of recreational 'frolics' among doctors, surgeons and dentists, followed by personal trials. In an era where the scope of laboratory medicine was limited and experiments on human volunteers fraught with ethical concerns, it was normal for scientific researchers to use themselves as test subjects.[6]

In the case of psychoactive drugs, however, the argument for self-experiment was even stronger: altered perceptions and sensations can only be reliably established at first hand. A classic justification for the practice was given by the French psychiatrist Jacques-Joseph Moreau de Tours, the first Western doctor to present a full description of the effects of hashish intoxication. Moreau opened his influential monograph *Hashish and Mental Illness*[7] with a clear statement of principle:

> *At the outset I must make this point, the verity of which is unquestionable: personal experience is the criterion of truth here. I challenge the right of anyone to discuss the effects of hashish if he is not speaking for himself and if he has not been in a position to evaluate them in light of sufficient repeated use.*[7 p1]

For Moreau, self-experiment was not merely an indispensable methodology but the key to hashish's most exciting potential application. He was particularly interested in the drug's ability to manifest many of the familiar symptoms of mental illness (such as hallucinations, distortion of time and space and *idées fixes*); but his proposals for its use in therapy revolved around giving it not to the patients but to their doctors. The greatest handicap faced by the psychiatrist was, he argued, the inability to experience their patients' conditions; but hashish gave them a means to do so, safely and reversibly:

> *Can we be certain we are in a condition to understand these sick people when they tell us of their observations? [...] To comprehend the ravings of a madman, it is necessary to have raved oneself, but without having lost the awareness of one's madness.*[7 p17]

Moreau, like Davy, also sought understandings of the hashish experience from the wider world of art, literature and philosophy, and by 1845 he was instrumental in orchestrating the hashish *salons* that became known as the 'Club des Hachichins.' Meeting in the splendid frescoed rooms of the Hôtel Pimodan on the Ile de St Louis, they drew (or were rumoured to have drawn) most of the luminary figures of Paris' literary demi-monde. References to hashish soon appeared in the correspondence of Honoré de Balzac and Gustave Flaubert, and the published works of Alexandre Dumas, Gérard de Nerval, Théophile Gautier and Charles Baudelaire. At the powerful dose specified by Moreau—three or four grams taken orally—hashish is effectively a psychedelic, and the milieu of the Club des Hachichins offered the most substantial literary engagement with the psychedelic experience thus far.[8]

"A NEW ARTIFICIAL PARADISE": MESCALINE

During the late nineteenth century anxieties about psychoactive drugs became more widespread against the background of a growing Temperance movement, public campaigns to control or prohibit alcohol, and medical models that were expanding the new diagnosis of 'addiction' to label all intoxication as pathological and deviant. It is striking, however, that psychedelic researches continued with little controversy. The most extensive example is the western encounter in the 1890s with the peyote cactus, which progressed through the self-experiments of an ethnographer, a physiologist, a psychologist and an art critic, as well as the chemist who eventually succeeded in isolating its active alkaloid, mescaline.

The hallucinogenic properties of peyote had been observed by the early Spanish colonists of Mexico, but had been construed by Jesuit scholars as demonic possession.[9,10] They were first described in scientific terms by James Mooney, a Smithsonian Institute ethnographer who encountered peyote rites in 1890 while studying the pan-Indian Ghost Dance phenomenon. The use of peyote, he established, was relatively new to the northern Plains tribes, having been brought from its traditional home in Mexico and the south only during the previous generation. Mooney participated in the rites that would later become the sacrament of the Native American Church and described the role of the cactus for its Indian subjects as:

> *a panacea in medicine, a source of inspiration, and the key which opens to them all the glories of another world [...] the psychologic effect is perhaps the most interesting, as it certainly is the most wonderful, phenomenon in connection with the plant.*[11 p10]

The primary focus of Mooney's reporting was to influence government policy in preserving Native American traditions and maintaining the right to freedom of worship. However, a version of his report was published in the *Therapeutic Gazette* and drew the interest of medical researchers. By 1895 the Berlin toxicologist Lewis Lewin was already attempting to isolate the active ingredient of peyote (known to botanists at this point as the 'mescal' cactus), and a pair of physiologists from Columbia University, DW Prentiss and Francis Morgan, decided to make clinical trials on volunteers. Their first subject, within a couple of hours of ingesting four and a half cactus buttons, reported:

> *a train of delightful visions such as no human being ever enjoyed under normal conditions [...] my pleasure so far passed the more*

ordinary realms of delight as to bring me to that ecstatic state
in which our exclamations of delight become involuntary.[12 p580]

The second subject, however, had a markedly different experience, in which similarly intense visions led to mounting paranoid
anxieties. Prentiss and Morgan recorded:

A marked symptom was a feeling of great distrust and resent-
ment which he exhibited towards those who were making the
experiment with him. He realised his 'mental inferiority' and
believed that we were secretly laughing at his condition.[12 p581]

These wildly divergent responses highlighted a challenge to the
scientific investigation of psychedelics that had already emerged
in trials of nitrous oxide and hashish. Most drugs, even most psychoactive drugs, do not produce opposite reactions in different
subjects: amphetamines, for example, are not a stimulant for some
and a sedative for others. The effect of psychedelics in intensifying
both positive and negative responses made them hard to describe
within standard clinical methodologies. James Mooney, from an
ethnographer's perspective, was unsurprised by this paradoxical outcome. For the Native American, the peyote experience is
culturally primed and undertaken within an established ritual
context, while "in several of the medical experiments the patient
seems to have hastily swallowed a sandwich and plunged at once
into exciting action."[11 p11]

Science might establish the chemistry of the plant's effects,
and eventually even the precise mechanisms of its action, but it
could not supply its character or meaning. There was no reason
to expect 'civilised' subjects to have a similar experience to Native Americans, or indeed to one another.

The challenge of constructing a new, western and scientific
framework for understanding peyote was swiftly taken up. Despite
the rising cultural anxieties about the dangers of newly discovered drugs—cocaine use, for example, was escalating and clinics

beginning to witness their first compulsive injecting 'addicts'[8]— peyote intoxication was perceived as a lengthy and nauseous ordeal with little potential for abuse. Its reported effects were, however, of great interest to some specialists, and on 24 May 1896 one of the most distinguished figures in American psychiatry, Silas Weir Mitchell, intrigued by Prentiss and Morgan's paper, swallowed a dose and overcame "a sense of great gastric discomfort"[13 p1625] before going out on his consulting rounds.

After an initial couple of hours of unusual vigour, Mitchell was obliged to abandon his patients; he lay down in a darkened room, closed his eyes and spent an "enchanted two hours" absorbed in vivid eidetic imagery. He had undertaken the experiment with the idea that peyote might be useful in the therapy of nervous disorders, but he now realised that the ordeal would be too physically demanding for the patients he had in mind. He was struck, however, by its potential for cognitive and psychological insights, to "be able with a whole mind to experiment mentally upon such phenomena as I have described is an unusual privilege. Here is unlocked a storehouse of glorified memorial treasures."[13 p1627]

As with many of the early scientific encounters with psychedelics, first-hand experience changed the framework of meaning: approached through the lens of one discipline, peyote had come into sharper focus through another. The non-specialist background of the nineteenth-century scientist was conducive to this kind of interdisciplinary fluidity: Mitchell, for example, was not only a psychiatrist but a novelist interested in the processes of creativity. His report in turn inspired a subject who was not only a psychologist but an art critic. Havelock Ellis had just written his controversial study of homosexuality, *Sexual Inversion*,[14] when he became perhaps the first person to take peyote in Britain, in his rooms at the Temple in London. His essay, published in 1898 under the title 'Mescal: a new artificial paradise,' focused on the aesthetic qualities of the experience: searching for meaning not in physiological mechanism but in the play of the senses and the imagination.

He compared his visions to Maori architecture, the moucrabieh woodcarving of Cairo and the 'hyperaesthesia' of Claude Monet, and concluded:

> *If it should ever chance that the consumption of mescal becomes a habit, the favourite poet of the mescal drinker will certainly be Wordsworth [...] many of his most memorable poems and phrases can not—one is almost tempted to say—be appreciated in their full significance by one who has never been under the influence of mescal.*[15]

The sight of his cigarette box shining like an amethyst, or the back of his chair glowing like a ruby in the pulsating light of the gas lamp, awakened in Ellis a Wordsworthian sense of intimacy with even the most humble details of his surroundings: an awareness that humanity and the natural world interpenetrate, and indeed create one another.

Self-experimentation opened up new aesthetic and philosophical vistas, but it was equally valuable for the harder sciences. Lewis Lewin was still finding the active chemical in the cactus elusive: many different 'vegetable fractions' could be extracted by different processes, but it was not clear from external observation which was responsible for the consciousness-altering effects. Another chemist, Arthur Heffter of Leipzig University, resolved the problem in 1897 by ingesting small amounts of different extracts and thereby winning the race to identify the psychoactive alkaloid, which he named 'mezcalin.'

WILLIAM JAMES AND THE RELIGIOUS EXPERIENCE

By the dawn of the twentieth century, then, psychedelics had been studied through a wide variety of frameworks—medicine, chemistry, ethnography, philosophy, aesthetics—under the unifying assumption that direct experience was a necessary part of the process. Despite the rise of positivist and materialist conceptions of science,[16] subjective accounts had remained central to the investigation. Yet the scientific method remained, as eloquently argued by the psychologist William James, intrinsically limited when it came to understanding mystical and religious experiences. The claim of psychedelics is essentially materialist: that a chemical introduced into the human body is generating the experience. Yet the experience itself can directly contradict this premise, for example by announcing itself to the subject as direct communication with the divine. For James, this created an unresolvable paradox: how could one understand these forms of 'extraordinary consciousness' in their own terms, while also bringing them within the purview of science?

Inspired by Weir Mitchell's report, James attempted an experiment with peyote but found the nausea too intense: "I will," he wrote to his brother Henry, "take the visions on trust." (quoted in[17 p125]). Instead he inhaled nitrous oxide, and in its intoxication found a glorious reconciliation of opposites, and a resolution to the seemingly contradictory imperatives of religion and science.[18] In *The Varieties of Religious Experience*[19] he cited his self-experiments to argue that, however imponderable the insights derived from mystical states might be, the states themselves were psychologically real, and as capable as any rational state of generating meaningful thoughts, beliefs and actions. Whatever claims can be made of psychedelics follow from this essential fact:

> *Our normal waking consciousness, rational consciousness as we call it, is but one special type of consciousness, whilst all about it, parted from it by the filmiest of screens, there lie potential forms of consciousness entirely different... no account of the universe in its totality can be final which leaves these other forms of consciousness quite disregarded.*[19 p388]

James' classic formulation echoes Humphry Davy on nitrous oxide a century before in arguing that the psychedelic experience is not a degraded or impaired form of 'normal' consciousness, but a demonstration that normative assumptions fail to encompass the plurality of mental possibilities.

CODA: THE SUBLIME

During the nineteenth century, psychedelics were explored from multiple perspectives: arguably more, indeed, than the twentieth, during which the scope of scientific inquiry would narrow as anti-drug ideologies took hold. Many of these early frameworks for understanding the psychedelic experience have been rediscovered over the previous half-century, but others have been lost entirely. In conclusion, let us consider a largely forgotten paradigm from the eighteenth and early nineteenth centuries that was used to frame some of the earliest encounters: the sublime.

In his influential *Philosophical Enquiry into the Origin of Our Ideas of the Sublime and the Beautiful,*[20] Edmund Burke argued that the two categories are fundamental opposites. Beauty arises from a sense of cosmic proportion and harmony, but the sublime ruptures this harmony and submerges us in ecstasy, awe and terror. It is the result of a collision between the human scale in which we live our daily lives and the true scale of the cosmos: the unfathomable span of geological time, the infinite expanse of the universe, the inscrutable processes of evolution. This produces a frozen moment—in Burke's words, "that state of the soul, in which all its motions are suspended"[20 p101]—when we glimpse the impossibility of reconciling our individual human perspective with a cosmos that so vastly exceeds our grasp. Our sensorium is overwhelmed by perceptions that defy normal comparisons, and we are temporarily immersed in what William James described as "the blooming, buzzing confusion"[21 p460] of raw experience itself.

'Sublime' was a word frequently reached for by Humphry Davy and his associates in their attempts to capture the epiphanies of nitrous oxide. Like Robert Southey's formulation of 'the atmosphere of heaven,' it does not assume a divine origin for the psychedelic experience, but equally it insists that it is more potent than reason and not susceptible to it. It is not entirely a physical property, nor entirely a subjective sensation: it emerges from the ambiguous territory between the observer and the observed, describing the interplay between the mind and external reality and allowing their relations to be constantly recalibrated.[22] As such it transcends the fault line between materialist and spiritual interpretations of the experience: the two may never be entirely compatible, but perhaps both can agree that psychedelics are sublime.

1. Davy H. *Researches Chemical and Philosophical, Chiefly Concerning Nitrous Oxide and its Respiration*. London: J. Johnson; 1800.
2. Jay M. *The Atmosphere of Heaven*. New Haven and London: Yale University Press; 2009.
3. Abrams MH. *The Mirror and the Lamp*. New York: Oxford University Press; 1953.
4. Shulgin A, Shulgin A. *PIHKAL: a Chemical Love Story*. Berkeley: Transform Press; 1991.
5. Shulgin A, Shulgin A. *TIHKAL: the Continuation*. Berkeley: Transform Press; 1997.
6. Altman LK. *Who Goes First?: the Story of Self-experimentation in Medicine*. New York: Random House; 1986.
7. Moreau de Tours J-J. *Hashish and Mental Illness [Hachich et l'Alienation Mentale]*. New York: Raven Press (Barnett GJ, translator); 1970 [1845].
8. Jay M. *Emperors of Dreams*. Sawtree: Dedalus Press; revised edition 2011 [2000].
9. Escohotado A. *Historia de las Drogas Vol. 1*. Madrid: Alianza Editorial; 1989.
10. Cervantes F. *The Devil in the New World*. New Haven: Yale University Press; 1994.
11. Mooney J. *The Mescal Plant and Ceremony*. Therapeutic Gazette 1896;20:7–11.
12. Prentiss DW, Morgan FP. *Anhalonium Lewinii (Mescal Buttons): a Study of the Drug*. Therapeutic Gazette 1895;9:577–85.
13. Mitchell SW. *The Effects of Anhalonium lewinii (the Mescal Button)*. British Medical Journal 1896;2:1625–9.
14. Ellis H, Symonds JA. *Sexual Inversion*. New York: Arno Press; 1975[1897].
15. Ellis, H. *Mescal: A New Artificial Paradise*. The Contemporary Review 1898;73:130–41. Available from: http://www.erowid.org/plants/peyote/peyote_article1.shtml
16. Daston L, Galison P. *Objectivity*. New York: Zone Books; 2007.
17. Strafford PG, Golightly BH. *LSD: the Problem-solving Psychedelic*. New York: Award Books; 1967.
18. James W. *On Some Hegelisms*. Mind 1882;7:186–208.
19. James W. *The Varieties of Religious Experience*. New York: Penguin; 1985 [1902].
20. Burke E. *A Philosophical Enquiry into the Origin of our Ideas of the Sublime and the Beautiful*. London: Penguin; 1998 [1757].
21. James, W. *Principles of Psychology*. London: Little, Brown; 1926 [1890].
22. Shaw P. *The Sublime*. Chippenham: Routledge; 2006.

PSYCHEDELIC FORMATIONS IN LITERATURE

ROBERT DICKINS

Between 1954 and 1964 a number of books were published that described introspective, hallucinogenic drug experiences. These texts range a number of forms and styles including personal recounts, novels, essays, and even psychedelic guide books. Collectively speaking, however, it is the context of these drug experiences that is of interest here, rather than the fact of the experiences themselves. For the purpose of this essay then, the six primary texts have been selected because they specifically deal with psychiatrically-facilitated experiences, although it should be noted that a number of other works not included could easily be added.

This body of texts, which hereafter will be described as *psychedelic literature*, is the result of a boom in psychiatric research with hallucinogens during the same period. This research led to the development of a number of new theories and practises, primarily concerning the drugs d-lysergic acid diethylamide (LSD) and mescaline. The extent to which these methods, theories and practises share a dynamic with psychedelic literature is the point of examination here.

This essay will argue that the publication of psychedelic literature is an attempt to socially, and culturally, legitimise the new psychiatric practises, which arose in response to hallucinogen research and an increasing public interest. Also, it will be argued that as a body of work psychedelic literature demonstrates a period of territorialisation within the methodology of that research field.

The result of which was to create a distinct, literary assemblage, which, it is hoped, will lay the foundations for further literary criticism in the field of psychedelic studies.

In order to achieve this, the form and content of psychedelic literature will be analysed in regard to the psychiatric practises, mainly the *psycholytic* and *psychedelic*, with the aim of creating a cartography of their relationship. It is necessary first, however, to say something of the context in which these drugs were being utilised and how this broadly developed into literary form.

Having first synthesised LSD in 1938, Albert Hofmann famously became the first person to intentionally consume the hallucinogen on 19 April 1943. Then in 1947, when Sandoz Corporation, the company that Hofmann worked for, was satisfied with testing, LSD was marketed as a research chemical. It did so with the suggestion of two possible applications in clinical-medical human research. Firstly, LSD was introduced for use in analytical psychotherapy as a means of accessing repressed memory and the unconscious. And secondly, Sandoz marketed LSD psychotomimetically, which is to say the chemical was thought to condition a 'model psychosis' in users.[1] This essay will be structured by plotting the trajectories of these two research approaches through literature.

The practicalities of clinical psychiatry and psychoanalysis lent a certain form to psychedelic literature. The primary texts of this essay all take place over either one or several LSD/mescaline sessions, depending on the approach and, for the most part, are conducted in a single room with a trained psychiatrist as a sitter. For example, *A Drug-Taker's Notes*[2] by Richard Heron Ward. Structurally, the book is divided between eight chapters, the second to seventh of which detail his six LSD sessions, with contextual arguments making up the first and eighth chapters. The content of Ward's six sessions takes the form of notes taken during the experiences, which are then framed through retrospective comment. The model of clinical research not only provides a setting for these texts but also the form in which narratives are constructed. However, there was no single methodology that holds true for all texts and it is the variations therein that concern us here.

Initially, using LSD as an access to the unconscious made a degree of sense. Sigmund Freud's (1856–1939) psychoanalysis was developed in order to produce a certain knowledge as an explanatory field for conduct and experiences outside other intellectual disciplines, dreams for instance.[3] The visual and imaginative phenomena that LSD provided its users with were, firstly, uncharted territories and, secondly, the manifestations of its effects were, in part at least, analogous to dream data. Therefore, working on the assumption that the data did indeed provide clues to the state of one's unconscious, LSD held the promise of being a useful aid in therapy.

In 1952 Dr. Ronald Sandison (1916–2010) became the first individual on record to bring LSD, which he acquired from Sandoz, into Britain. As well as being trained in psychiatry, Sandison was also versed in Freudian and Jungian analysis.[1] In 1954 Sandison published a paper in the *Journal of Mental Science* that stated:

> *Our clinical impressions have convinced us that LSD when used as an adjunct to skilled psychotherapy, is of the greatest value in the obsessional and anxiety groups accompanied by mental tension.*[4]

Sandison's pioneering research led to the development of what he termed *psycholytic therapy,* a method of interpreting LSD data that had its roots in Freudian and Jungian analysis, dealing with unconscious pathologies and imagery.

My Self and I[5] was written by the American Thelma Moss but was published pseudonymously under the name Constance A. Newland. Moss underwent psycholytic therapy in the practice of two Freudian therapists called Arthur Chandler and Mortimer Hartman working in the United States. According to the book Moss went through the psycholytic therapy course in order to cure herself of 'sexual frigidity.' Obviously, a rather dated and misogynistic prognosis of neurosis, but one that hits at the heart of Freudian pathology.

Dr. Ronald Sandison wrote the book's introduction, which demonstrates the spread of his psycholytic therapy to the United States. However, to what extent has this new therapy adopted the models with which it was originally conceived? Sandison is clear about this: "Freud not only gave us a theory, he also gave us a method of treatment. The theory has proved to be the most adequate, the tools of treatment the least adequate."[5 p15] With this in mind then, it can be said that the Freudian theory of the unconscious provides the context for her visions (i.e., the unconscious), and plays a role in the nature of the content in *My Self and I*:

> *Yes. Unconsciously I had equated the enema nozzle with the penis: both were instruments of torture which would, if I were to feel anything, explode me into a long scream in a tunnel. At long last, I had uncovered the classic Freudian "trauma" responsible for my sexual difficulty: one too-strong, too-hot enema, received when I was two and a half years old. It was preposterous. Yet undeniable.*[5 p149]

However, if Freud is providing the context, what is the method of treatment that structures the manner in which her visionary experience is explained in the text? "Jung gave us the method of active fantasy which the author has used with great effect during her treatment sessions."[5 p15] Sandison goes on to write that the role of the therapist is not to suggest or advise but rather encourage the patient to live out the 'fantasies.' This very fact underlines the faith that psycholytic therapists had in LSD's ability to reveal elements of the unconscious. It is seen as such an intrinsic value in the drug that the therapist need only facilitate the process by using Jung's method of 'active fantasy.'

In terms of form *and* content an interesting occurrence takes place between the Freudian and Jungian influences; the two approaches are segmented, both qualitatively and quantitatively as sections of the book. Part II, 'The Case History,' deals largely with childhood memory and trauma related to her sexual neurosis; the shorter Part III, 'My Self and I,' from which the title is taken, is concerned with *integration*, not simply rediscovering a memory. Moss wanted to "resolve the battle of her two sexes" by going "beyond Freud's personal unconscious into the collective unconscious of Jung—a realm of which I had only the vaguest knowledge at the time" and thus be able to "achieve a fusion between my self, and me."[5 p208-9]

The segmentation of the unconscious through the delineation of Freudian and Jungian spaces demonstrates the territorial limits of the psycholytic method in psychedelic literature. During her first 15 sessions Moss explored the space of her personal unconscious and a certain criteria of Freudian pathology; during the subsequent seven sessions she explored a Jungian space, characterised by integration and archetypes. The psycholytic method clearly played an important role in lending form and content to *My Self and I* and the successful therapy it described can be said to be a social validation. However, the segmenting of the psychedelic territory in the theoretical approaches to hallucinogens had begun some eight years before. To explore this segmentation and the manner in which it contributed to the formation of psychedelic literature, it is necessary to describe the *psychotomimetic* approach.

Doctors Humphry Osmond, John Smythies and Abram Hoffer, in Canada and the UK, began the 1950s investigating the connection between mescaline and schizophrenia.[6] Their approach to understanding the effect of hallucinogens is called *psychotomimetic*. Psychotomimetic means 'to mimic psychosis' and was first coined by Kurt Beringer in 1927 in reference to the effects of mescaline.[7] This ties their research directly into the second possible application Sandoz gave for LSD when it first marketed the drug in 1947. Though the doctors would soon turn their attention to LSD, a meeting between Osmond and the California-based, English author, Aldous Huxley (1894–1963) would produce the first example of psychedelic literature, one concerned with mescaline.

After collaborating with Smythies on a paper entitled *Schizophrenia: A New Approach*,[8] Osmond received a letter from Huxley who had recently read the paper. Huxley invited Osmond to come and stay with him in his Californian home and indicated that he would like to take part in a mescaline experiment.[9] As a result of Osmond's facilitation Huxley published two texts: *The Doors of Perception* and *Heaven and Hell*.[10] In regard to this present essay, it is a cartographical metaphor that Huxley employs in the latter book that is of importance:

> *A man consists of what I may call an Old World of personal consciousness and, beyond a dividing sea, a series of New Worlds—the not too distant Virginias and Carolinas of the personal sub-conscious and the vegetative soul; the Far West of the collective unconscious, with its flora of symbols, its tribes of aboriginal archetypes; and, across another, vaster ocean, at the antipodes of everyday consciousness, the world of Visionary Experience.*[10 p62]

Whereas for Sandison LSD's value lay in its intrinsic ability to reveal elements of the unconscious through a visual landscape, which the therapist need only facilitate, for Huxley the scope was wider. Instead of simply being a kind of key that gave one access to the unconscious, LSD was an experiential vehicle for manoeuvring around the psyche. Not only did this transform the psychiatrist into a guide, of sorts, but it posited the existence of segments of the psyche other than the unconscious. In the above quote, Huxley delineates them, the Old/New World, the Far West of Jung, and the 'world of visionary experience.' It is this final visionary space that Huxley primarily concerns himself with in the two books, and the discourse he invites has two major effects. Firstly, it opened a discursive, literary territory. And, secondly, it helped lead, through

Osmond, to the development of *psychedelic therapy*. Before exploring the relationship between this therapy and a number of texts, it is necessary to first mention how Huxley's visionary space became a point of discourse within literature.

Oxford professor Robert Zaehner (1913–1974) published his first response to Huxley's *The Doors of Perception*, an article entitled 'The Menace of Mescaline.'[11] He then expanded on his criticisms in the book *Mysticism Sacred and Profane*.[12] Broadly speaking, his argument revolved around whether or not a hallucinogenic drug had the capacity to produce a preternatural or religious experience and Zaehner's position, against that of Huxley's, was explicitly against this ability. Whatever the correct answer, however, the effect was to legitimise the question and it would come to play a role in therapeutic practise and all subsequent psychedelic texts. Moreover, this counter-position gave context to the first work of psychedelic literature dealing with LSD.

The writer, Richard Heron Ward, began a course of LSD sessions in the UK the same year the visionary space discourse between Huxley and Zaehner began. Three years later Victor Gollancz published Ward's account of his LSD experiences.[2] The book describes six LSD sessions the author undertook between 1954–1955 under the supervision of a female medical psychiatrist, only identified as Dr. X. The purpose of the doctor's research was to study the effects of LSD on mentally ill patients and Ward's role was as a control subject. Ward writes that he volunteered because "I wanted, in a word, help for my unbelief, who already believed that consciousness is not a constant."[2 p13] Interestingly, it is possible to identify the influence of the visionary discourse from both sides of the argument. On the one hand, Ward follows Huxley's belief in the different dimensions of the psyche but does not believe that LSD can take its user to the visionary, or religious, space.

The progression from dreamless sleep to wakefulness may be said to be a progression upwards through several degrees of consciousness. But need we take it for granted that the progression cannot be continued from wakefulness into a consciousness of yet another quality?[2 p14]

What is possible to understand from this was the establishment of a segmentary psyche within the discourse of, not only the psychiatric practise, but in the literature as well. Furthermore, while the ability for accessing personal, and collective unconscious, spaces with LSD had become legitimate research areas, the contentious new one, the psycho-spiritual, began to establish itself. Partially in response to this new therapy, *psychedelic therapy*, was developed.

Famously, the friendship of Osmond and Huxley gave birth to the word psychedelic and, moreover, it gave birth to *psychedelic therapy*, which aimed at manifesting a mystical or religious experience in those who underwent it. On the surface, this may seem to be a million miles away from the psychotomimetic reading, however, they do share a certain value, namely the ability to *manifest* a state of consciousness, as opposed to revealing pre-existing pathologies and the unconscious, as in psycholytic theory.

Psychedelic therapy was developed in the hope that doctors could use "chemicals to trigger new perceptions of the self"[6 p31] in patients. Whether the subject's own approach to the experience was philosophical, spiritual or epistemological "people regularly believed that the LSD experience fundamentally modified their being."[6 p31] As such, it is argued here, psychedelic therapy was partially developed in response to Huxley's identification of the visionary space and its implications for the potential for mystical and religious experience.

The therapy usually involved higher doses of LSD; drug-free discussions of the patient's life and spiritual/philosophical orientation; statistically fewer sessions than the psycholytic, usually between one and three; and with the purpose of correcting emotional disorders by integrating the experience into the patient's life.[13]

This approach is exemplified in psychedelic literature by Malden Grange Bishop's *The Discovery of Love—A Psychedelic Experience with LSD-25*.[14] Chapter one details how Bishop came to know about LSD and his reasons for taking it; chapter two are his answers to a questionnaire about his life and beliefs; chapter three his preparation prior to the session; four, his experience; and five details the post-experience. The structural format clearly delineates the methodology of psychedelic therapy/territory, but what of the content?

Bishop's psychedelic therapy session was administered by the Institute of Psychedelic Studies in San Francisco. Osmond sat on the board at the institute, which demonstrates the move of psychedelic from descriptive term to therapeutic method and Osmond also contributed the foreword to the book:

> *Those of us who are working with these strange substances trying to find the best way of using them, both in the treatment of illnesses and for the exploration of the human mind, need men like Bishop to come forward and explain that our purposes are serious and good, to emphasize that this is not a diversion, an amusement or an attempt to relieve people of their spare cash.*[14 p9]

At the outset of this essay it was proposed that psychedelic literature was an attempt to socially and culturally legitimise the use of hallucinogens, and in many ways the above quote exemplifies this. It is possible to identify three reasons for this proposition: 1) In response to a rise in public interest, which at the time was increasingly being governed by negative media coverage; 2) to legitimise the newly developing psychedelic theory within the scientific context; and 3), in order to add weight to the theoretical debates that surrounded the identification of the visionary space. In other words, through cultural, scientific and philosophical discourse.

The Discovery of Love addresses all these points in various ways and it is well worth outlining a number of them. Bishop wrote:

> *Trying to explain an LSD experience is like trying to explain*

love, or the experience of being in love. What I really discovered under LSD is love. Some call it God, and I like this term too. It is God; it is love.[14 p14]

There are three relevant implications to draw from Bishop's experience. Firstly that it was a successful treatment and the claims of psychedelic therapy are ratified within the social, literary space. Secondly, not only does this challenge the prevailing negative news trends in the social, by exploring the positive aspects of LSD, it does so while upholding the psychedelic discourse within psychiatry, sanctifying its use scientifically. Thirdly, Bishop contributes to the debate, as defined by the Huxley-Zaehner argument, so far as he posits a religious discourse. Bishop's position is very critical of organised religion and its claims over the mystical experience; whereas the direct, personal, religious experience through LSD is lauded, just as it was by Huxley.

Interestingly, it is possible to read Bishop's text as an amalgamation of psycholytic and psychedelic approaches so far as the content of the author's visions are heavily reliant on his personal memory and relationships. The biographical details act as the raw content of consciousness that are sieved through in order to reach the mystical experience. To utilise Huxley's cartographical metaphor, Bishop moves through the Old World, New World and Far West in order to reach the Antipodes, in which he found the experience of God/Love. The two techniques become part of the same progression, or territory, within the text.

The fabric of the visionary space also changed with the impact of ideas from outside the psychiatric research domain. *Exploring Inner Space*[15] by Adelle Davis (1904–1974)—published pseudonymously under the name Jane Dunlap—is a cogent example of this. Davis underwent five sessions of LSD under the research project of Dr. Oscar Janiger (1918–2001) who was investigating the effects of the drug on writers and artists.[16] Her impetus for taking part in the study, however, came from a magazine article.

Robert Gordon Wasson (1898–1986) was a banker and amateur mycologist.[17] In 1955, along with 'society photographer' Allan Richardson, Wasson met the curandera (female healer) María Sabina (1894–1985) who agreed to hold a ceremony in which the two could eat sacred mushrooms (teonanácatl). They became the first Westerners on record to intentionally consume a hallucinogenic, *Psilocybe* mushroom.[17] An article Wasson wrote for *Life* magazine entitled 'Seeking the Magic Mushroom'[18] had a widespread cultural impact and Davis directly cites it in *Exploring Inner Space*: "The mushrooms, he [Wasson] wrote, caused persons eating them to have visions and mystical experiences."[15 p11]

Arguably the finest post-Huxley text, in terms of literary skill, discussed in this essay, *Exploring Inner Space* is the story of the author's own mystical experience unfolding. In the words of her friend Robert S. Davidson, a clinical psychiatrist and colleague of Dr. Janiger, who wrote the introduction to the book, it was written "partly as a scientific document and partly as an inspiration to people who still believe in the intrinsic spiritual power of the universe."[15 p10] It was intended, therefore, to promote the spiritual use of LSD within society and, via the influence of Wasson, became further literary evidence for the visionary value of LSD.

In conclusion then, it is certainly possible, through a literary examination, to portray a reasonably accurate account of the way in which psychiatric research with LSD developed its own methodologies and the manner in which they constructed a specific understanding of the action of hallucinogens generally. This cartography mimics the theoretical territory that was marked out through understandings of the psyche in psycholytic, psychotomimetic and psychedelic approaches and, furthermore, the texts can be read as explorations of the segments they created. Psychedelic literature evidences the shared dynamics of not only the individual texts and psychiatric practise but of the manner in which their discourse entered into the social as well and can thus be read as culturally-contingent.

Finally, there are a number of other texts, not included because of essay constraints, which could also come under the label psychedelic literature, Huxley's novel *Island*[19] and Timothy Leary, Ralph Metzner and Richard Alpert's *The Psychedelic Experience*[20] for example. These texts variously demonstrate a move out from the clinical setting. As tension about hallucinogens grew in homes and the media, and governments began the process of outlawing the drugs for both the general population and human research projects, their social value was called into question anew. The literary response, however, came from elsewhere. Instead of any increase in the publication of psychedelic texts, it was largely scare-story novels and New Journalism that took up the hallucinogenic mantle in the decade that followed.

1. Roberts A. *Albion Dreaming*. London: Marshall Cavendish; 2008.
2. Ward RH. *A Drug-Taker's Notes*. London: Victor Gollancz; 1957.
3. Frosh S. *The Politics of Psychoanalysis*. London: Macmillan; 1987.
4. Sandison RA, Spencer AM, Whitelaw JD. *The Therapeutic Value of Lysergic Acid Diethylamide in Mental Illness*. Journal of Mental Science 1954;100(419):491–507.
5. Newland CA. *My Self and I*. New York: Coward-McCann; 1962.
6. Dyck E. *Psychedelic Psychiatry*. Baltimore: Johns Hopkins University Press; 2008.
7. Hintzen A, Passie A. *The Pharmacology of LSD*. Oxford: Oxford University Press; 2010.
8. Osmond H, Smythies J. *Schizophrenia: A New Approach*. Journal of Mental Science 1952;98(411):309–15.
9. Huxley A. *Moksha*. Rochester: Park Street Press; 1999.
10. Huxley A. *The Doors of Perception and Heaven and Hell*. London: Flamingo; 1954.
11. Zaehner RC. *The Menace of Mescaline*. New Blackfriars 1954;35(412–13):310–23.
12. Zaehner RC. *Mysticism Sacred and Profane*. London: Oxford University Press; 1957.
13. Grof S. *Realms of the Human Unconscious*. London: Souvenir Press; 2010.
14. Bishop MG. *The Discovery of Love*. New York: Torquil; 1963.
15. Dunlap J. *Exploring Inner Space*. New York: Harcourt, Brace & World; 1961.
16. Dobkin de Rios M, Janiger O. *LSD, Spirituality and the Creative Process*. Rochester: Park Street Press; 2003.
17. Letcher A. *Shroom*. London: Faber and Faber; 2006.
18. Wasson RG. *Seeking the magic mushroom*. Life 1957;May 13:100–20.
19. Huxley A. *Island*. London: Chatto & Windus; 1962.
20. Leary T, Metzner R, Alpert R. *The Psychedelic Experience*. London: Penguin; 2008.

DROP ACID NOT BOMBS: PSYCHEDELIC WEAPONS AT PORTON DOWN

JONATHAN HOBBS

Today, it is hard to imagine the military taking an interest in LSD as a weapon. It is considered to have "a lack of accepted safety for use" even under medical supervision[1] and has been prohibited under international law since 1971 due to "reports of serious damage to health being caused by LSD and similar hallucinogenic substances."[2 p175,3] Nowadays, almost all psychedelic substances are in the UK's most restrictive drugs classification and it is hard to imagine the government approving psychedelics for any use, let alone in warfare.

However, from the late 1950s until the end of the 1960s, British defence researchers experimented with using psychedelic chemicals as weapons at Porton Down, a military research centre specialising in chemical warfare (CW). Despite this seeming absurd nowadays, significant resources were invested in developing psychedelic compounds at Porton and hundreds of experiments were conducted over several years.

SHAPING DEFENCE POLICY: THE RISE AND FALL OF NUCLEAR WEAPONS

The proliferation of nuclear weapons had an enormous effect both directly and indirectly on defence policies worldwide and in 1957,

FIGURE 1: Bertrand Russell speaking at a Committee of 100 rally at Trafalgar Square, London on 25 February 1962. From Bertrand Russell fonds courtesy of McMaster University Libraries.

the UK's offensive CW efforts were scrapped.[4–9] However, nuclear weapons began to fall out of favour in the 1960s in light of popular anti-nuclear protests (Figure 1) and because the nuclear deterrent had been rendered impotent by the promise of mutually assured destruction.[10–12]

In Britain, the Defence Research Policy Committee was frustrated with being kept in the dark regarding nuclear research. By carefully manoeuvring information flows, it shifted the research emphasis to chemical weapons in order to secure more power and funding and to maintain a research network with the US.[6,7,13,14] Another factor was the self-perpetuating 'mirror image effect.'[15] The lack of intelligence about CW capabilities between the West and the USSR resulted in assumptions that the other side must be developing new weapons and, therefore, that more defensive and offensive research was necessary.[8,13,16,17] In the UK, this threat was largely constructed and mobilised by a tightly organised and politically influential alliance of scientists, military officers and the chemical industries who marshalled the uncertainty to gain funding and influence.[5,7,17–19] The result was that, by the 1960s, CW was a high priority at Porton Down.

"HUMANE" WAR: THE EMERGENCE OF INCAPACITANTS

However, due to horrific stories about the use of mustard gas during World War I, the public's distaste for CW largely discouraged British research in this area.[19] Gas warfare evoked revulsion as it was thought to "render bravery superfluous" and be "the ultimate destroyer of individuality, more indiscriminate than a machine gun."[20 p15]

Opposition to the horrors of chemical warfare meant that a new class of weapon was a necessary response to public, political and legal pressures.[15,21] Thus, incapacitating agents were developed. These were designed not to kill the enemy. Instead, they would be temporarily disabled but would make a full recovery— CW advocates promoted a new "non-lethal" concept for fighting.

In 1959, the Chemical Defence Experimental Establishment at Porton was ordered to prioritise three types of incapacitating agent above any lethal chemical agent.[22] They investigated hundreds of substances and, during the period between August 1961 and December 1963, 240 new compounds were received for testing as potential incapacitating agents while the political and military benefits were continually stressed.[23,24]

MEDIA CAMPAIGN AND NETWORK BUILDING

Supporters of non-lethal CW still had to persuade politicians of its benefits and the MOD maintained that incapacitants would provide a humane form of warfare.[25] The media were a key instrument and in 1959, *The Times* noted that, while "the natural revulsion against the use of gas after the First World War still persists," chemical weapons "caused proportionally fewer permanent

FIGURE 2: "Now we've got a chance to try the new Gas of Peace on somebody!"

injuries and still fewer deaths" and incapacitants could be "the most humane weapon yet devised."[26] The article also predicted futuristic nerve gases in a way that epitomised the technological optimism that had characterised much of the 1950s and 1960s (Figure 2). Politicians and the public had already been impressed by the wartime impact of penicillin, radar and atomic power— with two deadly World Wars in living memory, the aspiration for war without death was founded on scientific progress.[27] Milburn[28] argues that a complementary discourse causes science fiction to become science fact just as the concept of incapacitating gases and a war without death is actually realised.

Notably, contingencies and uncertainties in the presentation of this new technology were manipulated as they were promoted to two radically different audiences. To military chiefs and government officials they were marketed as alternative weapons of mass destruction. To the public at large they promised conflicts without casualties or wars without fathers who did not come home.

The great potential of incapacitants was not only their military effectiveness but also the way they could be represented to actively shaping arms development.[18]

A key aspect of this was the emphasis of a sharp boundary between lethal and non-lethal chemical weapons in order to justify work on incapacitating agents. Even though it is impossible to make a technically meaningful demarcation between them,[9,17,30,31] through interpretation and reinterpretation, the conception of incapacitants as distinct from potentially-lethal chemical weapons, was constructed and consolidated as an immutable 'fact.'[32]

Psychochemicals were soon singled out as being especially promising as the mentally incapacitating effects are usually independent of the lethal effects that come from physical incapacitation.[19,33] There was particular interest in LSD due to its high margin of safety and because it could cause "considerable psychological disturbance" with "little or no physical effect."[34,35 p2,36] It was preferred to other known psychedelics such as mescaline as its potency made it more practical.[20,34,37]

Other perceived benefits for incapacitating agents against other forms of CW were the ambiguity of their legal status under the Geneva Convention, their potential for use in 'graduated warfare' in areas densely populated with unprotected civilians, or to drug foreign leaders rather than risk all-out war.[7,10,38,39]

FROM BICYCLE DAY TO WIDESPREAD MILITARY INTEREST

Another reason the Porton staff were so enthusiastic about investigating psychedelics as weapons was that they were already the focus of a major research field.[40] After Sandoz made LSD available for research, there was substantial interest in psychedelic drugs in the psychiatric community. In England, pioneering research was taking place at Powick Hospital near Worcester. Ronald Sandison and his team worked on LSD therapy between 1953 and 1965 and discovered that LSD could help bring unconscious material to the surface in neurotic patients.[41,42]

By the mid-1960s, over 40,000 patients had taken LSD and psychedelic research had produced over 1,000 scientific papers and books as well as several international conferences.[43] Because of the attention psychedelics were receiving in medical circles, they inevitably appeared in Porton researchers' literature reviews and, within this context, the idea that they could have a viable use in CW was far from unwarranted.[44]

Furthermore, there was not the stigma that is now associated with psychedelic drugs. In the early 1960s, they were primarily a serious therapeutic prospect rather than a recreational drug associated with counter-culture politics and dropping out of established society.[45] There was also little medical evidence to suggest that they might pose a danger to health. Sidney Cohen, a medical expert on psychedelics declared them to be "astonishingly safe"[46 p27] and Abram Hoffer proclaimed that his worked showed LSD was "as safe as aspirin."[47]

Porton was far from unique in its investigation of psychedelics for military purposes. In 1947 the US Navy began studies looking for a truth serum and also assessed mescaline's role as a potential interrogation agent.[48] The Chemical Corps started to investigate how psychochemicals could be used to cause hallucinations, psychoses and convulsions in 1951.[20] The Army's interest in LSD was high at first, spurred by Major General Creasy's persuasive presentation to Congress in 1957 in which he captivated his audience with the idea of a cloud of LSD that could disable well-trained troops without causing them physical harm. Expectations and vivid representations were manipulated to affect important decisions regarding weapons policy and Creasy secured a tripling of the Chemical Corps' budget. Experiments ran at the Army base that would later be known as Edgewood Arsenal from 1955 until about 1972.[49] LSD was seen as a strategic weapon which could redress the imbalance in manpower between East and West. A later investigation revealed that thousands of US soldiers were involved in field trials of LSD.[50,51]

Even the CIA was interested in psychedelics and ran a parallel programme, formally approved in April 1953, called "Project MK-ULTRA" which was intended to investigate whether it was possible to modify an individual's behaviour by covert means. The CIA considered LSD to be of such promise that, in November 1953, they sent two agents to Basel, Switzerland with $240,000 in cash to buy Sandoz's entire supply and to convince the pharmaceutical company to keep them apprised of any other organisations that were requesting the drug.[52] The CIA were especially interested in LSD's extremely low active dose and that psychiatric reports suggested it could break down familiar behaviour patterns; raising the possibility of reprogramming or brainwashing.[39,48] The Warsaw Pact countries also considered psychedelics to be potential weapons and, in 1962, a British firm brokered a deal whereby China bought 400 million doses of LSD from a Czech company.[16,53]

PSYCHEDELIC RESEARCH AT PORTON DOWN

Recently-declassified documents at the National Archives in Kew reveal much of what actually happened at Porton. While it is important to be aware of potential conflicts of interest and the agenda that official records aim to promote, archived discussions regarding the resources devoted to experiments show that psychedelic substances such as LSD were a high priority in CW research at Porton.[54]

In 1958 information from Tripartite Conferences suggested that psychedelic substances could be used as chemical weapons. The very next year, Porton's Chemistry Committee reported that "an early start should be made" on the investigation of psychedelic drugs as war agents.[23,55]

By 1960, medical literature reviews had been conducted indicating that LSD (known within Porton as *T3456*) and related substances had potential as incapacitating agents. It was also known to be very potent with an active dose of as little as 50 µg and research suggested that it could be distributed as an aerosol.[9,23,56]

Soon whole series of psychedelic homologues were being synthesised *en masse* at Porton. These and other psychedelic chemicals such as psilocin and psilocybin (the active compounds in *Psilocybe* mushrooms) and mescaline were evaluated for their potential as incapacitants through "Hall's Open Field Test."[57,58] By 1962, 180 compounds had been screened and indoles and tryptamines (both structurally related to LSD)[B] had been identified as promising classes of chemical.[59-62] It was then decided that the next stage of assessment would be tests on human subjects.[56]

In 1963, the UK officially resumed its CW programme and research into psychedelic incapacitating agents continued at a steady pace. A target was set to have prototypes available for training in 1965 and a limited retaliatory capability ready by 1967.[63] In January 1964, 75 µg of LSD was given intravenously to eight volunteers and in April and October further doses were given to 15 observers. Later experiments showed that it was necessary to give at least 100 µg of the tartrate salt of LSD to incapacitate men to an obvious degree and that it was still active when taken orally.

By 1965, it had been decided that Porton should concentrate on psychedelics as they showed the most promise as incapacitating agents. In January that year, the first outdoor field experiment involving LSD was conducted.[38,61] Dubbed "Moneybags," the exercise consisted of three operations on separate days undertaken by a detachment of 17 Royal Marines. On one of the mornings prior to heading out into the field, 13 of the Commandos were given 200 µg of LSD orally and one additional man was given 75 µg—they were not told on which day they were to receive the drug. The experiment showed that "after about an hour they were totally incapacitated" (Figure 3) and that their response to the enemy was "sluggish and inadequate." The military umpire concluded

FIGURE 3: A Royal Marine struggles to contain his "inappropriate hilarity" while conducting an exercise under the influence of 200 µg of LSD.[64]

that "there can be no doubt that the agent employed could prove of immense value to our forces."[34 p30]

The results also suggested that LSD's effects were truly temporary and reversible. The report claimed that "none of the men showed any ill-effects 48 hours after exposure" and that they were then able to "complete an exercise with 'text-book' precision." Overall, it was thought that LSD "might make an ideal incapacitating agent."[34]

Despite this, given that the target of a working retaliatory capacity was fast approaching, we should question how "ideal" LSD really was at this stage. Given that the internal Porton report describing the Moneybags trial was designed to demonstrate concrete progress and to maintain the notion that psychedelics would soon be effective chemical agents, LSD's utility could have been exaggerated. Furthermore, despite its perceived safety, the dubious ethical position of administering prospective chemical weapons to friendly troops would be better justified if the effects were fully reversible.

In September 1965, a second field trial with LSD was conducted called "Exercise Recount." This time a dose of 1 µg/kg was used and only 16 of the 36 troops involved received the drug in order to determine whether undrugged men affected the performance of those under the influence of LSD. Again, the Porton report emphasised that LSD only had a transitory incapacitating effect as there was "no deterioration of efficiency" 24 hours after its administration.[36 p4] Furthermore, the assertion that "at no time was there any suggestion of a grave psychological reaction to the drug" and that no medical treatment was required demonstrated that LSD fitted the requirements for a chemical incapacitating agent.[36 p5] While it is difficult to dispute the material facts reported in these documents, emphasising the safety of LSD was certainly beneficial to those conducting research into its use as a chemical agent.

More research into psychedelic agents was conducted at Porton including 28 laboratory experiments on humans from August 1966 until March 1967 and a third field trial performed in January 1968.[65–67] In total, the Defence Evaluation and Research Agency reported that between 1962 and 1968, there were 136 experiments involving the dosing of volunteers with LSD.[68]

CONCLUSION

Today, the British government views psychedelics as dangerous recreational drugs that are tightly prohibited due to their alleged capacity to harm. However, for about ten years, dozens of psychedelic compounds were screened at Porton Down and were administered to hundreds of volunteers precisely due to their perceived safety and lack of long-term effects. In order to understand how and why psychedelics became the subject of CW research at Porton Down we must recognise *all* the reasons they were taken so seriously as well as why they had such significant resources devoted to their examination.

Firstly, it is imperative to appreciate how CW came to be a defence priority in a world previously dominated by the nuclear bomb. Foreign threats and local concerns were marshalled to successfully effect a change in defence policy and an increase in CW funding without which research into psychedelic agents would have been very unlikely.

Another aspect that is vital to a full understanding is the way in which incapacitating agents were promoted in the context of the unpopularity of CW. Government memos make explicit reference to the political benefits of waging war without unnecessary casualties. Public opinion toward CW as a whole was manipulated by exploiting alternative representations to interested parties with propaganda campaigns describing a new 'humane' form of war.

Finally, by recognising that the conception of psychedelics was very different in the 1950s and 1960s compared to today, we have a better appreciation of how they became seen as potential chemical weapons. The story of psychedelics in the military only makes sense with the realisation that politics, public influence, and actively manipulated contingencies affected chemical warfare policy far more than science or 'facts.'

A. From the film *Things to Come* (1936), prior to the attack on the fascist warlord by Wings Over the World. HG Wells imagined an incapacitating gas that was used in a hostage rescue mission but, presciently, it caused an unexpecetd death. Courtesy of Alexander Kora and William Cameron Menzies. Korda A, producer; Menzies WC, director. *Things to Come* [motion picture]. United Kingdom: United Artists; 1936.
B. LSD is technically an ergoline but it is structurally related to the indoles and also has a tryptamine 'backbone.' It is also chemically similar to mescaline as it contains the phenethylamine structure.
1. United States Code. Title 21, Chapter 13, Subchapter I, Part B Section 812. *Schedules of Controlled Substances*, 2008.
2. UN. *Convention on Psychotropic Substances.* United Nations Treaty Series. 1971;1019(14956):175.
3. UN Economic and Social Council. E/RES/1968/1294(XLIV). *Urgent control measures for LSD and similar Hallucinogenic substances.* 1968.
4. Schmidt U. *Medical Ethics and Human Experiments at Porton Down.* In: Schmidt U, Frewer A, editors. *History and Theory of Human Experimentation.* Stuttgart: Steiner; 2007. p. 283–313.
5. Balmer B. *Britain and Biological Warfare: Expert Advice and Science Policy, 1930–65.* Basingstoke: Palgrave; 2001.

6. Agar J, Balmer B. *British scientists and the Cold War. Historical Studies in the Physical and Biological Sciences.* 1998;28(2):209–52.
7. TNA DEFE 5/131. Ministry of Defence: Chiefs of Staff Committee: Memoranda Nos 401–440; 1962.
8. TNA DEFE 10/490. Defence Research Policy Committee: memoranda 1–48; 1962.
9. TNA DEFE 10/382. Defence Research Policy Committee: memoranda; 1960.
10. Balmer B. *Keeping Nothing Secret: UK Chemical Warfare Policy in the 1960s.* Journal of Strategic Studies. 2012 Dec 17, 33(6): 871–893.
11. Donovan BT. *Zuckerman: Scientist Extraordinary.* BioScientifica; 2005.
12. Zuckerman S. *Scientists and War.* Harper & Row; 1967.
13. TNA CAB 131/28. Cabinet: Defence Committee: Minutes and Papers (DO, D and DC Series); 1963.
14. Balmer B. *A Secret Formula, a Rogue Patent and Public Knowledge about Nerve Gas: Secrecy as a Spatial-Epistemic Tool.* Social Studies of Science. 2006 Oct 1;36(5):691–722.
15. Carter G. *Porton Down: 75 Years of Chemical and Biological Research.* HMSO; 1992.
16. Harris R, Paxman J. *A Higher Form of Killing: The Secret History of Gas and Germ Warfare.* London: Arrow; 2002.
17. Coleman K. *A History of Chemical Warfare.* Basingstoke: Palgrave Macmillan; 2005.
18. Hedgecoe A, Martin P. *The Drugs Don't Work: Expectations and the Shaping of Pharmacogenetics.* Social Studies of Science. 2003 Jun 1;33(3):327–64.
19. Furmanski M. *Military interest in low-lethality biochemical agents.* Geneva, Switzerland; 2005.
20. Evans R. *Gassed: Behind the Scenes at Porton Down.* House of Stratus; 2000.
21. Davison N. *The Early History of "Non-Lethal" Weapons.* Bradford: University of Bradford; 2006.
22. TNA WO 195/14656. Chemical Defence Advisory Board: research for new agents; 1959.
23. TNA WO188/710. CDEE/CDRE half-yearly progress reports; 1960.
24. TNA WO 195/15273. Biological testing of incapacitating agents; 1961.
25. TNA DEFE 13/440. Ministry of Defence: Private Office: Registered Files: Minister's Office: Chemical warfare; 1960.
26. *Chemical Warfare. The Times.* 1959 Aug 10:9.
27. Sandbrook D. *White Heat: 1964–1970.* Abacus; 2007.
28. Milburn C. *Nanowarriors: Military nanotechnology and comic books.* Postprints. 2005:1828.
29. *Things to Come* [Film] Directed by WC Menzies. UK: London Film Productions; 1936.
30. Pearson A. *Incapacitating biochemical weapons.* The Nonproliferation Review. 2006;13(2):151–88.
31. Hersh SM. *Chemical and Biological Warfare.* Panther; 1970.
32. Rappert B. *Non-lethal Weapons as Legitimizing Forces?* Routledge; 2003.
33. Dando M. *A New Form of Warfare: The Rise of Non-Lethal Weapons.* Brassey's; 1996.
34. TNA WO 195/16137. Applied Biology Committee: Porton Technical Paper number 936; 1965.
35. TNA WO 195/16429. Review of concepts of incapacitation; 1967.
36. TNA WO 195/16312. Exercise RECOUNT: preliminary report on field experiment (trials involving use of LSD); 1966.
37. TNA WO 195/16524. Biology Committee: note on biological actions of LSD 25; 1967.
38. TNA DEFE 6/97. Chiefs of Staff Committee: Reports of the Joint Planning Staff and successors: Nos 28–65; 1965.
39. Marks J. *The Search for the Manchurian Candidate.* Times Books; 1979.
40. Robinson JP. *Disabling Chemical Weapons.* Den Haag/Noordwijk, Netherlands; 1994.
41. Sandison RA. 'Psychological aspects of the LSD treatment of the neuroses.' *Journal of Mental Science* 1954 Apr;100(419):508–15.
42. Sandison RA, Whitelaw JD. 'Further studies in the therapeutic value of lysergic acid diethylamide in mental illness.' *Journal of Mental Science.* 1957;103.
43. Crockett R, Sandison RA, Walk A, editors. *Hallucinogenic drugs and their psychotherapeutic use: Proceedings of the Quarterly Meeting of the Royal Medico-Psychological Association in London 1961.* London: H K Lewis; 1963.

44. Robinson JP, Leitenberg M. *The Problem of Chemical and Biological Warfare*. Stockholm: Almqvist & Wiksell; 1971.
45. Dyck E. *Psychedelic Psychiatry: LSD from Clinic to Campus*. Johns Hopkins University Press; 2008.
46. Cohen S. 'Lysergic Acid Diethylamide: Side Effects and Complications.' *The Journal of Nervous and Mental Disease*. 1960;120(1):30–40.
47. *LSD as safe as aspirin*: Hoffer. Varsity. Sep 25 1967:2.
48. Lee MA, Shlain B. *Acid Dreams: The Complete Social History of LSD*. Grove Press; 1994.
49. Ketchum JS. *Chemical Warfare: Secrets Almost Forgotten*. Sanata Rosa, CA: ChemBooks; 2006.
50. Tendler S, May D. *The Brotherhood of Eternal Love*. 2nd ed. Cyan Books; 2007.
51. Moreno JD. *Undue Risk: Secret State Experiments on Humans*. 1st ed. Routledge; 2000.
52. Stevens J. *Storming Heaven: LSD and the American Dream*. Grove Press; 1998.
53. Rozsa L. *A Psychochemical Weapon Considered by the Warsaw Pact: A Research Note*. *Substance Use & Misuse*. 2009;44(2):172.
54. Dockrill ML. *British defence since 1945*. Blackwell; 1988.
55. TNA WO 195/14759. Chemical Defence Advisory Board: annual review of the work of the Board for the year ending September 1959; 1959.
56. TNA WO 195/15012. 1960 review of Chemical Defence Advisory Board: area scanning methods to detect C W agents in atmosphere; 1960.
57. TNA WO 195/15170. Biological testing of incapacitating agents: Pt 2 results; 1961.
58. TNA WO 195/15180. Progress at CDEE on new agent research; 1961.
59. TNA WO 195/15491. Advisory Council: report for 1962; 1963.
60. TNA WO 195/15322. Progress in chemical aspects of new agent research; 1962.
61. TNA WO 195/16213. Summary of work on lysergic acid diethylamide [LSD]; 1966.
62. TNA WO 195/15388. Current investigations in search for new CW agents; 1962.
63. TNA DEFE 5/142. Chiefs of Staff Committee: Memoranda: Nos 276–306; 1963.
64. IWM MGH 4464. A Trial of an Incapacitating Drug; 1965.
65. TNA WO 195/16529. Progress report on T3456 laboratory experiments; 1967.
66. TNA WO 195/16694. Applied Biology Committee: SMALL CHANGE [field trials with an incapacitant] (ABC.54); 1968.
67. TNA WO 189/1503. Small Change: a brief preliminary report on the efficiency of soldiers carrying out military tasks under the effects of T3456; 1968.
68. House of Commons Hansard Written Answers for 18 Apr 1996 (pt 6).

SEASON OF THE WITCH: 1966 AND THE VILIFICATION OF LSD IN BRITAIN

ANDY ROBERTS

"Certainly no drug has been produced which has caused greater trouble in this world than LSD."

Lord St Just, 30 June 1966[1]

Prior to 1966 the British government largely ignored LSD. The Secret Intelligence Services and the MOD had conducted experiments with it during the 1950s and early 1960s. These trials found that LSD was too unpredictable for use either as an interrogation tool or battlefield incapacitant. Otherwise, government files on LSD for the period 1952–65 suggest that no research took place that had any bearing on the criminalisation of LSD in 1966.

LSD was virtually unknown to the British public until 1966, when it became a household name through constant media attention. Yet, until 1963 the few media stories on LSD were, without exception, positive reports of medical use. In 1960, one journalist even suggested that an LSD cocktail would be used to "Curb the boss's tantrums!"[2] After its arrival in Britain in late 1952, at least 50 psychotherapists had begun to use LSD in their practice and a dedicated LSD therapy unit, under the auspices of Dr. Ronald Sandison, existed at Powick hospital in Gloucestershire.

During a House of Commons discussion on 11 December 1958 the Secretary of State for the Home Department was asked if he was aware of the properties of LSD and whether he proposed to bring it under the Dangerous Drugs Act (DDA). Rab Butler's response was negative in that there was no evidence LSD was addictive. Butler was also concerned that placing LSD under law would only serve to draw attention to it and stimulate demand.[3]

Until 1966 LSD was listed as a poison under Part 1 of the Poisons List and could only be sold by prescription. This, however, did not restrict its use to psychotherapy. LSD could be obtained for recreational use through a friendly doctor.[4] Widespread black market distribution and use of the drug in Britain was well underway as early as 1959 and throughout the early 1960s a rapidly developing British LSD subculture became established in London.

In 1963 a steady trickle of lurid LSD stories in American print media began to reach Britain, and *The Times* reported that a London doctor had drowned while under its influence.[5] Wider global medical and political reservations were raised in 1964 when the World Health Committee's Expert Committee on Addiction Producing Drugs expressed concern about the increasing recreational use of LSD. This disquiet may have prompted the brief House of Commons debate on LSD and other hallucinogens in May 1964 when George Thomas stated in the House of Commons there was "no evidence at present of misuse of these substances, but a close watch was being kept on the situation."[6]

The early 1960s was a halcyon period for the British LSD subculture as no one had yet been arrested or charged with any offence connected with it. It was a time of high quality and easily obtained LSD and there was experimentation without fear of legal repercussion or social opprobrium. Its use ranged from experiencing the sheer synaesthetic joy of the psychedelic experience, to deeper explorations of the human psyche and the spiritual realms, which seemed accessible and limitless when under the influence of this enigmatic drug.

Then, in 1966 everything suddenly and radically changed. By October a swarm of political, media and social forces, unwittingly aided by the folly of naïve elements within the LSD sub-culture, had conspired to demonise LSD. The drug was made illegal, outlawed for personal use and disapproved of as a psychotherapeutic aid.

No government file exists to explain why LSD was made illegal. Therefore, the drug's vilification and its path from obscurity to illegality must be traced through contemporary media, and such official documents that are available. It is also necessary to posit the influence of 'The Establishment,' which refers not only to "the centres of official power—though they are certainly part of it—but rather the whole matrix of official and social relations within which power is exercised."[7] The cumulative evidence indicates that the British Establishment—leading politicians, senior civil servants, police chiefs, governors of the BBC, media moguls and journalists—exerted influence in order to create a political and social climate in which LSD could be swiftly legislated against in 1966.

By the autumn of 1965 Timothy Leary's emissary to Britain, Michael Hollingshead, had established his World Psychedelic Centre (WPC) on London's Pont Street. The flat was a focus of LSD use and sale, visited by the core of London's psychedelic scene including Paul McCartney, Donovan and Julie Felix. On 25 January 1966 the police began their assault on London's psychedelic culture and raided the WPC. No psychedelic session in progress nor distribution quantities of LSD were found but they did arrest Hollingshead for possession of heroin, morphine and cannabis.[8]

Police action in early 1966 was too late to prevent the spread of serious recreational use of LSD. The drug was now so embedded that reference to it was appearing in pop songs. The Rolling Stones' '19th Nervous Breakdown,' released on 4 February, 1966 featured the words "On our first trip I tried so hard to rearrange your mind." To those in the know the meaning of the lyric was obvious but, unlike later records that refer directly to the psychedelic experience, it evaded the Establishment's attentions.

On 22 February Flying Squad officers stopped Russell Page in Covent Garden and found him in possession of four LSD laced sugar cubes he was selling for £1.50. He told the police his supplier was poet John Esam who lived in South Kensington. There, they found Esam and Frederick Klein hiding a tin containing LSD. All were charged with conspiring to distribute LSD.[9]

The media now had LSD firmly in their sights. In mid-March, *London Life*, the quintessential swinging London magazine, heavily trailed its forthcoming LSD exposé.[10] The editor had secured an exclusive interview with WPC co-founder Desmond O'Brien. He and Hollingshead saw this as their golden opportunity to expound their LSD philosophy to a wider audience. But they failed to understand that the press, no doubt emboldened by lurid American LSD stories, now wanted sensationalism, not philosophy.

The *London Life* interview was published on 19 March. 'The Drug That Could Become A Social Peril' opened with O'Brien rather unwisely introducing himself as 'Mr. LSD' and boasting that he and his colleagues, with "10 grams introduced into the water supplies at Buckingham Palace, Whitehall and other key centres in the country would enable us to perform a *coup d'état* in Britain." Elsewhere in the piece "a leading psychiatrist agreed" that LSD could be a weapon in the hands of anarchists.

O'Brien's attempts to describe LSD's positive effects, its potential for causing personal change, and the WPC's philosophy were subsumed by this threat of psychedelic terrorism. O'Brien's comments possibly did more damage to the reputation of LSD than many of the subsequent media assassinations. The editorial helped to further taint the drug's reputation: "there is a very real danger of this dangerous drug spreading, as purple hearts did, among wider sections of the population. Who knows what moral lethargy could result?"[10]

On the day following the *London Life* exposé, *The News of the World* and *The People* entered the debate. *The People* had infiltrated the WPC and, far from finding it a peaceful and purposeful acid ashram for the transformation of minds, portrayed it as a degrading centre of chaotic drug use with "hypodermic syringes, empty drug ampoules and a variety of pills" scattered around the floor.[11] *The News of the World*'s Charles Sandell noted that Scotland Yard's Drug Squad had been compiling a dossier on LSD use in West London.[12] An unnamed detective was quoted as saying LSD "presents a much bigger threat than marijuana and purple hearts," although just what this threat was remained unclear. Sandell also indicated that Home Secretary Roy Jenkins was going to bring the drug under "strict control," although there had been no indication of this in either the press or in parliament. It is hard to avoid the conclusion that in the first half of 1966 there was considerable behind-closed-doors communication, if not actually collusion, between the press, police and politicians with the intention of undermining the LSD subculture. The Establishment appeared to be at work preparing the way for draconian legislation.

In an attempt to trace where the supply of recreational LSD was coming from, Sandell contacted Sandoz, the Swiss chemical manufacturer who supplied the drug. A spokesman confirmed that although they had tight controls of their product he believed "there are unofficial supplies coming into Britain."[12] As yet, no underground British LSD laboratories existed, but substantial quantities of the drug were now coming into Britain by post and by couriers. LSD could be bought easily at clubs, coffee bars and from drug dealers. Mainly available on sugar cubes, the drug also came on blotting paper and a powerful dose of around 200 micrograms could be bought for between £1.50 and £5.00.

Concerns that LSD use could be promulgated via the medium of pop music arose in late March when the media alerted the public to the Pretty Things B-side 'LSD.' The lyrics were ambiguous, opening with "Everybody's talking, about my LSD," with a repeated chorus of "Yes I need my LSD." The Pharmaceutical Society commented they were "hoping this kind of thing would not happen. We are actually very much opposed to the idea of publicising this drug, which we consider is one of the most dangerous and frightening to date. It is wrong that teenagers should go to the extent of singing about LSD." Once again the negative aspects of LSD were being stressed by elements of the Establishment with no clear justification.

Phil May, the song's co-writer, commented:

The words have a double meaning and if you take them to mean pounds, shillings and pence, then it's all right. If you understand them to mean this drug which everyone seems to be talking about these days, then you obviously know about it anyway we have done no harm to anyone.[13]

Pressed for a statement, a Home Office spokesman opined, "We cannot comment on the implications of it at this stage, but we are keeping ourselves informed of its progress." A few days later the Home Office clarified its position. "Following a report in the *Evening Standard* on Wednesday we have contacted Philips Records and they are sending us a copy of the words."[14]

Increasing governmental concern about LSD was evidenced when the Home Secretary asked all suppliers of morning glory seeds to suspend sales pending tests to determine whether the lysergic content (the active constituent of LSD) of the seeds could be dangerous. Seeds were removed from shops and garden centres and much was made of an Easter greetings card containing a packet of the seeds. "More than 100 salesmen employed by Hallmark Cards" were despatched to remove the cards from display. The ban was lifted on 21 June but the press furore and the government's hysterical reaction only added to public fears about LSD.[15]

Left-wing journalist William Connor, writing as Cassandra in the *Daily Mirror,* was among the first heavyweight journalists to attempt a serious analysis of LSD's impact on Britain. Connor was clearly aware of the literature about its potential for transforming consciousness. Nevertheless his interpretation of LSD's effects was negative:

The mind, not the body, is the victim [...] The person under the influence of LSD becomes withdrawn and will crouch or huddle on the floor staring at any commonplace object like a chair, an electric lamp or the pattern of a carpet, and perceives in their shape and design a triumph of exquisite achievement.[16]

Connor went on to suggest that "murders and suicides and acts of total recklessness, regardless of the consequences, have occurred." He also suggested that a complete change of personality for the worse was an automatic consequence of LSD and that users saw "ordinary life" as "like death (and) normality is unendurable."

But Connor also caught a glimpse of the potential and far reaching changes of LSD when he quoted Leary:

present social establishments had better be prepared for the change. Man is about to make use of that fabulous electrical network he carries round in his skull. Our favourite concepts are standing in the way of a floodtide, two billion years building up. Head for the hills.[16]

Yet, Leary's and Connor's views were diametrically opposed and in his unsubstantiated closing comments, Connor put the seal of doom on LSD with "They don't mention the epilepsy, the convulsions, the lunacy and the final extinction that can be released within the sweetness of a lump of sugar."[16]

April 1966 also saw the publication of several more LSD 'scare' stories from America. In one, a five-year-old girl was said to have accidentally eaten an LSD soaked sugar cube and in another a man claimed he had been on LSD when he committed a murder. These and other similar stories made national headlines and, coming on the tail of the British press exposés, only added to the rapidly forming popular opinion that LSD was a dangerous drug that would forever change the lives of the nation's children.

These media exposés and minor panics all influenced public perception of LSD. A once obscure drug now enjoyed notoriety.

In the 20 years since World War II, Britain had successfully re-built its economy and society. The future looked bright and the last thing Britain wanted was a drug influencing its children to turn on, tune in and drop out, as Leary invited. And while the media exposés turned public opinion against LSD they had also alerted thousands of young people to an experiential culture they now desperately wanted to be part of.

On 15 April, after considerable deliberation and sensing their reputation was at stake, Sandoz announced that due to "unforeseen public reaction" they would stop selling the drug.[17]

The People ran another exposé in April when it gate-crashed an LSD party at London socialite Christopher Gibb's Cheyne Walk flat. The party, filmed for the BBC's *24 Hours*, was described as being a bacchanalian orgy, "men danced with men—women danced with women [...] a mass of male and female forms lying on the floor [...]Many of them were embracing." They implied that LSD caused immoral behaviour. Further, some of the alleged quotes—"I'm high on LSD. I'm a baby again"—did no favours to the LSD subculture. In the eyes of the public this could well have represented the beginning of the "moral lethargy" which the *London Life* editorial predicted.[18]

Britain saw its first successful LSD related prosecution in late April. Roger Lewis received a conditional discharge for possessing 13 sugar cubes containing LSD and a £25 fine for aiding and abetting its sale. Interestingly, although probably disingenuously, Lewis blamed the influence of the *London Life* article for getting him interested in the drug.[19]

In the House of Commons on 11 May the Joint Under Secretary of State, Lord Stonham, was queried whether LSD was to be brought under the Dangerous Drugs Act. Stonham replied that, "we have no evidence [...] to suggest the matter has got out of hand, whatever may have been suggested in some press reports. We are watching the position very closely" and that any additions to the Act were contingent on the decision of the United Nations

Narcotics Commission.[20] This echoed John Ryman, who for the prosecution against Esam and his co-accused noted that "We are dealing with the use of a type of drug not considered by the courts to any great extent."[21]

Other representatives of the Establishment lent their weight to the campaign against LSD. The influential *British Medical Journal* (*BMJ*) ran an editorial calling for LSD to be outlawed, citing cases where users had developed prepsychotic states or definite psychotic attacks as being "enough to warrant the proscription of so dangerous a drug."[22] Though the *BMJ* subsequently published critical letters from psychotherapists using LSD to successfully treat psychiatric patients, the *BMJ*'s editorial was taken seriously by the medical establishment and used in parliamentary debates as evidence that LSD was dangerous.

The subject of LSD was raised again in the Lords on 30 June when Lord St Just claimed "Certainly no drug has been produced which has caused greater trouble in this world than LSD," an astonishing statement, as besides a handful of media stories the world knew very little indeed about LSD. Lord Stonham contradicted his colleague by stating "There is no reliable information about the extent of its use in the United Kingdom," noting that the Home Secretary was considering whether to bring LSD under the control of the Drugs (Prevention) Act (1964) or the Dangerous Drugs Act (1965).[23] This exchange, the contradictory debate in the *BMJ*, and the stream of sensational press articles, underline the fact that opinion and not evidence appeared to be driving LSD's journey toward legislation.

On 21 July the Home Secretary laid before Parliament a draft Order which, when approved, would bring LSD under the Drugs (Prevention) Act (1964) in the form of the Drugs (Prevention of Misuse) Act 1964 Modification Order, 1966. The Order was approved in the Lords on 4 August amidst a discussion about the imagined effects of LSD. The general consensus was that LSD was a drug of illusion and hallucination, taken by people who wanted to forget their circumstances. Reference was made to dubious media stories about people re-living their births or wanting to fly, to which Lord Stonham commented, to much laughter, "LSD is not the only substance that can create that illusion: I have known people who thought they could fly on four pints of bitter." The Order was approved a day later in the Commons, once again in the context of a discussion that mixed half facts with full fictions about LSD's effects and usage. LSD's fate was now sealed and the press moved in to deliver the final blows.[24]

On 8 September, the eve of LSD being banned, London's *Evening Standard* ran a feature titled 'To LSD and Back Again.' Journalist Jonathan Aitken, later to be a disgraced Conservative Member of Parliament, took 200 micrograms of LSD and recorded his experience. After the usual pleasant symptoms of the drug's onset, Aitken experienced traumatic images of war and bloodshed. The *Evening Standard* notably quoted, "Get the message across that no one must ever use this drug again [...] it's terrifying what I'm seeing [...] this drug needs police, the Home Office and a dictator to stamp it out." As Aitken had previously covered the conflicts in Vietnam and Biafra, his experience was unsurprising. Though he did acknowledge that LSD had given him some personal insight, the whole experience was reported as negative, showing Aitken's ignorance of the drug's effects.[25]

October's British edition of *Reader's Digest* (published in September) published a damning swan song to the drug's impending criminalisation. Sweeping and unsubstantiated statements such as "LSD often gives people a powerful urge to jump out of a window, perhaps under the impression they are snowflakes or birds" along with references to incidents of murder and suicide under LSD's influence formed the bulk of the article. Although some positive effects were mentioned they were re-framed in a negative context. With a British circulation of 1,350,000, and a significantly larger readership, *Reader's Digest*'s pejorative and uninformed reports of LSD would have influenced many people's opinions about the drug as it passed from quasi-legal status to full illegality.[26]

On 9 September 1966 LSD became illegal in Britain. Manufacture, distribution and possession of the drug was now punishable by fines and imprisonment, the opinions of LSD psychotherapists who were achieving success with their patients notwithstanding. The Establishment's continued hounding led to the cessation of legal LSD psychotherapy in Britain in 1967.

Yet, legislation did not deter the use of LSD by those who believed in it as an agent of personal and social change. The drug's new status merely complicated and increased the risk of its acquisition and affected supply and quality. The Establishment's unspoken fears about how LSD could affect individuals and society were borne out after 1966 when, despite the draconian legal strictures on manufacture, distribution and possession, an underground LSD subculture arose in Britain. Through its network of squats, communes, events and communications it formed the basis of the 1970s Free Festival movement that was also targeted by the Establishment, resulting in the smashing of the Operation Julie LSD manufacture and distribution network and the eventual outlawing of free festivals.[27]

Whether the burgeoning psychedelic community, had it been more organised or coherent, could have prevented or minimised LSD's fate is unlikely. Contemporary society legislates against all drugs which affect consciousness. But the manner and haste with which LSD was brought within the law indicates how much the drug, and its potential to radically change consciousness, was feared by the Establishment. Opinions, and subsequently laws, were formed without recourse to fact or due consideration of the rights of the individual to alter consciousness in accordance with choice. An air of mystery will forever attend the Establishment's attitude to LSD in 1966, perhaps best summed up in the words of William Braden: "You can't reason people out of an opinion they did not arrive at by reason to begin with."[28 p209]

1. Hansard. London. June 30 1966. Available from: http://hansard.millbanksystems.com /lords/1966/jun/30/drug-taking-by-young-people.
2. Bedford, P. 'Cocktails will curb the boss's tantrums.' *London Times*. 1960 October 17:5.
3. Hansard. London. December 11 1958. Available from: http://hansard.millbanksystems .com/commons/1958/dec/11/mescalin-and-lysergic-acid-diethylamide#S5CV0597 p0_19581211_HOC_26.
4. Moorcock, M. *Moorcock's Miscellany*. 2 January 2007. Available from: http://www .multiverse.org/fora/showthread.php?t=4892.
5. 'Doctor's death mystery.' *Daily Mirror*. 1963 February 19:19.
6. Hansard. London. May 11 1964. Available from: http://hansard.millbanksystems.com /lords/1966/may/11/control-of-drugs#S5LV0274 p0_19660511_HOL_55.
7. Fairlie, H. 'Political Commentary.' *The Spectator*. 1955 September 23.
8. Hollingshead, M. *The Man Who Turned On The World*. London. Blond & Briggs Ltd; 1973.
9. 'Britain's first 'vision of hell' drugs case.' *Daily Telegraph*. 1966 April 4.
10. 'LSD: The Drug that could become a social peril.' *London Life*. 1966 March 19:7–10.
11. Gabbert, M. 'The men behind LSD—the drug that is menacing young lives.' *The People*. 1966 March 20:14–15.
12. Sandell, C. 'Menace Of The 'Vision Of Hell.'' *News of the World*. 1966 March 20:9.
13. Housego, M. 'Group plugs LSD and wins a rebuke.' *Evening Standard*. 1966 March 23.
14. 'LSD song: Home Office studies words.' *Evening Standard*. 1966 March 25.
15. 'Morning Glory 'drug' sold in Easter Cards.' *The People*. 1966 April 3.
16. 'Cassandra. The Cost Of LSD.' *Daily Mirror*. 1966 April 4:5.
17. 'US firm to stop sale of LSD drug.' *Manchester Guardian*. 1966 April 15:1.
18. Kempson, T. 'BBC In A Wild 'Drug Party' Sensation.' *The People*. 1966 April 17:1.
19. 'LSD Drug Charges Man Convicted.' *London Times*. 1966 April 28.
20. Hansard. London. May 11 1966. Available from: http://hansard.millbanksystems.com /lords/1966/may/11/control-of-drugs#S5LV0274 p0_19660511_HOL_55.
21. 'Drug case said to be 'trend setter.'' *London Times*. 1966 May 11.
22. 'Effects of LSD.' *British Medical Journal*. 1966;1(5502):1495–6.
23. Hansard. London. June 30 1966. Available from: http://hansard.millbanksystems.com /lords/1966/jun/30/drug-taking-by-young-people.
24. 'Government move to stop misuse of the 'fantasy drug.'' *Manchester Guardian*. 1966 July 22:1.
25. Pickard, C and Aitken, J. 'To LSD And Back Again.' *Evening Standard*. London. 1966 September 8:7.
26. Young, W. 'The Truth About the Dream Drug.' *Readers Digest*. 1966 October:186–190.
27. Roberts, A. *Albion Dreaming*. London: Marshall Cavendish; 2008.
28. Braden W. *LSD and the press*. In: Cohen S, Young J, editors. *The Manufacture of News, Social Problems, Deviance and the Mass Media*. London: Constable and co Ltd; 1973. p.195–209.

BREAKING CONVENTIONS IN POLICY AND SCIENCE

AMANDA FEILDING

My purpose in setting up the Beckley Foundation was to break the prevailing taboos that constrain drug policy and drug science. Policy is strangled by a fixation on criminality, and science is blocked by the fear of using controlled substances to investigate consciousness.

It is 50 years since the nations of the world assembled to sign the 1961 UN Single Convention on Narcotic Drugs. Declaring themselves concerned "with the health and welfare of mankind," the signatories set themselves lofty and admirable aims: to tackle the health, social and economic problems associated with drugs while ensuring an adequate supply of medicines essential for relief of pain and suffering. How has the international drug control regime measured up to its stated objectives in the past half century? Do people have access to the drugs they need for pain relief? Has the UN's prohibitionist regime succeeded in bringing about a significant reduction in drug use, problem use, crime, violence, corruption and drug-related deaths? I fear the answer is no. Some 80% of the world's population have no access to the medicines indispensable for the relief of severe pain. Drug use has ballooned since the 1960s, and the latest UN data show no fall in use or problem use over the last decade.

It was to try to counteract these obviously failing policies that in 1998 I established the Beckley Foundation. Its aim was to undertake policy research and provide an evidence base for policy decisions, initiate political and academic debate on drug policy reform, and stimulate and carry out scientific research into the potential therapeutic applications of psychoactive substances. The Beckley Foundation is the only organisation to engage in both pioneering scientific research and rigorous policy analysis. We have developed collaborations with over 15 of the world's leading universities and institutions, including Imperial College London, University College London, the Institute of Psychiatry, the University of Oxford and Johns Hopkins University, USA. The Foundation has published over 30 books, reports and proceedings documents as well as many peer-reviewed academic papers.

The word 'Conventions' in the title of this chapter refers in part, of course, to the UN Conventions which collectively govern national and international drug policies around the world. But it also refers to the societal norms and taboos that have grown up around altered states of consciousness, drug use, drug policy and the science of psychoactive compounds. Challenging these taboos is difficult: they are ferociously protected by layers of misunderstanding. It is also rewarding: the study of consciousness and its altered states touches on that which makes us human and, since the first stirrings of our cultural history, has been at the very centre of human development.

At long last, the political and scientific tide shows signs of turning. Incumbent presidents are starting to be brave enough to say the unthinkable, that we might perhaps even *debate* creating a regulated legal market that would take profits and power from the criminal cartels and put the world's third-largest industry into the hands of governments.

THE BECKLEY FOUNDATION SCIENTIFIC PROGRAMME

In my opinion, understanding consciousness and how one might enhance the function of the human brain must be among the most important areas of human exploration. By using psychedelics as tools to alter conscious experience we can learn an enormous amount about consciousness itself by correlating personal experience with changes in cerebral circulation and brain function as observed through brain-imaging technology. The fact that for the last half-century this area of research has been taboo is close to insanity. Indeed it was to break this misguided convention that I set up the Beckley Foundation. I was lucky in having a father who advised me early on, "whatever the Government tells you, do the opposite!"

Since the late 1960s, I have wanted to investigate the changes in cerebral circulation that we hypothesised took place after the ingestion of psychedelic substances. In 2008, working in collaboration with David Nutt, we set up the *Beckley Foundation Imperial College Psychedelic Research Programme*. Robin Carhart-Harris, a Beckley fellow, acted as the principal investigator. Using the most advanced brain-imaging technology (fMRI), we observed the brains of volunteers as they received an intravenous dose of psilocybin, the active principle found in magic mushrooms, in three separate studies.

I had long worked under the hypothesis that the use of psychedelics increases the volume of blood in the capillaries of the brain, and hence brain activity, thereby expanding conscious awareness. To our surprise, our research instead showed that psilocybin *decreased* blood flow, particularly to regions of the brain that act as 'connector hubs'—major junctions with large numbers of connections to other brain regions.[1] These hubs seem to be critical in allowing different parts of the brain to communicate efficiently. But the hubs also *constrain* brain activity by filtering out the majority of input so that our experience of the world is orderly and manageable. Psilocybin appears to reduce the censoring activity of these centres by depriving them of blood, allowing a freer and more fluid state of consciousness, which is also associated with creative thought. The description of the brain as a 'reducing valve' whose filtering activity is lifted by psychedelics was originally proposed by Aldous Huxley in the 1950s, but has never before been scientifically demonstrated.

The findings raise important possibilities for the therapeutic use of psilocybin. For instance, one of the hub regions whose activity is suppressed by psilocybin (the medial prefrontal cortex or mPFC) is *over*-active in depression. Our results imply that, in depressed patients, psilocybin may bring the activity of the mPFC down to a more normal level. This exciting possibility has already generated funding from the Medical Research Council for a clinical trial of psilocybin's potential as an antidepressant.

Another region that we identified as being suppressed by psilocybin is the hypothalamus, which is over-active during 'cluster headaches,' a particularly agonising and debilitating form of recurrent headaches, colloquially known as the 'suicide headache.' Again, psilocybin could have a therapeutic use in this condition. Certainly there is strong anecdotal evidence from cluster headache sufferers that LSD and magic mushrooms are among the few treatments to provide effective relief.[2]

In another Beckley-Imperial study, subjects were given cues to recall positive events in their lives.[3] With psilocybin, their memories were extremely vivid, almost as if they were seeing the events rather than just imagining them. The subjective experience correlated with an observable change in brain function; subjects who were performing memory recall under psilocybin (but not without psilocybin) activated brain regions used for processing visual and other sensory input. These findings too have potential therapeutic applications. They suggest that psilocybin may be a valuable adjunct to psychotherapy, helping patients trapped by repressed trauma to access distant autobiographical memories and thereby work through them.

This research provides a neuroscientific foundation for the research the Beckley is currently undertaking with Roland Griffiths and his team at Johns Hopkins University. This is the first investigation in modern times to use a psychedelic to assist in overcoming addiction, in this case to nicotine. Participants are long-term smokers who have tried to quit several times unsuccessfully. So far, the results have been incredibly successful as psychedelics sometimes give rise to distinctive, insightful experiences that can produce enduring positive changes in attitude, mood and behaviour.

Our successful studies with psilocybin have now led to further studies with MDMA, which are already under way. We have also prepared the protocol for a study investigating the effects on the brain of LSD, which we hope to start soon.

The Beckley Foundation has recently launched a research project into the efficacy of medical marijuana, working with Harborside Health Center, a licensed dispensary of medical marijuana in California, with access to a cohort of over 100,000 patients. Importantly, our study is not treating all cannabis as identical. Instead, we are measuring the chemical compositions of various strains so that we can look at the medical effects of each strain in relation to the concentrations of a range of active ingredients. We are correlating the chemical data with responses to online questionnaires completed by patients. Our colleagues at University College London, led by Valerie Curran, will carry out the statistical analysis. We hope to build the first large-scale database of the comparative effects of different strains of cannabis in treating different conditions. The research will also generate information about the positive and negative side-effects of cannabis and about its efficacy in comparison with conventional pharmaceutical treatments.

The recent findings from our scientific research programmes demonstrate, unequivocally, that the therapeutic potential of psychotropic drugs is worthy of further study, breaking the convention that dictates that all use of these drugs is 'problem' use. Ultimately, perhaps, people will come to re-recognise what humans have known for millennia: that psychotropic substances can be central in overcoming diseases of mind and body, catalysing the solution of problems, and bringing about profound insights into the nature of the self and our place in the world.

THE BECKLEY FOUNDATION POLICY PROGRAMME

The same societal taboos or conventions that hamper our scientific work are responsible for the irrationalities in drug policies that have resulted in the failures of the prohibitionist approach characterised by the War on Drugs, an approach that has desperately exacerbated the problems associated with drugs over the past 50 years.

Drugs policies all over the world are cast from the same mould. Three UN Drug Conventions, signed in 1961, 1971 and 1988, bind the drug control legislation of all Parties to the same model and severely restrict independent policy experimentation.[4] The 1961 *UN Single Convention on Narcotic Drugs* consolidated previous treaties into the first unified global declaration of drug prohibition, banning the production, trading and possession of controlled substances with the exception of drugs destined for medical or scientific use. The 1971 *UN Convention on Psychotropic Substances* expanded the scope of the control measures to a larger number of psychotropic drugs and their precursors. When the 1988 Convention was signed, all parties became obliged to treat the unlicensed production, distribution and *possession* of drugs as a criminal offence (*use* is also effectively criminalised, as it is impossible to use a drug without possessing it). Thus the War on Drugs became a war on users.

The UN's own evidence consistently shows that the Conventions have failed to achieve their stated aims. During the 1980s, global production of opium tripled and cocaine manufacture quadrupled.[5] The average retail price of cocaine in Europe fell by over one-half in real terms between 1990 and 2008; for opiates, the price dropped by nearly three-quarters.[6] Producer and transit countries have been reduced to war zones. Between December 2006 and September 2011, over 47,000 people have been killed in Mexico alone in drug-related violence.[7]

The Conventions have fared no better in their aim of ensuring a sufficient supply of indispensable medicines. The WHO estimates that 80% of the world's population do not have access to treatment for severe pain, and that some of the half-million women who die each year in childbirth could be saved if the medicines they require were available.[8] The problem is not expense or the lack of *potential* global capacity. Rather, the necessary pain-killing and obstetric drugs are subject to strong control and often rendered inaccessible because of their status as scheduled substances under the UN regime.

In a 2010 report, UN Special Rapporteur Anand Grover stated:

> *The primary goal of the international drug control regime [...]*
> *is the 'health and welfare of mankind,' but the current approach*
> *to controlling drug use and possession works against that aim*
> *[...and results in] countless human rights violations.*[9 p2]

Some countries routinely apply the death sentence for drugs offences, sometimes targeting foreign nationals disproportionately and executing young 'mules' in order to send a message to major traffickers.[10] The litany of horrors that have arisen as collateral damage from the misguided ideology of prohibitionism is overwhelming. Forty years after President Nixon declared the War on Drugs, it is clear that it has failed.

How might countries be enabled to move beyond this state of affairs? The UN's noble concerns with the health and welfare of mankind and the relief of pain and suffering are still valid. But since the 1961 Convention was adopted, the world has changed, and so too must our responses. The Conventions are not Holy Writ, inscribed in stone; they should be flexible and responsive to evolving knowledge and circumstances. In 1961, cannabis was used in traditional societies as a social and religious substance, and by a minority of intellectuals in Western capitals. Now the use of cannabis is a rite of passage for youth around the world, and accounts for 80% of all drug use. AIDS did not exist in 1961; now nearly one-fifth of injecting drug users in the world are living with HIV, while half have hepatitis C.[11] Drug use must be seen as a health issue rather than a crime, and must be dealt with by public health institutions rather than the apparatus of criminal enforcement.

I have convened nine Beckley Foundation international drug policy seminars, mostly held at the House of Lords, which have brought together top scientists and politicians to discuss new research, debate the successes and failures of current drug policies, and explore new policy options. The most recent of these seminars was the two-day launch in November 2011 of the Beckley's *Global Initiative for Drug Policy Reform*,[12] where high-level representatives of 14 countries gathered to discuss the future of global drug policy. For the *Initiative*, I commissioned two new reports: "Rewriting the UN Drug Conventions," by Robin Room and Sarah MacKay, and the first-ever "Cost-Benefit Analysis of a Taxed and Regulated Cannabis Market," by Stephen Pudney.[13]

"Rewriting the UN Drug Conventions" offers a clear roadmap to how a country or a group of countries would set about amending the UN Conventions in order to achieve two important policy options:

> *i. to clearly decriminalise the non-commercial possession and use of any or all drugs within their national boundaries, while maintaining their international obligations;*

> *ii. to establish a legal, regulated market in any or all drugs for non-medical use.*

There is already a degree of latitude within the wording and interpretation of the Conventions, but its limits are unclear, and it can cause 'net-widening,' where the powers of the police are extended. Countries such as the Netherlands, Portugal and the Czech Republic have taken advantage of the wriggle room within the Conventions, but their reforms also reflect the restrictions imposed by the Conventions. For example, in the Netherlands, the purchase of small quantities of cannabis in 'coffee shops' is tolerated (although technically still an offence). However, there is no such policy of toleration for large-scale cultivation and trade. Therefore, the supply of cannabis to the coffee shops should officially be prosecuted. This 'back-door' problem puts the police in a very awkward position.[14]

The Czech policy likewise operates in a legally grey area, although the results are very positive. Like many other reform-minded nations, the Czech Republic has been challenged by the International Narcotics Control Board (INCB), the UN's quasi-judicial monitoring body on drugs, which frequently acts beyond its original remit as a tribunal to block change. The INCB notes in its most recent report:

> that [in] the Czech Republic, the possession of drugs for personal consumption in amounts below defined thresholds is an administrative offence... The Board has entered discussions with the Government to examine whether that legislation is in conformity with... the 1988 Convention, which requires the establishment of such acts as criminal offences.[15 p11]

However the room for manoeuvre is delineated; some policy options are unquestionably beyond the pale. The creation of a legal, regulated, non-medical market for a controlled drug falls into this category. The *Global Commission for Drug Policy* has consistently called for the need to experiment with such a market. However, because of the Conventions, no country has yet been able to do so. This means that there is no evidence base for the effectiveness of such a policy option, at either national or sub-national levels. The exception, ironically, is in those 17 states in the USA that have established regulated markets under the guise of medical marijuana. It may be worth noting that the USA, which acts as the dominant force against reform, has the potential to override the Conventions, since under US domestic law Congress may overrule international agreements![16]

As described in *Rewriting the UN Conventions*, one way of achieving reform is for a country to *denounce* (withdraw from) a Convention and then seek to *re-accede* (re-join) with *reservations*, in other words with an opt-out from specific parts of the Convention. This is the option currently being pursued by Bolivia, which has an indigenous tradition of coca-leaf chewing stretching back millennia. Coca leaf is one of the substances proscribed by the 1961 Convention (although in its raw state it has no history of harms); its growth, preparation and distribution are prohibited. In 2011, Bolivia denounced the 1961 Convention with the intention to re-accede with a reservation for coca-leaf chewing. This is an option that Bolivia has every right to pursue, and the notion of denunciation and re-accession has been successfully used for other international treaties. However, the INCB is highly critical of Bolivia's actions. Nonetheless, Bolivia will most likely be allowed to re-accede with its reservation; it is privately acknowledged that it is preferable to have Bolivia within the Conventions rather than outside. The Bolivian President, Evo Morales, made it very clear at the meeting of the Commission on Narcotic Drugs in Vienna in March 2012 that although the Bolivians intend to permit the growth of and use of raw state coca leaf, they do not intend to permit its growth for the manufacture of cocaine, and are doing everything within their power to stop it.

A limitation of denunciation and re-accession with reservations is that it allows only for *deletion* of treaty wording. A country cannot use this method to *change* the wording of the Conventions; it is merely opting out of certain specific sections. Therefore there are certain policies that cannot be achieved using this method. The report also outlines the ways in which the wording of the conventions would need to be *changed* to bring about policy options that cannot be realised simply by *deleting* wording. The diplomatic methods by which a country or group of countries could achieve these changes are complicated, but the report lays them out clearly so that if a country has the will to change, a roadmap has been drawn up showing how to get there.

THE TURNING OF THE TIDE

To coincide with the launch of the *Global Initiative* in November 2011, the Beckley Foundation published an open letter in *The Guardian* and *The Times*.[17] The letter was signed by 60 of the world's best and brightest, including 12 Nobel Laureates and nine former presidents. "The War on Drugs has failed," they stated, "it is time for a new approach."

Until very recently incumbent politicians have been reluctant to put their names to calls for reform—societal conventions get in the way. But the tide seems to be turning, and change is being led by Latin America. In 2011, President Santos of Colombia, a close ally of the USA, said, "I am not opposed to any formula that is effective, and if the world decides to legalise and thinks that that is how we reduce violence and crime, I could go along with that."[18] In February 2012, Guatemala's newly elected president, Otto Pérez Molina, also called for legalisation to be considered—a remarkable statement from a former general elected on an uncompromising 'firm hand' platform. The leaders of Brazil, Mexico, Honduras and Costa Rica have all joined the call for a new approach.

There is definitely a shift taking place in world opinion. Over the last 14 years, it had been my primary intention to use the Beckley Foundation to educate 'thought leaders.' Now I feel that most thinking people realise that the prohibitionist approach to the control of psychoactive substances is deeply flawed. What is lacking is political will and courage. In the UK for example, David Cameron supported a debate around legalisation and regulation, both in 2002 as a member of the Home Affairs Select Committee enquiry into drug misuse and in 2005 as a Conservative leadership contender. Now that he is Prime Minister, the Government is sadly taking a very different line. This is largely due to the tabloid

newspapers such as the *Daily Mail*, and fear that the elector-
ate demands a tough stance on drugs. The public should realise
that prohibition leads to a totally *unregulated* market controlled
by criminal cartels. Our children would be better protected by an
approach of *strict regulation*, where the Government is in charge,
not the criminal underworld. In order to bring about this change,
there must be a demand from the 'bottom up' for our politicians
to adopt more evidence-based, health-orientated policies. To help
stir that demand, the Beckley Foundation is currently setting up
a new campaign website with the support of the *Global Commission on Drug Policy*, Virgin and Avaaz.

Let half a century of repression give way to a new era where
common sense, rationality and scientific evidence join to bring
about a safer, healthier and more humane world.

1. Carhart-Harris RL, Erritzoe D, Williams TM, Stone JM, Reed LJ, Colasanti A, et al. *Neural Correlates of the Psychedelic State as Determined by FMRI Studies With Psilocybin.* Proceedings of the National Academy of Sciences, USA. 2012;109(6):2138–43.
2. Sewell RA, Halpern JH, Pope HG Jr. *Psilocybin and LSD in the Treatment of Cluster Headaches.* Neurology. 2006:6:1920–22.
3. Carhart-Harris RL, Leech R, Williams TM, Erritzoe D, Abbasi N, Bargiotas T, et al. 'Implications for psychedelic-assisted psychotherapy: functional magnetic resonance imaging study with psilocybin.' *British Journal of Psychiatry.* 2012;200(3):238–44.
4. Available from: http://www.unodc.org/unodc/en/treaties/index.html. Accessed 27 April 2012.
5. United Nations Office for Drug Control and Crime Prevention. World Drug Report 2000. Oxford: Oxford University Press; 2001.
6. Avaiable from: http://www.unodc.org/documents/data-and-analysis/WDR2010 /AllPrices.pdf. Accessed 27 April 2012.
7. Available from: http://www.pgr.gob.mx/temas%20relevantes/estadistica/estadisticas.asp Accessed 27 April 2012.
8. World Health Organization. Improving Access to Medications Controlled Under International Drug Conventions. Available from: http:/www.who.int/medicines/areas /quality_safety/ACMP_BrNoteGenrl_EN_Feb09.pdf. Accessed 27 April 2012.
9. Grover A. *Report of the UN Special Rapporteur on the Right of Everyone to the Enjoyment of the Highest Attainable Standard of Physical and Mental Health.* United Nations. 2010;A/65/255.
10. Gallahue P. *The Death Penalty for Drug Offences Global Overview 2011: Shared Responsibility and Shared Consequences.* London: Harm Reduction International; 2011.
11. United Nations Office for Drug Control and Crime Prevention. World Drug Report 2011. Oxford: Oxford University Press; 2012.

12. Available from: http://reformdrugpolicy.com. Accessed 27 April 2012.
13. Both reports are published on the Beckley Foundation website, www.beckleyfoundation .org, and elsewhere.
14. Wiarda J. *The Truth Has Sometimes to be Suspended.* In: Beckley Foundation, editor. *Global Drug Policy: Future Directions.* Oxford: The Beckley Foundation; 2005.
15. International Narcotics Control Board. Report of the International Narcotics Control Board for 2011. New York: United Nations; 2012.
16. Kirgis FL. International Agreements and US Law. American Society of International Law; 1997. Available from: http://www.asil.org/insigh10.cfm. Accessed 27 April 2012.
17. Available from: http://reformdrugpolicy.com/partner/public-letter. Accessed April 27 2012.
18. Smith P. *Colombia's Santos Open to Drug Legalization.* Drug War Chronicle. 14 February 2011;671. Available from: http://stopthedrugwar.org/chronicle/2011/feb/14/colombias_ santos_open_drug_legal. Accessed 27 April 2012.

RELIGIOUS FREEDOM AND THE EXPANSION OF AYAHUASCA CEREMONIES IN EUROPE

KEVIN FEENEY & BEATRIZ CAIUBY LABATE

Since the late 1980s, itinerant South-American shamans and congregations of the Brazilian ayahuasca religions, Santo Daime and União do Vegetal (UDV), have appeared throughout Europe. At the heart of these traditions is the consumption of ayahuasca, a psychoactive brew containing dimethyltryptamine (DMT), a Schedule I substance under the United Nations Convention on Psychotropic Substances (CPS). The legality of ayahuasca under the CPS has been interpreted differently throughout the world, as has the religious nature of these traditions.[1,2] While freedom of religion is protected in Europe under the European Convention on Human Rights (ECHR), this protection depends on the recognition of a religion's legitimacy, and whether particular practices may be deemed a threat to public health, safety or morality. In the case of indigenous itinerant shamans, or contemporary psychotherapeutic practitioners, the legal issues are even more complex. This chapter seeks to examine the status of these ayahuasca traditions in Europe, and to investigate the role and significance of the ECHR in shaping the discourse on religious liberty and ayahuasca.

A BRIEF HISTORY OF AYAHUASCA TRADITIONS IN EUROPE

Early European experiences with ayahuasca generally took the form of workshops, or ceremonies, adapted from their original cultural contexts to cater to European tastes and the interests of the New Age movement,[3] however, it was not long before structured religious groups like the Santo Daime and UDV began to take hold. In 1989, a Santo Daime delegation from the Centro Ecléctico da Fluente Luz Universal Raimundo Irineu Serra (CEFLURIS) arrived in Spain for the Easter Holy Week, which became the first official visit of the Santo Daime to Europe.[4] By 1992, a branch of the Santo Daime appeared in The Hague, Netherlands.[2] An early Santo Daime/New Age hybrid developed in Germany in 1993, and was soon followed by more traditional congregations of the Santo Daime.[2] Informal practicing groups arose in Spain in the early 1990s, and by the mid-1990s branches of the Santo Daime had emerged in France and Italy.[2] Currently, congregations of the Santo Daime can be found in a number of European countries, including: Austria, Belgium, the Czech Republic, England, Finland, Greece, Ireland, Portugal, and Switzerland, among other small nuclei. Chapters of the UDV appeared later in the 1990s, and can now be found in Spain (first appearing in 1993), the UK (1994), Switzerland (1994), Italy (1998), and Portugal (2003).[5]

With a presence in Europe exceeding twenty years, and with congregations in numerous countries, much can be investigated regarding the history and formation of ayahuasca religions in Europe. So too the trajectories of shamans and therapeutic practitioners who have visited or established practices in Europe. Here we focus on the legal and social challenges these traditions have faced in the European community, and provide some conjecture as to how these groups might assimilate in a continent wary of both minority religions and of increasing cultural diversity, particularly when the global War on Drugs continues to have a strong hold worldwide.

There are three primary legal barriers that adherents of ayahuasca traditions face in order to practice their ceremonies in Europe. The first regards the legality of ayahuasca, which contains DMT, an internationally controlled substance. The second regards whether the Santo Daime, UDV, and other ayahuasca drinking modalities, are viewed as legitimate religious practices deserving protection under the ECHR, or whether they are seen as problematic cults, which should be prohibited. Finally, if these traditions are recognised as religions, there remains the question of whether ayahuasca poses a significant threat to public health, morals or safety. Such threats would permit individual states to prohibit religious uses of ayahuasca under Article 9(2) of the ECHR. Each of these issues will be explored below in order to provide an overall picture of the circumstances faced by different ayahuasca traditions within the current European legal and political climate.

LEGALITY OF DMT AND AYAHUASCA

The Single Convention on Narcotic Drugs, adopted in 1961, was an attempt to unify a number of international drug control treaties under one umbrella, and currently provides the foundation for international cooperation in the War on Drugs. The Single Convention can be viewed as establishing a three-part division of controlled substances, which includes plants (opium poppy, coca, cannabis), specific compounds (i.e., cocaine, dihydromorphine, hydrocodone, etc.), and preparations containing specified quantities of controlled substances. This division is significant since the Single Convention is the only modern drug convention to specify plants requiring control, and because ayahuasca is a plant-based product.

DMT, one of the active compounds in ayahuasca, didn't come under international regulation until the CPS was adopted in 1971. This convention added a variety of chemical compounds to the list of scheduled substances, but did not address the regulation of any additional plants. While no plants are specified for regulation, the CPS introduced a new definition of "preparation," referring to "any solution or mixture, in whatever physical state, containing one or more psychotropic substances."[6 Article 1(f)] In order to clarify the CPS, a commentary was subsequently published which stated that beverages and infusions made from plants were excluded from coverage,[7] but no further guidance was provided about the definition of "preparation." As a result of these ambiguities in the CPS, there have been conflicting opinions regarding whether ayahuasca can be considered a controlled substance.

This issue was cause for dispute in a Netherlands court case where Santo Daime members were charged with use and distribution of DMT in violation of the CPS.[2,8] In order to clarify the legality of ayahuasca, an opinion was solicited from the International Narcotics Control Board (INCB), a quasi-judicial body of the UN drug control system. In response, the Secretary of the INCB clarified that, "no plants (natural materials) containing DMT are at present controlled under the 1971 Convention," and that "preparations [...] made of these plants, including ayahuasca, are not under international control."[9] Nevertheless, the Dutch court determined that it was not bound by the INCB's interpretation, and found that ayahuasca qualified as a preparation under the CPS because a combination of plants (*Banisteriopsis caapi* and *Psychotria viridis*) is required to produce the desired hallucinogenic effect.[8]

This interpretation, however, has not been universally accepted. Courts in both France and Italy have determined that ayahuasca is a derivation of uncontrolled natural products, and, while containing DMT, not specifically prohibited.[2,10,11] In France, charges against a branch of the Santo Daime were dismissed after several years of intense court battles (1999–2005) because the plant components (*B. caapi* and *P. viridis*) were not specifically prohibited under the CPS or French law.[2] Following the dismissal the French government moved quickly to schedule both plants as illicit "sectoidal" products,[12] an issue we will return to later.

In Italy, the argument that ayahuasca is an uncontrolled natural product was initially rejected in 2005 by a Court in Perugia, which ruled that ayahuasca is a preparation because it is a mixture of more than one plant. The Supreme Court of Cassazione overturned the ruling as inadmissible, citing a lack of evidence concerning how ayahuasca is actually prepared.[13] The case was returned to the Court of Perugia to hear evidence regarding the preparation of ayahuasca, and to determine whether ayahuasca contained a "surplus" of alkaloids when compared to the alkaloid content of its component plants. At the rehearing, the Santo Daime provided expert testimony that ayahuasca is a decoction of two plants, and that the final product has an alkaloid content comparable to that of the original plants.[11] In light of this testimony, the court rejected allegations that ayahuasca was a prohibited preparation, and charges against the Santo Daime were dismissed.[2]

Due to ambiguities in the CPS, the legality of ayahuasca and its plant components will likely continue to be determined on a state-by-state basis. If a particular country determines that ayahuasca is subject to government control, however, ceremonial use of ayahuasca might still be protected under the right to religious freedom as guaranteed by the ECHR.

EUROPEAN CONVENTION ON HUMAN RIGHTS

The foundation for religious freedom in Europe was established in 1950 with the drafting of the ECHR. Of primary importance to our discussion is Article 9, which protects the individual's right "to manifest his religion or belief, in worship, teaching, practice and observance."[14 Article 9(1)] Under the ECHR, individual states may proscribe certain religious activities in pursuit of one of several "legitimate aims," which include restrictive measures "in the interests of public safety, for the protection of public order, health or morals, or the protection of the rights and freedoms of others."[14 Article 9(2)] The measures taken by the state in pursuit of legitimate aims, however, must be "necessary in a democratic society,"[14 Article 9(2)] a phrase which has been interpreted by the European

Court of Human Rights (ECtHR) to mean that limitations must be in response to a "pressing social need," and that the measures taken are "proportionate to the legitimate aim pursued."[15 §50] This standard is similar to the one established in the United States under the Religious Freedom Restoration Act, which favoured the UDV and Santo Daime in the USA.[1]

RELIGIOUS RECOGNITION OF AYAHUASCA TRADITIONS IN EUROPE

Many European countries have developed rules regulating the recognition of religious groups. These regulations have been occasionally used to deny recognition to, and ultimately prohibit, certain religious practices. The ECtHR has recognised the right of states to regulate religions, stating that "states are entitled to verify whether a movement or association carries on, ostensibly in pursuit of religious aims, activities which are harmful to the population."[16 §40] However, it requires that any restrictions on religious practices be justified and "proportionate to the legitimate aim pursued."[16 §44]

The Santo Daime has successfully procured recognised religious status in the USA, Canada, Italy, the Netherlands, and Spain, while the UDV has, so far, procured official status in the USA and Spain. The processes necessary for religious recognition, however, are often bureaucratic and ideological, and tend not to favour minority religions. In Spain, for example, the road to recognition for the Santo Daime and UDV was onerous. Both groups were initially denied recognition based on insufficient proof of their religious character. Fortunately for the Santo Daime, the government's denial was not generated within the requisite time period, which resulted in default recognition by the Spanish government.[2] The UDV redrafted its documents and changed the name of its congregation to Church Virgen de la Concepcion, an important religious reference in Spain, before re-applying in 2005. The group was denied a second time, necessitating an administrative appeal.

Registration was eventually granted to the UDV in 2008, seven years after their first application.[2]

While states undoubtedly have a variety of motivations in limiting recognition of religious groups, it is necessary to recognise that much of Europe views 'New Religious Movements' (NRMs) suspiciously. The European experience with cults, such as Sun Myung Moon's Unification Church and the Order of the Solar Temple, has led governments across Europe to attempt to curb the influence and practice of NRMs, efforts that often appear to categorise religious minorities as a social problem.[2,17] To limit the activities of NRMs, many countries have not only implemented strict regulations on religions, but have also adopted legislation outlawing brainwashing, variously referred to as "the deceitful abuse of a state of ignorance or a situation of weakness," or "the crime of mental manipulation."[17 p153-4]

The movement to regulate and restrict the activities of NRMs has been strongest in France, culminating in the passage of the About-Picard law in 2001, which criminalised "the fraudulent abuse of a state of ignorance or weakness."[18 Article 20] Under this law, the government can hold a whole religious group responsible for the illegal activities of its leaders, activities that, if repeated, allow the government to permanently dissolve a religious organisation. By outlawing the plant components of ayahuasca, the French government has positioned itself to permanently dissolve the Santo Daime Church.

The classification of *Banisteriopsis caapi* and *Psychotria viridis* in France as 'sectoidal' products is unique and requires further explanation.[12] This legislative move was essentially an attempt to associate these plants with brainwashing and sects, a derogatory term for some NRMs in France. The sectoidal classification likely stems from an essay that claimed a preparation of *B. caapi* and *P. viridis* may produce "chemical submission" in users.[19 p77] By labelling these plants as 'sectoidal,' the French government has implicitly taken the position that there is no legitimate use of ayahuasca, and that the religious use of these plants poses an unacceptable threat to individual liberty. This position implies that adherents to the Santo Daime and UDV are not volitional participants in their religion, but rather are victims of some type of hallucinogen-based brainwashing. Thus, in France, the stereotypical notions of hallucinogens and sects have been drawn together in a way that clearly demonises ayahuasca practices.

While procuring religious recognition in various countries poses difficulties, particularly where anxieties about NRMs are high, another important consideration regards the centrality of ayahuasca to these practices. The issue of centrality is duly illustrated by a lesser-known case from the Netherlands, where two ayahuasca drinkers claimed protection under Article 9 of the ECHR.[20] The following statement by one of the appellants, "I can practice my religion without the use of ayahuasca," was a key consideration for the Supreme Court in determining that the risks to public health posed by ayahuasca outweighed the religious interests of the appellants.[20 §3.3] Significantly, court cases in the Netherlands involving the Santo Daime religion—where daime (ayahuasca) was recognised as a fundamental sacrament to their religious practice—have found the religious interests of the Daimistas to be greater than the government's interests in protecting public safety.[8,21] Taken together, these court cases suggest that the centrality of ayahuasca to a particular religious practice may be key to a successful claim under the ECHR.

Although official religious recognition by a state is not necessary to invoke Article 9 of the ECHR, which protects both freedom of religion and freedom of thought, both government recognition and showing that the sacrament is central to the religious practice should help solidify religious liberty claims under the ECHR. The pervasive suspicion of NRMs has created problems for minority religions, and is perhaps the biggest barrier to acceptance for new religions in Europe. Nevertheless, states must be able to justify restrictions on religious activities under ECHR Article 9(2) as measures that are pursuant to a "legitimate aim," and which are "necessary in a democratic society."

LIMITATIONS ON RELIGIOUS FREEDOM

The interests of public health, morals, and safety, are all considered legitimate and permissible reasons to limit freedom of religion under Article 9 of the ECHR. Thus, if a particular state considers ayahuasca to be a controlled substance, either nationally or internationally, then it may restrict its use, as long as ayahuasca can be shown to pose a threat to these legitimate government interests. However, restrictive measures must be deemed "necessary in a democratic society" and be proportional to the state's aims. As a result, an overview of potential outcomes is warranted.

Health and safety played a curious role in the prosecution of two members of the Santo Daime who were charged with importation of illicit drugs, with intent to distribute, after bringing ten litres of daime into Spain in 2000.[2] The confiscated beverage was analysed in order to determine whether "dangerous" levels of DMT were present. The result of the toxicological analysis, which failed to take into account the potentiating effects of harmala alkaloids, determined that the DMT content in the confiscated beverage was too low to produce inebriation, based on DMT's known oral activity. The judge, relying on the conclusions of the toxicology report, dismissed the charges, finding that the daime could not be considered a threat to public health given the low levels of DMT found.[1,22] Additionally, the judge considered that the ayahuasca was intended for private consumption by a group of individuals with a history of ayahuasca use rather than for general distribution; a fact that supported a finding of limited public risk.[22] It is interesting to note that the court reasoned that the Santo Daime was some sort of insulated "addict community," using ayahuasca only among themselves, rather than considering it as a religious group with potential liberty interests. This approach differs substantially from the way these groups understand their sacramental use and results in a sort of 'ironic victory.'

In Germany, a court determined that the mere presence of DMT was sufficient to find that ayahuasca posed a threat to public health, and justified prohibiting its religious use.[2] This ruling is questionable under the ECHR. The German government was never required to demonstrate that the limitations on religious use of ayahuasca served a "pressing social need,"[15] nor that the restrictions placed on DMT were proportional to the government's goal of protecting public health.[23] Germany's justification for prohibiting religious ayahuasca use, based on its mere illegality, would likely be seen as an insufficient application of the ECtHR's test, which requires examining not only the basis but also the means used for restricting particular religious activities.

A British court similarly dismissed application of this test when hearing an ECHR defence of marijuana possession by a Rastafarian. The court, while recognising Rastafarianism as a legitimate religion, determined that prohibition of cannabis under the Single Convention was sufficient proof of a "pressing social need" to justify restricting religious use. Additionally the court rejected the defence's arguments that the prosecutor be "required to conduct a trial, hearing evidence as to the merits or demerits of cannabis."[24 §31] One significant difference between cannabis and ayahuasca, however, is that cannabis is clearly controlled under the Single Convention, whereas the legality of ayahuasca under the CPS is much murkier. While different countries are likely to come to different conclusions about the threats posed by ayahuasca, each state must still meet the requirements for limiting religious freedom as outlined by Article 9(2). In situations where the outcomes appear inconsistent with the ECHR and ECtHR case law, as in the German and English cases mentioned here, the ayahuasca groups might consider applying to the ECtHR for review. The ECtHR has yet to hear any cases dealing with the religious use of psychoactive substances, and such a case may help to clarify how restrictions on religious activities are to be examined under Article 9(2).

CONCLUSION

In this chapter we have attempted to outline the three main barriers to the practice of ayahuasca religions, shamanisms, and therapeutic activities involving ayahuasca in Europe. While the questions of legality, religious legitimacy and perceived risks of ayahuasca use are the same questions asked in each country, how they are answered varies considerably. Despite the presence of international conventions aimed at unifying drug control laws and creating universally recognised human rights, Europe remains a diverse continent with varied political and cultural interpretations of international and European law. The CPS and ECHR might best be seen as providing broad guidelines within which individual states must manoeuvre. As we have seen, the Santo Daime and UDV have had some preliminary success in establishing themselves as official religions in several countries; however, the members of these religions, and other ayahuasca practitioners, continue to face persecution in Europe and elsewhere. This persecution needs to be understood, not only in light of the continuing influence of the worldwide War on Drugs, but also in view of the generalised anxiety toward NRMs in Europe.

The cases discussed here show that having a recognised religious use, in contrast to recreational or other use, is desirable. Nevertheless, obtaining recognition of new religious groups can be complicated and often involves facing hostile and ethnocentric definitions of what qualifies as a legitimate religion. For practitioners who are outside of the more conventionally recognised syncretic-Christian ("religious") modalities of the Santo Daime or UDV, the situation is even more challenging. Shamans, either indigenous or New Age, or persons such as licensed psychologists holding therapeutic ayahuasca ceremonies, are less likely to be protected as religious practitioners under the ECHR.

While it is unlikely that any new convention will be able to standardise drug control or religious rights, the gradual state-by-state recognition of the Santo Daime and UDV may help build a foundation of legitimacy upon which these groups may seek to gain broader acceptance. In the future, however, it may be necessary for these groups to apply to the ECtHR on religious freedom grounds in order to obtain a clear precedent regarding their right to use their sacrament. While such a move runs the risk of a negative outcome, the result could also lead to a more uniform application of the ECHR. For now, ayahuasca religions, itinerant shamans, and therapeutic practitioners, continue to face a patchwork of regulatory schemes throughout Europe, with only a few countries recognising the validity of these traditions and their right to use this controversial Amazonian brew.

1.   Labate BC, Feeney K. Ayahuasca and the process of regulation in Brazil and internationally: Implications and challenges. *International Journal of Drug Policy*. 2012; 23(2):154–61.
2.   Labate BC, Jungaberle H, editors. *The Internationalization of Ayahuasca*. Zurich, Switzerland: Lit Verlag; 2011.
3.   Balzer C. Ayahuasca rituals in Germany: the first steps of the Brazilian Santo Daime religion in Europe. *Curare*. 2005;28(1):57–70.
4.   Groisman A. *Santo Daime in the Netherlands: An anthropological study of a New World religion in a European Setting*. University of London; 2001.
5.   CEBUDV. *Linha do Tempo 1922–2011*. In: Agenda 2011. Brasilia, Brasil: CEBUDV; 2011.
6.   *Convention on Psychotropic Substances*. 1019 United Nations Treaty Series 175; 1971, entry into force 1976 Aug. 16.
7.   United Nations. Commentary on the convention on psychotropic substances, done at Vienna on 21 February 1971. New York: United Nations; 1976.
8.   Rechtbank Amsterdam. 13/067455–99, AB1739 , AB 2001, 342; 2001 May 21.
9.   Schaepe H. Letter from the Secretary of the INCB to R. Lousberg, Inspectorate for Health Care of the Ministry of Public Health in the Netherlands. 2001 Jan. 17.
10. Cours d'appel de Paris. 10ème chambre, section B., Dossier N° 04/01888; 2005 Jan. 13.
11. Tribunal Perugia. n. 1391/05; 2006 Jan. 13.
12. Order of April 20, 2005. Journal Officiel de la République Française n°102, page 7636, text n°18; 2005 May 3.

13. Corte Suprema di Cassazione. n. 1616; 2005 Oct. 6.
14. European Convention on Human Rights. European Treaty Series No. 5; 1950, entry into force 1953 Sept. 3.
15. Sunday Times v. United Kingdom. ECtHR; 1991 Nov. 26.
16. Manoussakis and Others v. Greece. ECtHR; 1996 Sept. 26.
17. Richardson JT, Introvigne M. "Brainwashing" theories in European Parliamentary and Administrative Reports on "cults" and "sects." *Journal for the Scientific Study of Religion.* 2001;40(2):143–68.
18. About-Picard Law. Law No. 01–504 of June 12, 2001. *Journal Officiel de la République Française* n° 135, p. 9337; 2001 June 13.
19. Pépin G, Duffort G. Ayahuasca: spirit liana, shamans and chemical submission. *Annales de Toxicologie Analytique.* 2004;16(1):76–84.
20. Hoge Raad. LJN: AZ2497; 2007 Jan. 9.
21. Rechtbank Haarlem. 15/800013–09, LJN BH9844; 2009 March 26.
22. Juzgado Central de Instrucción, número 3 de Madrid. T.S.J., 60/2000; 2000 Oct. 10.
23. Handyside v. United Kingdom. ECtHR; 1976 Dec. 7.
24. R. v. Taylor. England & Wales Court of Appeal (Criminal Division) 2263; 2001 Oct. 23.

INTRODUCTION TO THE
MDMA DEBATE

BEN SESSA

Breaking Convention 2011 was an important event for so many reasons. It was the first time since the 1960s that an international conference dedicated entirely to psychedelic research had been held in the UK. It was a show-casing of work for academics, scientists, artists, writers and performers and it was, above all, a truly magical experience in which a tremendous atmosphere of togetherness and participation pervaded the whole weekend.

My main academic responsibility for the weekend was the organisation of the medical and clinical speakers; the pinnacle of which was this MDMA Debate. The debate was conceived partly as a means to invite as many MDMA experts as possible without having the time to give them all a lengthy slot of lecture-time, so I decided to lump them together to share the stage. But it became something much more than that. This debate represents the first time these experts—some of whom have debated one another over the years in the scientific literature—have met head-to-head like this in an open forum. The result was a fascinating display in which the audience was treated to a live discussion of some shared and some refreshingly divergent views on the subject of MDMA. Thankfully it was not simply an exercise in sycophantic similitude, but rather a real contest, the kind of discourse that's essential for this subject.

The use of clinical MDMA—and especially its old nemesis ecstasy—throws up a whole raft of pharmacological, moral, political, legal and social questions. What better group of people to debate these issues than Val, Rick, Peter, Andy and Jon? I am grateful to them all for their courage and expertise and also to the audience who also contributed and made this event another of the great aspects of Breaking Convention 2011.

Finally a word about what some people went through to bring this transcript to you: Enormous thanks must go to Cameron Adams for single-handedly travelling to Lithuania to retrieve the elusive hard-drive on which this MDMA debate video was stored, then further thanks goes to those squirrelling folk at MAPS for transcribing the film. I have made only minimum edits to improve the flow and prose. Apart from that, what follows is how it went. Enjoy.

THE MDMA DEBATE, UNIVERSITY OF KENT, CANTERBURY, UK. 2 APRIL 2011

Jon Cole[1] (JC), Val Curran[2] (VC), Andy Parrott[3] (AP), Peter Oehen[4] (PO), Rick Doblin[5] (RD). Moderated by Ben Sessa (BS).

BS: 3,4-methylenedioxymethamphetamine: Killer drug? Saviour of mankind? None of the above? All of the above? The UK has a particular interest in MDMA. We have had 23 years of heavy ecstasy use here, with over 100 million tablets of ecstasy consumed in this country every year for 23 years. Are we right to talk about MDMA recreationally and MDMA therapeutically? Can we compare the two? Do the morbidity statistics of recreational ecstasy use have anything whatsoever to do with MDMA being used clinically? Is there a future for MDMA psychotherapy? What do we think about the politics and classification of MDMA? What do we think about children taking MDMA?

What we have here is a collection of experts in the field. From psychology, politics, from psychopharmacology, risk management and psychotherapy, people who have published some similar articles and some very different perspectives about MDMA.

Today we want a stimulating and rousing debate. Each speaker will have five minutes to set out their stall and then we will open the floor for questions from the audience and hopefully the panel will ask questions of one another too.

Thank you all for coming to this event. I think this debate is long overdue in this country. Let's get started.

JC: Essentially I'm going to ask you some questions, this is very interactive. If I were a researcher looking into the safety of MDMA and I applied to the government for some money, how many of you, if you were the government, would give me that money? [Audience raises hands.] That's way more than I thought. Okay, if I were to ask you, "would you give me money to look at the danger of MDMA?" how many of you think the government would put their hand in their pockets and give it to me? Such is the nature of research that you reverse what normally happens when I ask that question. Normally when I ask that question everyone thinks the government should put his hand in his pocket and pay to demonstrate that ecstasy or MDMA is dangerous and those people feel that the government should not pay to show that MDMA is safe. However those amongst you who know anything around the science, will know that the experiments to show the safety will be exactly the same. What it shows is that there's a financial imperative for us to discuss danger when discussing drugs like MDMA. This is why I call it the ecstasy paradigm. Therefore I've not got slides or discussions of research studies, simply because I don't think that's relevant. What I think is relevant is our discussion around the *narratives* of MDMA and related compounds and what we really need to discuss is why are we focusing on safety or danger when in reality the experiments are the same? What we're focusing on is our interpretation of them. So, therefore that's what I want to leave you with. The simple question: Is it the narrative? Or is it the danger? Thank you.

VC: I'm going to follow now by trying to summarise the main issues, which I hope will help stimulate the debate. I don't need to tell you a lot, but the benefits of MDMA are very clear. We recently used the Nutt framework to ask 1,500 drug users to rate the 20 most common drugs including alcohol and tobacco and other illicit drugs. MDMA came up highest of all 20 drugs in terms of acute benefits and second only to LSD in terms of chronic benefits. And empathy, as a clinical psychologist, is important for me; empathy in the therapy situation is hugely important. The drug has potential benefits. We've heard how it stimulates the release of neuropeptide oxytocin, which is the human bonding hormone. It's what bonds the baby and mother through the breast milk and through the whole process of birth. This debate, as Jon Cole has just talked about, has been based on harms, all sorts of political, economic and other reasons. The harms are in terms of what happens immediately after you have the drug: a few days later is the short term. The long term has been the main debate. And then something that we've been particularly interested in is what happens after you stop. So I want to challenge what the scientific evidence is on these things. Actually we've given ecstasy in a horrible old basement room in St Mary's Hospital and people love it even when you make them come in at 9 in the morning. They get a huge kind of empathy and they really enjoy doing the experiment. We have to turn people down we get so many volunteers. Just to be fair the science shows it does have some impairing effects. It impairs memory acutely. In this study we gave either ecstasy alone, ecstasy plus alcohol (2–3 units of alcohol), alcohol alone, or just a double placebo drink and pill. And what you see clearly is that ecstasy, 45 to 120 minutes after you've taken it, does impair memory. It stops you from remembering words, but it also enhances your ability to control your impulses. A Dutch study shows this. And it focuses your attention and speeds up your psychomotor function. But you won't see *that* in the newspapers. You'll only see memory impairment. A few days after use, we showed a long time ago, you get a midweek dip in mood, a midweek low, but seven days later, that's gone. You're back to normal. So again it's only a fluctuating thing, which we think coincides with changes to serotonin in the brain. Long term there's been such rubbish written about this drug, such bad science. [Referring to the slide.] This is a paper from a very respected Dutch group who had done the only prospective study of MDMA. They took people from coffee shops before they'd used ecstasy and followed them through and did brain imaging, cognitive testing, after some of them had started using the drug. This is a memory test where you're shown related words and then you're asked to recognise 30 words. This got published in a highly prestigious journal, *Archives of General Psychiatry*. And what it shows is that kids that went on to use ecstasy, before they'd used ecstasy they remembered nearly all of the 30 words. After they'd started using ecstasy you'd still reckon their performance was pretty amazing. What they did was to show impairment. They said that in this group 22% of them had actually shown a slight decline, right, one word. Whereas in the group who'd never used ecstasy didn't show that. Only 6.7% showed the decline. The authors concluded that doses of ecstasy are associated with a decrease in verbal memory function. Which suggests ecstasy-induced neurotoxicity. You don't have to be a scientist to realise that is absolute rubbish. There have been an awful lot of very poor neuroimaging studies done in the field. The best one to date is one done in Canada by Steven Kish. And they did show a reduction in an index of your brain's serotonin function. Serotonin is an important neurochemical, especially in things like depression. But even though there was a reduction in current users, especially in memory areas, hippocampus, and in perceptual areas like the occipital cortex, nothing was abnormal in the ecstasy users. The overlap between the two groups was huge. No abnormality either in terms of memory or brain function in ecstasy users. The year before, using the same radio-ligands used to look at serotonin in brains, we found that when people have given up using ecstasy there was absolutely no difference in their brains compared to people who had used similar other drugs or no drugs at all. We've also shown no memory impairment a year after people have given up compared to people who use drugs other than ecstasy. And John Halpern has similarly shown in a paper recently out, no memory impairment in people who use ecstasy but were not using a load of other drugs like cocaine and amphetamine. No withdrawal syndrome has been identified. Since we've been researching ecstasy I've never met a single ecstasy addict. The American government, NIDA, are paying someone called Linda Grants to go out and show that ecstasy users fit the psychiatric classification for addiction. The only way she's shown it at all is by finding people, over half of whom also use heroin, so completely atypical of the ecstasy-using population.

AP: Thanks Ben for inviting me. I'm going to explain how I came to believe that ecstasy is far more damaging than when I first started doing studies. So my first studies were in 1993 to 1996, largely interview studies. And we got lots of positive subjective reports. And this is when it's called an entactogen. I published two to three papers during this period. And, like many people at the time, I believed it was quite different from many of the other psychoactive substances. It was an entactogen. However we also found initial reports of problems. We had people who said they had taken it and had bad experiences. One of the people in one of our interviews said they wouldn't touch it again because their experience with it was so bad. A few others said they'd had bad experiences, which were quite unlike earlier experiences they'd had on the drug. And also we saw recovery problems as Val pointed out in the previous slide. Many of our users recalled that they had mid-week blues, which has now been well replicated. We've looked about in a number of studies and found more problems mid-week. So, it's certainly a euphoric drug when taken, but it certainly has untold effects in recovery period. So if you asked me, then in 1996, would I recommend it for therapy, I'd be very neutral. I'd say, "Well it seems to have a positive profile but also it seems to have negative effects as well." So the overall profile from 1996 would have been neutral. We then found the first study of memory deficits compared with young matched non-users. This confirmed an earlier American study, which is more of a clinical report of nine users who also had psychiatric problems. This has now been confirmed in published studies. It's probably 30, 40, 50 studies, which have found deficits. Most of those studies controlled for other drug use including cannabis. Rogers undertook a big government sponsored meta-analysis in 2009. They had seven measures, which they had sufficient data on—they had been done in eight or nine studies or more—where they could do a meta-analysis. In seven of the measures they concluded that ecstasy was more damaging than poly-drug user controls. The control group was crucially other drug users not using ecstasy. One measure they didn't find a deficit was NART, which is a measure of intelligence. The other six measures were all memory measures. The meta-analysis concluded there were specific memory problems in ecstasy users. We've also looked at higher cognitive problems, particularly pre-frontal problems. The number of groups that find problems in higher executive deficits: problem solving, social intelligence. Again most studies these days need to control for cannabis in their statistical analysis or in the groups. You also find acute type reactions. One of the intriguing things about ecstasy is the wide variation in individual responses. Some people seem to be very robust. Many people have mild problems and some people have quite severe problems. We find this in the serotonin syndrome. Occasionally people develop quite a strong syndrome and a small proportion need hospital emergency treatment. If you talk to medics who work in emergency Saturday nights the past 10 to 15 years, they said they often have stimulant abusers/users (whatever you like to call it) in their hospitals. They're almost invariably treated successfully. People now know how to treat the hyperthermic reactions successfully and most people are released the following day, on Sunday morning, but it is certainly a severe bad reaction. The mid-week problems we've talked about...

In 1997 I found the first case of psychiatric problems. This is a young recreational user who reported phobic anxiety, which they attributed to being an ecstasy user. We then did some studies and we found raised psychiatric problems in lots of ecstasy users. Again, this is compared with other drug users as well. Other users also have problems—cocaine, amphetamine, methamphetamine—they're all associated with psychiatric distress. MDMA is not dissimilar from those. In 2006 I'd have said, "No, it wasn't a safe drug." More recently I've been looking at the effect of environmental co-factors and these seem to exacerbate the problems. If you look at dancing music, psychosocial factors, the theory is it's not just the drug alone. It's the concomitant stimulation which leads to the brain being over stimulated and this leads to a positive on-drug experience, but it also leads to negative recovery problems in the week afterward. We found people that danced the most report the strongest mid-week recovery when matched for drug use. It's a combination of drug and physical over-stimulation, which seems to be the problem. Further along, I'm writing a review on this at the moment and at low doses MDMA has very little effect on temperature. Visual defects: several groups have now reported subtle deficits in occipital cortex. Social intelligence, which I think is relevant to MDMA as a therapy, seems to be reduced in regular users. Neurotoxicity: in the Nell paper, Val Curran said, "the effects weren't particularly marked." Let's go over that. I'll talk about one error. In the occipital cortex 51% of the ecstasy user group had SERT levels below the lowest region of the control group. There was a lack of overlap. Many of the ecstasy users had quite strong deficits. In conclusion, I wouldn't recommend it.

PO: As a psychiatrist and psychotherapist I'm greatly frustrated by the number of people I encounter in my private practice who I'm not able to treat properly. There are multiple reasons why people are treatment resistant, not only PTSD and as Ben said in his introduction this afternoon we are desperately in need of ways of enhancing psychotherapy. Leuner, of psychedelic therapy in Europe once made the approximation that only 50% of people can be treated by psychotherapy, so we need something that's an enhancer. From my point of view, from what I've seen, MDMA can be this drug; can be one of the drugs. I strongly advocate to differentiate between the therapeutic use where you would administer one dose of 125 mg in a completely different setting, no physical exercise. It has been shown that, for example, the cortisol levels when exercising go way up and if you are lying down on the couch they are lower, much lower. Maybe that's one explanation for the damage that it could cause. We should investigate. We have the chance now with these studies going on to combine these studies with neurophysiologic studies. That would be really interesting and support evidence of damage or benefits. Thank you.

RD: Hello. First off, I'd like to thank Andy Parrott and all the other researchers that have looked at the risks of MDMA and of ecstasy. I think it's essential that we have a clear understanding of what the risks are. However I think it's been the case that the risk data has been exaggerated and the potential benefits have been denied. Whenever you're doing a risk-benefit analysis, if there are any risks and there are no benefits then you would conclude that it's not appropriate to use the drug. But if you look at Medline and you put in ecstasy or MDMA there are over 3,500 papers that have been published at a cost of over $300 million. There's only one paper on a completed study on the therapeutic benefits of MDMA and that's Michael Mithoefer's study. That paper, though, has fundamentally shown that there are benefits. I think Andy's data that he talked to us about, about he's now convinced that MDMA is unsafe for therapeutic use, it all comes from recreational use of MDMA. So, I think it's completely inappropriate. Although it's valuable, it's not enough. We need to look at the risks in a therapeutic context and we don't see the kind of risks that he's talking about. But, even if we did, you know Aspirin kills a lot of people. People are allergic to penicillin. We don't have to show or we don't have to claim that MDMA is this rare drug that has no risks and only benefits. The temptation in a way is for advocates to be boxed into that corner because the other side is saying there are all risks and no benefits. But what we're really looking for is an accurate comparison of risks and benefits and then a weighing of them from actual research in therapeutic contexts. I have seen over the years that the risks data has been used to suppress researching benefits. From 1985 when MDMA was criminalised to 1992 when the FDA opened the door to MDMA research, seven years went by with no possibility of permission to do MDMA research into therapeutic uses. That has now changed. Andy spoke about the first study of the neurocognitive consequences in nine subjects. That study was funded by MAPS. What you don't probably realise is that it was done by Larry Price and George Ricaurte. It was done at Yale. We are trying to be the leaders of the research into the risks of MDMA when used in a therapeutic context and also the benefits. I paid for the neuropsychologist to do the analysis. That particular study was doing other measurements, tryptophan challenge tests and things like that. I got this report from neuropsychologists and it said there's nothing here remarkable. There are a few changes, but it could easily be attributed to the fact that several of the subjects flew in from California, that they had just received tryptophan and their tryptophan challenge test. They're unusually intelligent. There's nothing here. And to my surprise, years later this turned into a paper with John Crystal and the neuropsychologist as coauthors. I called the neuropsychologist and I said, "How could you do this? I don't understand the difference between the report that you gave and the paper that was published." He said, "If you ever release the report I gave you I'm going to sue you." I was like, "This is my property. I paid for it. How could you possibly do that?" You can see that there is a tendency to exaggerate the risks in order to get publications. So, I think the risk research is absolutely essential, but I think it's been highly biased by motivations coming from funders to justify cruel and counter-productive prohibition. I think that the potential patients who could be benefiting from this is a major social cost that usually is not weighed into any of these discussions.

I'd now like to switch and say that we have a series of phase II pilot studies all over the world. We're looking at a range of methodological questions that we need to address. What we're going to try to do is find out over the next two to three years: what is our method? How do we refine the method? How do we teach the method? How do we assure ourselves that therapists in different settings are actually adhering to the method? How do we develop a double-blind study with a powerful psychoactive drug like MDMA? Are there cultural differences and how do we figure out what they are and how to work around them? Is the cause of PTSD requiring a different treatment or can we enroll people that are victims of sexual assault and also combat related PTSD and also car accidents? Our working assumption is that the cause of the PTSD is irrelevant. Then we go to the FDA and we say, "Here's our data," and we propose a phase III study. If they accept the design and permit us to move forward then we move forward with that. It'll probably take us three years to get to the end of the phase II meeting, another five years and another $8–9 million to get to the end of phase III, then we submit to FDA and I'm anticipating that, in a decade, if we're fortunate, we will probably have MDMA as a prescription medicine. Thank you.

BS: Thank you, all of you first of all for sticking to those rigid time limits that we set of five minutes each. There's a number of things that we need to be cautious about: The difference between recreational use and clinical use, we need to appreciate that no drug is 100% safe and we're actually looking at risk versus benefit ratios. Who would like to pick up on some of the points of some of the other speakers first? Do we have in the audience any psychiatrists, clinical psychologists or other people who work clinically with patients? I'm interested to know whether or not people have come across morbidity associated with recreational ecstasy use in their clinical practice.

Audience member: Not really.

BS: I haven't either.

Audience member: I've sometimes felt brought down after I've been using it fairly extensively, but nothing that can't be corrected with amino acid supplements.

BS: So, you're describing a mild adverse effect. My question was really whether clinicians have found clinically relevant mental disorders associated. We are aware that it does have mild subjective negative effects in people. The point I was making: are these effects sub-clinical or are these at a level that are reaching the psychiatric clinics and hospital beds? My broad experience and speaking to other psychiatrists is that they are not of a clinical level. So, I just wanted to make that point.

RD: I don't tend to disagree with you Ben, but I am aware of someone who had taken MDMA and under the influence of MDMA had remembered a prior sexual assault, which had led to physical violence where she had almost been killed. Under the influence of MDMA it came up but she wasn't in a context where she felt she could really work it though. And so she ended up checking herself into the emergency room in a hospital to avoid committing suicide. Later she contacted me, this was in 1984, and I agreed to sit with her in another MDMA experience. It ended up helping her to confront it in a safer context. From that she decided she wanted to become a therapist. She now is a therapist and she's worked on our Spain MDMA/PTSD study. That's something that's now 26 years ago and she's had long-term positive effects. So, I think the context of MDMA is absolutely critical. It's possible to take MDMA in a setting where you end up feeling worse off sometimes for months. My question for Andy is: How can you really, in all good conscience, look at the risk data from non-medical, non-clinical settings and say that justifies a decision that MDMA research in clinical settings is too dangerous to conduct?

AP: Well, you've described one straight from 1984? If you look at the Greer and Talbot paper published in 1986, they had 29 clients. Now, these weren't psychiatric clients. They were friends and acquaintances, about nine of who had sort of psychiatric levels of problems. But they weren't psychiatric clients. Now two of those 29 had abreactions to the drug, which lasted more than a week. Many of the participants had abreactions that lasted a day or so, but these two had problems which lasted a few weeks. With one therapeutic administration, you can elicit, you can engender problems.

RD: Would you be influenced if I were to speak to George and say, find out how those two people are doing right now. If we could get that information and give it to you, would that in any way change your attitude about the therapeutic research with MDMA?

AP: Well, they actually describe this in the paper. One of the clients got better after a few weeks. The other was given free non-drug assisted psychotherapy for a year. So, the problems of that 29th person were really quite enduring. And so they needed a fairly prolonged period of therapy after one session. The problem with MDMA is it elicits all sorts of material, both positive and negative. Franz Vollenweider shown this, lots of other groups have. I've been involved in a study in Australia where we tested people in a laboratory and people had to drive simulated cars. We didn't get positive and it's probably because the environment wasn't positive. In other words, what happens with MDMA is it boosts all material. It's a CNS stimulant. If you're in the wrong environment you may well have negative material boosted. In my final slide I was going to say the crucial factor is the therapy not the drug. In fact,

Greer and Talbot said, "The primary thing is the therapy." So, my position is it's far safer just to give therapy.

BS: Can Val cut in here?

VC: Sorry, I just can't understand how you get different results from everyone else Andy. If you look across all the studies: Kuypers and Ramaekers, Dutch people—they have lots, we've done stuff, Harriet de Witt's done it, everybody gets these really positive moods. And as I've said we do our studies in the basement of a hospital. It's not at all a nice environment. I think there's something odd about your data. No one else gets it but you. I also think that in your chat with Rick Doblin, if you take any drug there's always going to be one or two or a few people who have a bad reaction, even alcohol.

AP: It's the new data we're most surprised at. We expected to get positive effects, so we were very surprised when we didn't.

VC: Are you sure it was ecstasy that you gave?

AP: [laughing] We buy from a Swiss pharmaceutical company. I guess Swiss sell pretty high quality, so it was 100 mg of laboratory MDMA. You mentioned Harriet de Witt. She and Bedi in New York published two studies where they didn't get positive effects. In both those studies the participants were given other tests in the laboratory. What we wrote about in the paper was the environment. If it's in a negative laboratory environment where you have to do lots of tasks, MDMA probably won't give you a positive experience. If you're experiential, sitting in an armchair, you've got supporting people around you, encouraging, you'll get a nice positive experience. It's the environment.

VC: We'll just have to agree to differ, because we do eight-hour studies. They come at 8:00 in the morning and we keep them all the way through. On the MDMA days they love it.

BS: Jon.

JC: I've got a slightly different take. If we look at all of the neuro-toxicity studies, we look at the brain imaging studies, the studies where tryptophan was being administered, if you look in the participants section it clearly says none of these people had a psychiatric problem. In all of the studies that have been quoted around whether they've got neurotoxicity or not, none of them had a psychiatric problem. So, how do we get this notion that all of the psychiatric problems observed in people are due to MDMA and they're due to neurotoxicity? Because people who are clearly demonstrated, according to the papers, to have neurotoxicity, don't have any psychiatric problems. And I've reviewed plenty of these papers as a scientist. One of the things that I didn't want to say because it's potentially libellous and there's a camera pointing at me, is how about the problem that, when challenged, the authors refused to draw the attention of the reader to that fact. I did it in every review and every time when the paper was published it was not there. I think that what we've got to accept is that whilst there's a large amount of research, as Val has pointed out, a lot of it's done very poorly, but there's also a huge publication bias and we have to take that into account when we consider that research.

BS: Can we have a question? Robert.

Robert Forte (audience): This isn't so much a question as a brief account. From 1981 until 1985 I was a graduate student at the University of Chicago and I had embarked upon a quasi-formal investigation of MDMA where I had handed it out to hundreds of people. Me and my associates... this is actually how Rick got his first MDMA. When I had collected over a hundred written reports of this experience I took it to Daniel X. Freedman, who was the president of the American Psychiatric Association and editor of the *Archives of General Psychiatry*. And I said, "This is a new drug that hardly anyone knows about that is extraordinary and it may be the best thing that psychiatry has ever had." He referred me to Charles Schuster, who at the time was the director of the University of Chicago Drug Abuse Research Unit. I gave him and his assistant some. Then in 1985 I was about to give a lecture at the University of Chicago on the curative effect of MDMA. This was the morning that the DEA declared their emergency scheduling of the drug and Schuster and Dr. Seiden were written up in the *Chicago Tribune* as the experts on MDMA that said it caused this brain damage, this damage to serotonergic receptors. I was astonished because just two weeks earlier he was supporting my formalising my research at the University of Chicago. I went to his office and I said, "How could you do this? This is just what happened with LSD. A rumour is introduced and now there are still people who think that LSD causes brain damage." He took me into his office and he explained to me, and this is exactly what he said, he said, "Look. I have a nice setup here." He had a whole floor at Billings Hospital at the University of Chicago. He said, "The government gives me a lot of money. Sometimes I just have to do what they say." Two years later he was appointed to head NIDA, the National Institute of Drug Abuse. I think this story indicates that there is a kind of crisis of legitimacy in this whole MDMA debate from the very beginning. That this brain damage stuff is kind of contrived and misleading to justify a political position of the government. In this case in the US.

Audience member: Excuse me. Can I add something?

BS: Yes, please.

Audience member: I'd just like add a little bit to the neurotoxicity part of the ecstasy story. Both Parrott and Curran referred to the Kish study showing a decrease in the serotonin transport binding in ecstasy users. I would just like to add a little bit to that story, because it's very difficult to assess toxicity in the living human brain of course. This is part of the reason why we can argue from here to eternity about if it's toxic or not, because actually it's impossible to show. It's not possible to come up with any measurement to really show it. In a paper that we will publish in two months we have also mentioned the serotonin transporter, which some people view it as a marker of toxicity. We don't necessarily do that because it could also just be an effect of that state of serotonin depletion, if this serotonin transporter down-regulates. But what I think is important to say is that one thing that we see and also that third study that has not come out yet from the New York group. We see the same thing. We see a quite severe decrease in serotonin transporter binding in the cortex, especially in the occipital cortex. It's not necessarily reversible, from the data that we have and also the same is seen in this New York group. The jury is still out to see if there's actually severe changes in heavy users, especially, heavy recreational users of ecstasy, if there's changes in the serotonin system or not.

AP: Can I respond?

BS: Yes, please.

AP: In the Kish study they found variation in reduction of the serotonin transporter. What they also found is it correlated with two things. One was lifetime dosage. So heavier users had less of the transporter. The second thing that correlated was memory impairment. So the loss of serotonin transporter was correlated with poorer performance on their cognitive tasks.

Audience member: Yes, we actually see the same. We also see an effect, the more lifetime use of ecstasy, the lower the serotonin transporter. We see the same, the New York groups see the same. So, there's some kind of lifetime dose-responses relationship. But, what we also see and what the Kish paper refers to, and actually did mention, because that might be as important, is that they see also a relationship, and we see that, time since last use adds the binding. And that points to a possible reversibility of the findings, so that the serotonin transporter might down-regulate, but it might get back up if you take a break and don't use ecstasy. In our data that will come out, it looked like after 200 days of abstinence the serotonin transporter is back in business, especially in sub-cortical regions. We don't see that in the cortex.

JC: Can we just be very clear. Ecstasy and MDMA are not the same thing.

Audience member: What's the difference, please?

JC: The difference is ecstasy is the illegal drug in tablet form that very rarely contains MDMA. Most street ecstasy in the UK at the moment contains benzylpiperazines as tricor butyl-piperazine or meta-coro-phenyl-piperazine. They do not contain 3–4-. I can point to a sign up there that's embarrassing. I recently analysed the confiscated tablets in the bins at [a large rave club in the UK], Creamfields. There wasn't much MDMA apart from in crystallised form. Let's just be clear ecstasy is a street drug, which may or may not contain MDMA. Therefore we cannot say using it 500 times equates with the exposure to a known dose of MDMA. That's just nonsense.

VC: That's interesting to know that you've got more data. Kish quotes our study where we've looked at people who've given up ecstasy for at least a year, that was an inclusion criterion. And we found no differences whatsoever. And the other interesting thing about Kish is he found no differences in the striatum, which is where you would expect the differences to be. I think we all agree, it's the time since last use. Reneman's data agrees as well. I think eight out of the nine studies that have looked at people reducing or stopping do show an association between recovery of SERT and times since last use. Our study took two years to do to find the controls. We couldn't find British people who had used stimulants and other things the ecstasy users had used. There weren't anyone. If you'd used ecstasy you'd also used coke and whatever else. So we ended up getting volunteers from South Africa and Australia or New Zealand because the ecstasy movement started later there. I think it's really important how your controls are matched. And you're saying about heavy users showing non-reversibility. I would worry about the effects of lots of other drugs on SERT. Heavy users are going to be using lots of other drugs as well.

RD: I'd like to make just one point, too. It's that the real issue I think is functional consequences. The assumption is if there's a change somehow or other that's bad. We're already talking about, and Peter talked about it, how there are changes associated with therapeutic benefits. So first off, this assumption, that any kind of change is bad. Then there's just this focus in our particular study, we did neurocognitive tests with people who got three doses of MDMA, 125 mg plus 62.5 mg after two hours, and there was a slight gain in neurocognitive performance after the MDMA treatment, which is not to be unexpected, because people's emotional issues: their anxiety, depression, PTSD, affect their performance on neurocognitive tests. If we can help people with their PTSD we would assume that their neurocognitive performance would go up. Now the placebo people who also had a 20-point drop in their CAPS, not as much as the MDMA people, they got better as well, slightly in their neurocognitive tests. I think the key point is: What are the functional consequences? I would like to remind people... I don't know how many people have recently heard that—it was about six months ago—George Ricaurte and Una McCann came out with a new paper saying that MDMA causes potentially fatal sleep apnoea. That was in the title: potentially fatal sleep apnoea. And it just doesn't get the press that it did, anymore, that it used to. You know, there's just this exhaustion in a way with the effort to try to show that MDMA has these fatal consequences. That's why I say again to Andy, that we really need to look at risks in a therapeutic context and we are doing our best to study neurocognitive performance. We're going to start doing some sleep measures. We don't really believe there's potentially fatal sleep apnoea from MDMA. I think we need to really look at pure MDMA in a therapeutic context and then evaluate it in a comprehensive way.

AP: One comment needs to be said... Serotonin is important for breathing. When you breathe at night, that's controlled by serotonin. If you're an MDMA user you're damaging your serotonin system. That's what Ricaurte and McCann reported. You had young, fit people who weren't overweight. Sleep apnoea is usually associated with males who are overweight. It's a disorder where you stop breathing in the night. What was happening was youngsters in their mid-twenties who weren't overweight... was it 25% of their sample?—had sleep apnoea.

JC: So, how many have died then, Andy? Surely, if we've got millions of ecstasy users and sleep apnoea surely we should have a fatality count in the thousands. Sorry. Does anyone else see the logic of the fact that there are no dead people?

AP: I'm not defending the title. I'm just trying to talk about the...

JC: Where are the dead people? This is nonsense. I'm sorry.

BS: I'd like to ask a question about the way in which neuro-cognitive testing is carried out. Can the panel enlighten me: How many of these studies that demonstrate neurocognitive deficits include urine drug testing on the day of test? Because of course, nobody's disputing that acutely intoxicated with MDMA one can be somewhat disturbed neurocognitively. That is after all why people take it. One man's neurocognitive deficit is another man's party. If you want to bring someone into a laboratory and do neurocognitive testing on them and they are ecstasy users and we've already asked the question: whatever the hell an ecstasy user is, because we don't even know what ecstasy is. Have we got some good studies that really control on the day of testing for any concomitant drug use?

VC: Well yeah. I think both our group and John's group used hair as well as urine so that we could see previous drug use. The hair is like a tree. Each centimeter of hair grows in a month. You can look at drug use in your hair. In those studies we found no difference between poly drug users and ecstasy users in neurocognitive function. In better-controlled studies I think, Andy will probably disagree, show a lack of difference really.

BS: So, when it's well controlled for, you don't see the neurocognitive deficits?

VC: That's my take on it. When they are better studies, they are bigger studies, they are better matched for all the drug use, and then, you know, I think, you don't see it.

AP: You're probably not going to be surprised by this. In the Kish study they took hair samples and they proved that they were MDMA users. MDMA was present in their hair. They also took urine samples to control for recent drug use. The Kish study... if you want to see a good paper... many of the earlier papers were flawed. It's an extremely difficult area to do research in. There are lots of potential confounds. The Kish study—I think many people like Val said it—is now seen as pretty much a gold standard. And Elizabeth Franklin's group in Holland have done lots of very good research. But the Kish study was quite remarkable in the number of things they tried to control. They did find memory deficits.

BS: Can we take that question from the floor? Is that OK?

Audience member: Given that we are noticing that there's some seeming depletion of serotonergic transporters, how can we consider other means of increasing that? I've recently come across a study of the UDV members that JC Calloway and Dennis McKenna were part of as well, where they found that they were psychologically integrated. I believe they also found that they had more serotonergic receptor sites developed in the brain. I believe that's to do with the advanced neuro-inhibiting function rather than the psycho...[inaudible] release. Is there any work being done into how you might address the problem of serotonergic?

RD: I have to say that, in our clinical studies, we've explicitly decided not to try to co-administer any other substances with MDMA because we want to try to get a complete picture of what MDMA does by itself. We think it's way premature to conclude that in a therapeutic setting there is some neurotoxic problem at all, anyway. Then to try to do multiple drugs administered at the same time, it's just really too complicated and not necessary. So, we've not seen a need to do that in clinical studies.

BS: Torsten has a question.

Torsten Passie (audience): I would like to introduce a study that was done ten years ago by Tomasian et al. It was a government-financed study and I only want to give a short introduction. It was five groups... one without any drug use, one with drug use but without ecstasy, and three ecstasy-using groups. One was 50–100 doses, one was 100–500 doses, and one 500–2,500 doses, but with other drugs used similar. I mean at the same point of time, which is different from Halpern's new study. This study was showing that the group with the lowest range of accumulative dosage of ecstasy use haven't had any deficit in any parameter and they have done a very thorough study with even PET scans and neuropsychological batteries and everything. The funny thing is that the results of this study were published as a book because it was an end report of a government-financed study. The publications that came out afterward in the international literature, in the English language, they were putting all the ecstasy-using groups together so that under the line everybody got the damage. And not so many people are aware of that study but I guess Mr. Parrott, as a specialist should be aware of that. What does he think about the low-range ecstasy-using group and about these results even with other drugs used at the same point in time at rave parties, etc.?

AP: Yeah. I'm aware of the publication—those papers I wasn't aware of his chapter in the book.

Torsten Passie: Okay, okay. So, this is the thing, how they fitted it together. At one conference...I may mention that for just a second.... Yeah, I can show you... The funny thing is when Mr. Tomasian was presenting his results at the scientific conference, I was putting my finger up and asking him, "What about that group?" and he told the people, "Yes, you're right. They hadn't had any deficits. But I don't want to mention that because I get funny questions then." [Laughing].

BS: The chap in the back there waving. Yes please...

Audience member: Some recreational ecstasy users claim that they use 5-HTP the day after and delay the mid-week blues. Does anyone on the panel know anything about 5-HTP's effects with ecstasy?

Another audience member: We've experienced it once.

Audience member: Have you looked at the comedown effects and differentiating between MDMA and ecstasy? We're obviously talking about a drug which, you know in my experience, we should claim gives a happy sensation irrespective of context. People have associated it with very severe downhill feelings afterward, once the effects have worn off. As a prescription for people with psychiatric disorders how would you justify that?

BS: Okay, thank you. I wonder whether Peter might be able to come back up on this? Can we justify therapeutic use of MDMA when there are these anecdotal experiences of negative comedown effects when used recreationally?

PO: In a therapeutic setting people are instructed about possible comedown effects and, if they are, they take it more easily. They can access help if they need it. People in recreational settings—that's what I see often—do not know about this and they are not very well educated about possible negative effects such as anxiety or depressed mood or when they get into a crisis because subconscious material comes up. So, there is definitely also a need for more education about these things.

Audience member: So, you're saying education is the reason? If people are educated enough about drugs that they realise MDMA isn't dangerous?

PO: It's all about mindset, set, and setting. You can compensate...

Audience member: So it's the same with an alcoholic drink, for instance?

RD: I'd just like to add that in our therapeutic context—first off that it's not been a substantial issue—but secondly the way in which we conduct the studies is that the people take the MDMA in the morning. They don't take it at night. So they first off don't lose any sleep. They spend the night in the treatment centre and then they have non-drug integrative psychotherapy the next morning. Then we release them to go home and they're called every day for a week on the phone to check-in, to see how they're doing. Then they come back for non-drug psychotherapy on a weekly basis before their next MDMA session three to five weeks afterward. Then we repeat that two to three times, depending on our different studies. There are some times when people have opened up such painful emotional material that they're struggling to deal with it for a period of time. But it's not the idea that that is somehow or other such a problem that the therapy shouldn't be done.

BS: A question from Sue.

Susan Blackmore (audience): First a comment and then a question to Andy. My comment is: I'm feeling so horribly naïve and upset about this publication bias, publication suppression business. I mean I feel naïve because I didn't really believe it but you've told me enough stories here. It bothers me very much, not just in the context of drugs, but in the context that in other ways I'm always defending science against people who say, "Science is just making it up." I mean the potential harm of this is not just to drug legalisation to a better world in terms of drugs, but to the whole respect for science in general. And that really bothers me. Anyway, I'm going to go home and digest this and worry about it. My question to Andy concerns—it's a very small one— it concerns this business about the cofactors of dancing and so on. You concluded that the people who dance more or do various other things more, have worse effects. Am I right in assuming this wasn't a real experiment? I mean in a real experiment you take a hundred users and you tell these many to dance this much and this many to dance this much. Presumably you're asking them after the fact how much they danced and they could be different people or they could be induced to dance more because of things going on in their brain, that cause and effect could be the other way around.

AP: We've done a few studies. I've described one of them. We've got 11 ecstasy users who agreed to go clubbing to their normal club.

Susan Blackmore: Ecstasy users or MDMA users?

AP: I'll reply to that as well. They were ecstasy users. They agreed to go dance clubbing in the same venue, in the same group of friends, on two different occasions. On one they take drugs as normal. We weren't allowed to say, "take ecstasy," but the ethics committee allowed us to say they could take their normal whatever it was. On the other they agreed to abstain from ecstasy or any other stimulant. They didn't take any stimulants. We also took saliva samples and the saliva confirmed MDMA presence in all 11 people when they danced on MDMA. It confirmed their abstinence when they danced the same weekend, the same group of friends, off drug.

We have tested this. We've also tested surveys, Internet surveys of people and asked them how much they danced etc. That's where the data comes on the more memory problems. Those that report they dance more report more problems.

Susan Blackmore (audience): Yeah. That's exactly my point. It's they reported they danced more. Now why does dancing more have a greater effect? It could be because it's the dancing, but it could be that they're caused to dance more. You can only make that conclusion if you've actually manipulated this as an experimental variable, can't you?

AP: If I can reply again? They also had wrist things, which are called actographs, so we recorded their physical activity. They had the same, similar levels of physical activity dancing—they danced both occasions. We also measured cortisol. The cortisol increase when they're abstinent was very little. When they're on MDMA the cortisol increase was 800%, which is massive. They also got 0 change in testosterone, whereas they got a 75% in testosterone when they danced on ecstasy. It's not dancing per se it's the combination of the dancing and the MDMA, which is problematic.

Audience member: Is it MDMA now? You said, "ecstasy."

AP: They were ecstasy users. We tested their samples, their saliva samples, and all 11 had MDMA in their saliva.

BS: Okay. We've got a lot of hands up. Amy.

Amy: What's ecstasy and what's MDMA? If you were to take laboratory MDMA in a club, recreationally sorry, is that safe? If you took normal ecstasy in a recreational environment, what are your views on that?

JC: Well, how do you define safe?

Amy: What are the risks you've been talking about and what effects would it have?

JC: If you look at alcohol, alcohol kills around 4,000 people through direct intoxication per year. And how many of us would consider going down to the pub after this talk to be safe? So, the question is, is the danger always lies—basic principle of toxicology —it's in the dose. So whenever somebody comes to me and says, "Is ecstasy dangerous?" I just go, "What are you talking about?" The thing is, it's the dose of MDMA which may potentially cause an adverse reaction. If we look at the medical statistics on adverse reactions, for drugs like MDMA, the overwhelming majority walk in to A&E and they walk out again. Usually the ones who come in on a gurney and die are the ones who are poly drug users. When we talk about the safety of MDMA in a clinical setting there is data dating back to when Rick started, to when Franz Vollenweider did his studies, all the way through to when Andy did his study in Australia. No one's dying. The key thing... the question that you're asking is: In the correct setting, with the correct dose, is MDMA safe? The fact that no one's died... now you could say, "Well okay, that's not an indication of safety." 100,000 people per annum die from doctor-administered drugs. We know that prescribed pharmaceuticals are incredibly dangerous. We also know about issues in the pharmaceutical industry. That's a matter of public record in terms of class-action suits, suppression of data, etc. So, I've just upset you [Susan Blackmore] even more. The key thing is: The question that you're asking is very difficult to answer. The question is whether it's relatively safe compared to the other things that you could do. So for example if we were to use Dave Nutt's example of horse riding or going up into Everest, lots of people do it. And lots of people die. But we don't sit around having debates like we're having now.

Amy: My point wasn't just that, as Peter emphasised, about the therapeutic setting. Is it really the context behind it or is it the actual drug itself? I'm confused as to what is most important: the context or the actual substance itself, the street version...

JC: I've looked into this. Basically, squaddies on route marches die of hyperthermia. They fall over, fall into hyperthermia. They die on the spot. The incidence is roughly equivalent to the instance you see in the ecstasy users. What's the link? Extended aerobic exercise, probably with poor hydration, probably reasonable nutrition. Similarly if you look at the serotonin function of marathon runners, it's roughly equivalent to that of ecstasy users. Again, what's the link? Extended aerobic exercise. The thing is, if you sit around having a good time listening to classical music, why would you die? There's enough studies indicating the physiology of MDMA in those environments and I think, for example, at the temperature rise of all of the clinical studies, most of them indicate a temperature rise of 0.5°C. If you look at animals, almost invariably you're looking at a 2°C rise in core temperature. The difference is they've got fur. We haven't. We're much more tolerant to the heat stress produced by this compound. It's got to be the setting. If you jump up... if you're going like an idiot for eight hours what do you expect? [Laughter.]

BS: I'd like to get to these questions. This lady here and then this chap in the back.

RD: What I just wanted to say is—Jon basically raised the question: How many people have died in clinical settings? But there's another measure, which is called the serious adverse event. All of the regulatory agencies in the world require the researchers to report if there's a serious adverse event. That could be going to the hospital because blood pressure has increased and they needed some special treatment or some psychological problem lasted for over a few days and they had to be hospitalised. There has never been a single serious adverse event in over 475 people who have used MDMA in clinical settings. That isn't to say that it's perfectly safe. I think what we have to constantly get back to is balancing risks and benefits. I think that's what has been suppressed for so long. MAPS is only a tiny non-profit organisation. We have a budget of a little bit over $1 million a year. We're the only people in the world paying for studies into the therapeutic use of MDMA. That's fundamentally wrong. There should be so much more government money, other major foundation money, so that in this context we've been forced to sort of argue about is there serotonergic neurotoxicity in the absence of any evidence about benefits? And that's finally emerging. I think you cannot look at the risk question without also looking at the benefits. I think if you talk to somebody, like Peter's person, who did those drawings. If you say to her, "If you remember one less word would you pay that price?"

BS: Thank you. You've had your hand up. And then there's a gentleman in the back. Yes, please...

Audience member: I want to make two short remarks and one question. First I want to congratulate Andy for coming. I think it's very good that somebody with a different kind of discourse attend a conference like this.

BS: I personally invited Andy and indeed all the panel because I have deep respect for all their work. Thank you for pointing that out.

Audience member: The other thing that I want to say is: as an anthropologist I kind of find some resonance with this therapeutic discourse, this kind of exemption for therapeutic use. I find resonance with the religious argument for exemption. There seems to be, sort of in the air, some kind of exclusivity that in this context things are different. And I'd like to go again for Charlie's talk in the morning. That we look into wider perspectives, because as an anthropologist I'm pretty afraid to take drugs with doctors. That's a little provocation, but I respect you a lot for the work of MAPS and what I'm interested in, what I find kind of this funny circuit system is that the whole proposal to study the efficacy of drugs is to try to see what is their effect, not counting expectations. You kind of make all these techniques double and nobody knows what they're taking and all this kind of 'neutral' context. But

I find this paradoxical, because we all know that taking drugs depends a lot on expectations. Isn't it important that we try to create these expectations that will heal us? How do you deal with that in scientific terms? Because it's very important that we have a... if you want to create the therapeutic official use you need an accompanying culture of belief in this cosmology and this idea that it will heal us because this is fundamental for healing. I think this kind of conference gives a kind of setting for this. That it's creating this cultural understanding for all of us. That we have some sort of thing we can relate to. That doesn't appear in the discourse. Everybody's trying to detach all these cultural elements to it. But shouldn't we bring it into centre stage? Instead of getting rid of it, try to elaborate on it, build on it.

BS: There's a guy at the back. He must have a very sore arm in the air for so long. So please, let's have your question.

Audience member: I was just worrying about the interchangeable use of the words ecstasy and MDMA. If ecstasy can be a combination of many different substances, then how does the term poly drug use come into there?

BS: I think we've covered that somewhat. That it is very difficult to make any reasonable comments about recreational ecstasy users and combine that with what we know about MDMA. Do we need to say any more on that?

Audience member: What's ecstasy?

BS: Exactly. I think we've already explored that.

Audience member: MDMA's being sold as well and that's adulterated so you get these interchangeable. You just don't know because of the illegality.

VC: I think one of the hard things to research over the years since I've been doing this sort of stuff, is that ecstasy has changed so much. There have been times when ecstasy was MDMA and now it's rubbish. I mean nobody's using it. In history it was good. There was good stuff around. If you're looking at the research over time, you think what if they were doing it ten years ago. Yeah, probably this is MDMA they are talking about. If they're doing it now, we have no idea. So that again creates a very odd literature and evidence base really. That's why we have to go with the studies that have been much more controlled and really checked what's in the pills and all the body fluids that show that.

AP: Yeah, I can agree. In my last two years in Swansea we've had difficulty getting ecstasy users. So if you are an ecstasy user and you're taking pure MDMA then please come along to Swansea and we'll test you. [Laughter.]

BS: This lady down in the front here.

Audience member: You were talking about the recreational use and I think this idea kind of leads me to the whole set and setting. Once we've got to take on board one's mindset, which is what you illustrated. Also I think the environmental factors that you were talking about doubting. In terms of where these people were dancing whether it was the environmental factors taken into consideration i.e., if the club had air-conditioning for example. If there was a garden, if there were safety measures in place for these people should they need it. Were they taking into the consideration the environmental factors?

AP: In our Internet survey we simply asked people. In the study I talked about where we had the people go dancing under two drug conditions.

Audience member: But did you ask them if the area where they were dancing was safe for them? Was there air-conditioning? Was there water available? You know... do you know what I mean? So that their setting was optimum. Because it's all well and good to be able to conduct these studies in a laboratory where the temperature's nice and you have all these things available, but what about in a recreational setting where it's unpredictable?

JC: We did a study in a nightclub and we did the ambient temperature of the dance floor and it was 25.9°C at about 1:00 in the morning. We also found no temperature rise in any of the participants. I think the thing is, we do need to be careful that that club had air-conditioning and it was turned on. I think that that's a very good point and people need to take that into account when they're assessing these studies, particularly if it's self-report on the Internet.

Audience member: I think we need to do some educating people who are going to take these substances as well.

RD: I just wanted to comment that the police have taken notice in the United States that some clubs will provide areas that are lower temperatures than the main dance areas and the police have used that as a reason to arrest the club owners and to try to take their properties, because it's a sign that they are aware that drug use is taking place in their facilities. There was a case in New Orleans where the DEA explicitly said that if there are rooms that are 15° or more lower than the dance areas that that is a sign that they can be prosecuted for having a club where MDMA is being used. The American Civil Liberties Union finally was able to fight that, but what we have is a perverse situation where the police have a harm maximisation strategy. That's what we have with impure drugs, with reducing harm reduction efforts, because they want to scare people from ever trying to do it. And that's the idea I think that worries me a little bit about this concern about suppressing research into therapeutic use. It sort of fits into this overall strategy: We're only looking at risks. We can't have honest drug education for young people because if there's benefits then what are we going to do? How do we explain that to them? And what do they then believe about the other studies? I think we have a perverse situation that we have to some way or another get around. I think to Bia's question about expectancy: For our research we really have one audience and it's not everybody here. It's the regulatory agencies. We have to speak their language. So, we must work within their context. Eventually maybe we can broaden out. That will be a bigger discussion. But for the next ten years or so we must speak directly to the concerns of the regulatory agencies.

BS: Okay. This chap here. Black t-shirt.

Audience member: I'd just like to make the point that having worked with survivors of sexual abuse, a very significant portion of those don't respond to therapy. Being a long-term survivor of sexual abuse and as clients which don't recover I think they think that the risk that they run on a day-to-day week-to-week basis is self-harm and suicidal ideation. They'd all think that the types of concerns we're discussing are minuscule. I think that they'd also think that, given the history of working with these substances and the successes that seem to be established, that waiting another ten years is appalling, especially if in fact it's on the level that we've just been talking about, about whether, you know, there's a slight problem with mood on Wednesday. [Laughter.] It just seems that the voices of the people that would benefit aren't here today.

BS: I think that's a very good comment from someone with a clinical perspective on the risk benefit argument.

AP: If you're going to have a drug, which severely depletes serotonin, which is the theory of the mid-week blues, and you've got somebody with suicidal thoughts, then that's a potential danger. They may well have very positive thoughts and good therapy with you on the session. The problem is: What's going to happen in recovery periods two to three days afterward? That's one potential issue which I think needs to be addressed.

RD: Let me just say that the FDA has reasonably noticed that with certain kinds of medications there's a low risk—certain antidepressant medications and also Chantix that's used for tobacco cessation—that there is a low risk of a very small minority of people either getting agitated or near potential suicide. So, now they have required all drugs that affect the central nervous system to include measures of suicidality. We have included that now in all of our clinical studies and we will be able to really have clear definite data about that risk.

BS: Question from Andy Roberts.

Andy Roberts (audience): In my professional life, the past 22 years I've worked managing hospitals dealing with young vulnerable homeless people usually between the ages of 16 and 25. I was working in hospitals; I worked during the ecstasy period in between 1985/86 and 1994. I saw hundreds of young people take ecstasy, people from tragic backgrounds who had no one to turn to. It revolutionised their lives to the point where they were transformed people. It's a bit like throwing the baby out with the bath water. Because look, the minuscule harms I've seen to young people working in hospitals have been far far outweighed by the positive experience in young people, many of whom have gone on to bright futures transformed by their ecstasy experience.

BS: Peter wants to make another point.

PO: I'd like to respond to Andy. If you give ecstasy... MDMA, sorry—MDMA to a subject who has a sexual assault history, it's not the same thing if he's in therapy or it's just recreational use. You will have a better therapeutic alliance with them and he will call you up and it'll probably be not just at whims of his serotonergic system, but it will have to do with the material that came up in the session. It's easier to deal with than just Wednesday blues.

BS: I think we should wind this up, mainly because otherwise it will not stop. [Laughter.] Firstly I just want to thank all of our panel and all of you lot for really making my day. It's been a tremendous afternoon looking at all of these issues and this debate has been the icing on the cake. It's really good to get everyone together; the audience and the panel. Thank you very much. Let's all take this forward. Let's bear in mind that we have to look at MDMA versus ecstasy, we have to look at clinical versus recreational, and we have to look at risk versus benefits, because otherwise we're going to get confused. Thank you all so much. Have a lovely evening.

1. Head of the Department of Applied Psychology in the Institute of Psychology, Health and Society of the University of Liverpool.
2. Department of Clinical, Educational and Health Psychology, Institute of Cognitive Neuroscience, University College London.
3. Department of Psychology, College of Human and Health Sciences, Swansea University.
4. Born in 1956 and raised in Canada and Switzerland. Medical school at University of Basel/Switzerland. Specialist degree in Psychiatry and Psychotherapy 1988. Psychotherapeutic training in Guided Affective Imagery Therapy, Systemic Couple and Family Therapy and in Psycholytic Therapy. In private practice since 1988. Special interest in altered states of consciousness and psychedelic substances for more than 20 years. Board member of the Swiss Medical Association for Psycholytic Therapy (SAePT). Principle investigator of the Swiss phase II MDMA/PTSD pilot study (since 2006).
5. Founder and executive director of the Multidisciplinary Association for Psychedelic Studies (MAPS). He received his doctorate in Public Policy from Harvard's Kennedy School of Government for his dissertation on the regulation of the medical uses of psychedelics and marijuana. His undergraduate thesis at New College of Florida was a 25-year follow-up to the classic Good Friday Experiment, evaluating the potential of psychedelic drugs to catalyse religious experiences. He also conducted a 34-year follow-up study to Leary's Concord Prison Experiment. Rick studied with Stanislav Grof and was among the first to be certified as a Holotropic Breathwork practitioner. His professional goal is to help develop legal contexts for the beneficial uses of psychedelics and marijuana, primarily as prescription medicines but also for personal growth for otherwise healthy people. He founded MAPS in 1986, and currently resides in Boston with his wife and three children.

POLY AND MONO: REFLECTIONS ON THE VALIDITY OF 'POLY DRUG USE'

AXEL KLEIN

During the mid 1990s a clinical psychologist freshly transferred to the municipal hospital in Vienna was puzzled by the classificatory conventions in place. The ward for patients with dependency problems was divided into two sections, one for 'Heroin Süchtige' the other 'Polydrogen Süchtige.' A quick review of the medical notes revealed a disturbing similarity—all patients were heroin injectors first and foremost, with a voracious appetite for all manner of other substances. The reasoning behind the label was explained by one of the nurses: the label did not signify anything regarding drug preference, but provided a euphemistic distinction for those with a fair chance of recovery (heroin) and those for whom there was little hope (polydrug). Giving them a pseudo-medical label allowed the hospital to hold on to these vulnerable patients and provide some basic care. Most would use the opportunity to rest, feed up and return to the streets within the space of a few days. The hospital provided a safer and more agreeable environment than the police station, and medicalising what was better understood as a behavioural or social problem was more humane than throwing people into prison. If all that was needed was coming up with a bogus category there was no question of what course of action medical practitioners should take. Oh, Felix Austria, other countries fight wars on drugs, while you simply change labels of drug-using patients.

A couple of decades on and that particular label from the back rooms of the psychiatric ward has leaked into the professional mainstream. Within the greater drug field poly drug use has become a concrete issue, the stuff on which universities with courses in addiction management offer dedicated programmes, and a subject worthy of technical analysis by the European Monitoring Centre on Drugs and Drug Addiction.[1] In Britain the Home Office has tasked the Advisory Council on the Misuse of Drugs to organise a panel of experts to investigate the problem.[2]

What it comprises is not in itself complex or controversial—the use of more than one drug either simultaneously or over a period where they are designed to interact. The ACMD phrases it thus, "the consumption of two or more psychoactive substances in one acute episode, such that at least two substances have not passed their acute effect half-life."[1 p5]

Nothing wrong with that, and as most 'experts' can testify, it is clearly something that happens. What is interesting for us then, is what lies beyond the tautology, in the collaboration of policy makers, researchers and treatment providers. These are three out of four interest groups critical in the construction of drugs as a 'social problem' requiring intervention (the fourth is law enforcement, with no interest in the details as long as there are popular substances to be controlled). And as the failure of prevailing policy becomes apparent and existing paradigms collapse under the weight of evidence, the only response is to repeat the erstwhile assertions but with reference to another signifier. There is already a clear tradition among drug war evangelists to parade ever-new, ever-more dangerous drugs. Cooked up ghetto size portions of cocaine did the trick in the 1980s, then as support for drug wars began to flag in the 1990s methamphetamine became the 'new crack,' and for a few months in 2010 the 'plant food' mephedrone was served up to titillate the public.

In each case the original arguments for drug control are restated: there is a substance out there that lures the innocent with a promise of exquisite pleasure, followed by agony, death and destruction. Policy makers rush to announce a suite of tough measures that usually involve more powers for the police and a generous dollop of public money. Within a few years the issue goes quietly away as the drug lives up to neither promise of paradise nor purgatory. It is in the end just another chemical concoction offering the user a fleeting high or low, a numbing of senses or a vivid aperture to novel sensations. For most users the medical consequences are insignificant, an unfortunate few part with health, liberty or wellbeing. For all concerned the measures so loudly announced make things only a lot worse.

There is a certain predictability to the drug scare, each stage in the cycle brings to the fore different players with a stake in the control system—the frontline worker fighting against the odds, the investigator bringing in the hot new story, the sober accounts by the expert. Polysubstance misuse ('Poly') allows for a replay of the drama without tying it to any one particular substance. Counterintuitive though this may be, it has developed into its strongest single feature. Previous drug scares always floundered on reality as drug and user became familiar. The warnings of one generation, be these about reefer madness-induced suicide attempts or crack babies abandoned in project dumpsters, became the bad jokes of the next. Even heroin has lost much of its venom, defanged by needle exchanges and growing information about regular yet non-addicted users.[3] In contrast to these drug-specific scares, then, Poly can run and run as ever-new combinations of mind-altering substances come to excite and haunt us.

In spite of the operational utility of the term, it suffers from an underlying analytical flaw, so obvious that even seasoned drug war myth decoders have failed to spot it. It is the implicit assumption on which the term rests—that because poly drug use is a new problem, the less or perhaps even non-problematic, traditional norm is *mono* drug use. But as even proponents of the term admit, the very suggestion of mono drug use is so ridiculous as to close the debate right down. What a closer probe of drug use patterns then reveals is the problematic with both parts of the term—poly and drugs. Because its unstated assertion that what we are talking about is illicit substances moves the classification and the debate back from the realm of pharmacology and medicine to that of policy and law. We leave behind the hallowed grounds of scientific objectivity to head towards sectarian moralism.

So what is a drug? Some commentators have suggested that we should best drop the term[4] or that it is part of our intrinsic way of ordering the world,[5] while others still have suggested widening the notion to embrace mind-altering substances regardless of legal status.[6,7] We may indeed want to follow Sherrat's advice and speak of 'Peculiar Substances,'[8] if it were not so long and awkward, and may indeed resort to Escotohado's definition of 'substances that overcome the body.'[9]

The rich discussion on classification recognises explicitly that terminology is political, important and difficult. Experts in the UK have assessed a range of substances and found that the physical risks associated with licit tobacco and alcohol are considerably higher than those associated with illicit MDMA and cannabis.[10] School education, sensibly, is increasingly focused on 'healthy lifestyles,' exhorting young people to realise their potential and happiness through activity rather than consumption—of any substance, legal or illegal. Yet, just as these incremental advances are being made, the uncritical application of the term 'poly' only serves to throw concepts, discourse and policy back by a decade.

So we are once again talking about 'drugs' as if this were an uncontested concept. But it refers to a potpourri of pharmacologically unrelated substances that happen to be illegal, or 'new legal highs' which are in due course going to be made illegal given the proclivity of governments to bring things under control, and the willingness of scientific advisors to appease.

Staying with the idea that anything taken to alter mind or mood for recreational rather than medical purpose constitutes a drug, we quickly realise that poly drug use—or drug combinations—is nothing unusual, novel or dangerous, but the norm. Survey information from ESPAD and BCS suggests that the most popular illicit substance used in the UK (as in all of Europe) is cannabis.[11,12] This being a versatile substance it lends itself to many different modes of administration. In India cannabis leaves are mixed into a drink known as bhang. Mixed with flour and sugar it can be baked into the hash cakes of hippie fame. From Herodotus we learn that the Scythians would use cannabis vapours to spice up their sweat lodge sessions, and pharmaceutical companies have even developed an 'under the tongue' spray full of cannabinoid goodness, but without any of the mind altering THC.[13] Yet the overwhelming majority of cannabis consumers in this country mix their herb or solid with cigarette tobacco before skinning it into a tightly rolled joint. As the novice passes through the cannabis-entwined gateway to illicit pleasure, 'poly' is blazoned on the portal.

Let us remember that cannabis, MDMA, cocaine and most other popular illegals are enjoyed in recreational settings, as substitute or accompaniment of legal substances. These (alcohol and nicotine) are so culturally embedded that they are usually not even recognised as drugs. There are subcultural reactions to mainstream consumption patterns, like the disdain of dance scene clubbers for 'beer monsters,'[14] or the rejection of Big Tobacco by some cannabis smokers. But many users are happy to indulge in a variety of pleasures on either side of the legal boundary.

This line is far more blurred than would appear at first sight, as most people start experimentation with drugs during their teens, when alcohol and nicotine are by law unobtainable. In some places it may even be easier to source controlled substances by recourse to the informal sector. One of the unintended consequences of restrictive tobacco and alcohol policies designed to protect the young is to push them towards alternatives. From the perspective of a minor the acquisition and use of vodka or cannabis are equally transgressive. Yet, the controlled substances are not only available on cool and sometimes friendly underground circuits, they also provide more bang for the buck. Cannabis, particularly, packs much more punch per pound than vodka or cider.

Combining drugs for maximum, synergistic effect, to stretch a precious substance or dilute a powerful one is part of drug culture pure and simple. With the accelerating circulation of goods and people drugs like khat, ayahuasca, iboga or kava that were once confined to particular cultures are becoming available on global markets. Human ingenuity, unleashed in laboratories the world over, is continuously coming up with formulas for new substances or novel ways of using old ones. How these affect the health of individuals and public is naturally a subject of concern. Yet reifying the established method of combination into a new syndrome is dangerously misleading.

Where does it stem from? We suggest that at its root lies a fudge, not so different from the one reported from Vienna earlier on. Our contention is that during the 1980s and 90s drug treatment services in the UK evolved in response to problematic heroin use. Though the majority of illicit users were messing around with cannabis, MDMA, amphetamine, prescription medicines, alcohol and tobacco, the main object of concern was heroin. People using other drugs rarely considered themselves as having a problem that required medical interventions, a judgment with which many treatment professionals and courts would concur.

The system, as it evolved at that time, was mainly directed at preventing the spread of infectious disease, or more specifically HIV/AIDS, and overdose deaths. To that end they encouraged injectors to come into contact with services, offered counselling, free needles and after a short assessment, methadone. Billed as 'substitution therapy' methadone provided heroin users with an alternative fix while they were struggling to kick the habit. A powerful, stupefying, synthetic opioid it is hardly conducive to regular functioning, causes dependency, and has a range of adverse physical side effects, but can help people reduce their illicit drug use and the acquisition crime that it often triggers.

By the mid 1990s this modus operandi had become well established and was attracting funding under the New Labour drug strategy. With the money released by the Treasury came demands for accountability and a general interest in drugs, identified as one of the much critical 'causes of crime.'[15,16] Measures were imported from the US, including the creation of a Drug Czar (the UK Anti Drug Coordination Unit boss) and testing of arrestees in police stations—New England and Wales Arrestee Drug Abuse Monitoring shortened to the witty acronym NEW ADAM.[17] The data coming in showed that offenders were extremely promiscuous in their drug use, with weekly habits costing several hundred pounds, and a growing popularity of cocaine, and particularly its downmarket variant, crack. Drug workers conducting these assessments and hoping to recruit arrestees into their services found that the 'treatment' on offer—counselling sessions, group work, 'structured treatment'—was failing to attract this client group. Without the carrot of a substitution drug they found it hard to convince drug users to show up to their service, and more importantly to give up their favourite pastime.

Methadone prescription was working by bringing in people with a strong preference for opiates. But this 'treatment' was having little impact on their alcohol, nicotine or cannabis use. Yet this was rarely considered as an important treatment outcome, as long as the programme objective was set to reducing heroin use. Where heroin did not form part of the client's drug use repertoire, treatment providers were helpless.

While there was some scope for the different counselling techniques (cognitive behavioural therapy, psychodynamic interventions, psychosocial interventions) they were all marked by low recruitment, high drop out, and poor achievement of objectives. In the treatment community these setbacks were explained by the term 'relapse,' borrowed from other medical fields, to cover the fact that what is provided hardly meets the standards of treatment. All they were in fact able to do was to provide heroin users with a synthetic substitute that took the edge off of cravings they were no longer able to satisfy. Coming at precisely the time when the proliferation of training courses, and the creation of a dedicated agency under the Department for Health, were lending professional status to the sector, this was too painful a realisation to acknowledge. It threatened, furthermore, to staunch the flow of public funding just as it was coming on stream. By 2005 over £500 million were invested in treatment, up from a mere £61 million in 1994.[18] The field responded adeptly by redefining the problem.

Help was at hand in the form of a term that had been coined in the early 1970s as a 'political term, rather than a scientific term.'[19] Transferred to the UK it provided the treatment sector with a category for clients who had hitherto been wise enough to avoid both heroin injecting and treatment. As a label it provided an explanation for poor service outcomes, but preserved the idea of treatment efficacy. The sector depends, of course, on the interlocking myths of addiction as a disease that is curable by scientifically proven, medical treatments. Policy makers keen to appear tough on drugs will agree to budget allocations for services and treatment professionals in turn provide a fig leaf. Poor outcomes are damaging for all concerned, hence the importance of a technical explanation. The revival of 'poly drug use' therefore meets multiple needs. It explains away the low success rate, holds on to the idea that there is humanity and compassion in our drug policy and allows a sensation-hungry media to recycle drug myths and scare stories.

What is left unexplored, meanwhile, is where the drug use scene is trending, what informs the fashions in consumption, the combination of substances, and the assessment of risks by that large, silent majority of non-problematic drug users. To ameliorate these shortcomings, since the summer of 2011, a small team of researchers have been working their way through the chill out rooms of London night clubs, asking anyone prepared to talk about their recent intake.[20]

At the top of the list alcohol jostles with cannabis and MDMA for pole position, but the 2012 clubber has a wide range of pharmacological options to party up his weekend. Popular options include cocaine, amphetamine and poppers, while heroin does not get a mention. Mephedrone makes a good showing, but one year into the ban its popularity is waning. Ketamine scores high but views are divided. According to its fans, "everybody here does K," but for others it is simply "the worst drug ever." The term 'drug' itself holds no fear. Respondents feel neither shame nor fear about their drug use, but project a confident self-reliance. From experience and club lore they know how to combine—popping a couple of Es before going out, then into the evening a line or two of cocaine to work up the energy, and towards the end a spliff for winding down.

The clubbers are cool insiders, who project a general satisfaction with who they are, where they are and how they look. Conversation is laced with names of places that one has come from or is going to, the sharing or comparing of cognitive maps about town. Even the open courtyard where people are chilling is astir with energy, a positive dynamism of young people on the move. Requests for interviews are mostly met with bemused condescension. There is the occasional suspicion, or an inebriated inability to concentrate, but the predominant mood is friendly and the manner almost invariably polite. Hedonism has a human face that looks like the boy next door.

As 'hoovering' up powders, popping pills, or slurping liquids become an accepted part of the recreational repertoire the willingness to mix, match and experiment follows naturally. There is no sense of the marginal nor anything that feels overtly subcultural in these drug-using scenarios. There is no overt inversion of values or challenge to the mainstream. The poly drug-using club is merely the extension of consumer culture into the night-time economy. These markets may be supplied by criminal networks, but half a century of popular illicit drug use has habituated young people to breaking the law in search of pleasure. The popularity of 'legal highs' does testify a residual deterrent effect, but also opens opportunities for intermediary layers of friendly suppliers, dealers who start out 'sorting out' friends and are pulled upstream by opportunities. How these differentiate between substances opens up a new chapter of complexity. There are certainly ethical positions, with cannabis evangelists for instance, or dealers specialising in cocaine. But like any retailer, drug dealers are opportunistic in sourcing their wares and responsive to market signals. Yet the notion of a poly drug dealer has not as yet entered criminological vocabulary.

As morning breaks, the club disgorges a cohort of depleted dancers, heading for home and rest. *En route* their paths cross those of commuters heading for shops and offices in central London. At cafes and pit stops all along the public transport network both groups fuel up with drugs discovered in a different era. Exquisite as only culturally embedded products can be, the gifts of a colonial past have come to ease the transition from both home to work and play to home. Clubbers and commuters stir the sugar into foaming coffee, and where open spaces allow, inhale deep on tobacco. Britain's favourite soft drugs, so sublime they lie beyond recognition—poly, of course.

1. *Advisory Council on the Misuse of Drugs. Draft Report on Poly Substance Use.* London: ACMD; 2010.
2. *European Monitoring Centre on Drugs and Drug Addiction. Polysubstance use: Patterns and responses.* Lisbon: EMCDDA; 2010.
3. Warburton H, Turnbull, P, Hough M. *Occasional and Controlled Heroin Use. Not a Problem?* York: John Rowntree Foundation; 2005.
4. Seddon T. *Let's Not Talk About Drugs.* Drugs and Alcohol Today. 2010;10(3):21–3.
5. Ruggiero V. Drugs as a password and the law as a drug: discussing the legalisation of illicit substances. In: South N, editor. *Drugs: Cultures, Controls and Everyday Life.* London: Sage; 1999. p. 123–38.
6. Bancroft A. *Drugs, Intoxication & Society.* Cambridge: Polity Press; 2009.

7. Klein A. *Drugs and the World*. London: Reaktion; 2008.
8. Sherratt A. *Introduction: peculiar substances*. In: Goodman J, Lovejoy P, Sherratt A, editors. *Consuming Habits: Drugs in history and anthropology*. London: Routledge; 1995. p. 1–10.
9. Escohotado A. *A History of Drugs. From the Stone Age to the Stoned Age*. Park Street Press; 1999.
10. Nutt DJ, King LA, Phillips L. Drug harms in the UK: a multicriteria decision analysis. *The Lancet* 2010;376 (9752):1558–65.
11. Smith K, Flatley J. *Drug Misuse Declared: Findings from the 2010/11 British Crime Survey*. Home Office Statistical Bulletin; 2011.
12. Hibell B, Guttormsson U, Ahlström S, Balakireva O, Bjarnason T, Kokkevi A, Kraus L. *The 2007 ESPAD Report: Substance Use Among Students in 35 European Countries*. Stockholm: The Swedish Council for Information on Alcohol and Other Drugs; 2008.
13. GW Pharma Ltd. Sativex Oromucosal Spray. SPC; 2010. Available from: http://www.medicines.org.uk/EMC/medicine/23262/SPC/Sativex+Oromucosal+Spray. Accessed 8 May 2012.
14. Measham F, Aldridge J, Parker R. *On drugs: risk, health and hedonism in the British club scene*. London: Free Association Books; 2002.
15. Buchanan J. Drug policy under New Labour 1997–2010: Prolonging the war on drugs. *Probation Journal*. 2010;57:250–62.
16. Stevens A. *The Blair Experiment*. Druglink. 2010;25(6):20–1.
17. Bennet T, Holloway K. *Drug use and offending: summary results of the first two years of the NEW-ADAM programme*. London: Home Office Findings 179; 2004.
18. McGregor S, editor. *Responding to Drug Misuse: Research and Policy Priorities in Health and Social Care*. London: Routledge; 2010.
19. DuPont RL. Polydrug Abuse and the Maturing Drug Abuse Data base. *Annals of the New York Academy of Sciences*. 1976;281:311–20.
20. Ongoing research project, findings were published in 2012.

FROM META-SIN TO MEDICINE: A PROGRAMME FOR FUTURE RESEARCH INTO THE HEALING POWER OF PSYCHEDELICS

CAMERON ADAMS

In traditional societies around the world, psychedelic substances have been used for medicinal purposes. This has also been the case in Europe and America, until the psychedelic clampdown of the 1960s. Though there was a whole raft of arguments legitimising the prohibition of psychedelics, mainly focused around health concerns, scientific evidence at the time contradicted this. In fact continuing research shows that psychedelics are generally safe and humans have probably had a very long evolutionary relationship with them. It is not scientifically reasonable from a public safety perspective to make psychedelics illegal; very few, if any, people die using them and any negative long-term effects have failed to materialise.[1] If it was about safety, driving and bathrooms would be illegal, being far more dangerous than psychedelics. The former boasts 32,955 deaths in the past 11 years in the UK alone,[2] while in 2008 approximately 21.8 million Americans were injured in the latter.[3] Instead, this is frankly a moral issue. The illegality of psychedelics is based not on medical merits but on a concept of sinful behaviour. This essay is about where research can go when we exclude the concept of sin from psychedelics and accept the fact of their use.

Though psychedelic use ranges from recreational to sacramental, here I am concerned with psychedelics as medicine. I do not see this use as more important, it is just where my personal interest lies. Much of what I write here is speculative, educated guesses about potential avenues of future study. In other words it is a statement of a few hypotheses that could be tested when research with psychedelics is freed from paranoid control.

This idea of sin is better understood through the lens of biological citizenship.[4] This is the concept that citizenship requires engagement with socially defined rules, such as language, paying taxes, etc. Among these acts of engagement are biological factors; biology has ceased to be something fateful, and has become knowable, mutable, improvable and manipulable through procedures such as plastic surgery or genetic testing. If one has a family history of breast cancer, for instance, prophylactic mastectomy is now available;[5] a body part is removed because it *might* develop cancer. The birth process is heavily involved in biological citizenship where foetuses are regularly tested for genetic diseases and the parents are expected to make a choice about whether or not to go to term if any are found. Further, women seeking an abortion in some states of the US will now be legally required to receive a transvaginal sonogram administered via a phallic wand, which many women equate with rape.[6] So, we are becoming engaged in our biology in a way mandated by social and political forces. Biological processes cease to be exclusively biological; they become social or anti-social. In current Euro-American culture, psychedelics are seen to be anti-social. They are wrong, not because of any intrinsic properties, but because their use defines someone as either 'us' or 'them.'

As I have alluded to earlier, science has established that psychedelics, that is classic tryptamine and phenethylamine psychedelics, are exceedingly safe biologically, far safer than alcohol as measured by therapeutic index (the ratio between active dose and deadly dose). Remembering that the lower the number, the more deadly, alcohol's TI is approximately 10 while that of mescaline is 24. Generally, psychedelics are even safer than mescaline with DMT, LSD, and psilocybin having TIs of 50, 1,000 and 1,000 respectively.[7] Additionally, no psychological deterioration, and even increased psychological functioning, is found.[1,8–10] Finally, the abuse potential of these substances appears to be quite low as their most common pattern of use does not include frequent dosing.[11]

We are currently experiencing a re-emergence of the use of medicinal psychedelics. The most salient medicinal psychedelic, in popular media and in academic publication, is ayahuasca, though medicinal use is not limited to this decoction. One way of looking at psychedelic medicine, as understood through the work on ayahuasca, is that:

> *although referred to as a medicine, ayahuasca [and other psychedelics by extension] is clearly not used as an ordinary pharmacological medicament. Instead medicine alluded to more holistic concepts of being a sacrament or a healing plant.*[12 p200]

In fact, the users of ayahuasca said that it may or may not heal you and the results are unpredictable; we shouldn't think of ayahuasca as a pharmaceutical substance, but as a "psychological catalyst which unfolds within fields of sociocultural ideas."[12 p202] This is a fancy way of saying that healing is a function of set and setting. Ayahuasca enhanced the users' emotional and mental states so they could understand or even see the source of their poor health. The psychedelic influenced them in making positive changes in their lives which helped them heal. Much of the interpretation of psychedelics as medicine seems to be of this nature.

For example, If you look at the MAPS website of current psychedelic research[13] what you see is primarily behavioural and psychological conditions being studied. This is telling of how we have approached these medicines. It is our cultural bias as to how we think they work. To unravel and repair this bias we first need to know that disease and illness are not the same thing. One way of looking at them is, "illness is what the patient feels when he goes to the doctor and disease is what he leaves the doctor's office with."(Cassell 1978 in [14 p548]). Illness includes the signs and symptoms, and how you feel about what's going on with you. Disease is a structural or functional biological problem. Thus, they tend to overlap quite a bit but they are not the same thing. You can have either without the other. The classic example is asymptomatic high blood pressure. Until one is diagnosed and prescribed medicine, one is often unaware of the condition. One has a disease with no illness. You can also have illnesses without diseases. Illnesses are social whereas diseases are biological.

Now if we review the studies of psychedelic medicine, as exemplified by the ayahuasca study, we see that the bias is toward investigating the use of psychedelics for illness as opposed to disease. It could be said of the end-of-life anxiety study with psilocybin,[15] for example, that nobody has been healed. The fact that they have less anxiety about dying is irrelevant because they will still die. This is a rather narrow perspective. I would argue that the psilocybin trip cures the illness of dying but that we have not explored the substance's effect upon the disease. It is important to keep this in mind when studying psychedelic medicine, especially here at the beginning. There is this sense that they are best for psychological problems, often perceived to be more illness than disease. Yet there are biological factors of psychological issues. Thus, it is our cultural bias that leads us to study psychedelics in regards to illness alone.

Yet, psychedelics may do more. In the addiction literature, it is argued that exposure to new substances hijack our evolved reward centres of the brain and thus we develop pathological relationships to them. However, our relationship to psychedelics is probably not new as many are ancient and relatively simple in that they need no processing to be consumed.[16] Our long-term relationship with some psychedelics means that we must have evolved mechanisms to deal with them. Unlike with heroin or cocaine, which are recent arrivals to our consumption patterns, the use of psychedelics cannot be seen as simply maladaptive or bizarre. They may, in fact, become a kind of food.

We need food because we do not make all of the substances we need; that's what makes up the essential vitamins, minerals and amino acids. These are things that you have to get from outside; they are exogenous. Further, much of what we eat—garlic, basil, many herbs—is medicinal. We are continually taking low doses of these medicinal substances that are quite beneficial to our health. Likewise, coca leaf and khat have large amounts of many minerals, vitamins and amino acids while many alkaloids are based, chemically, on tryptophan or tyrosine. These essential proteins may become available after we eat them.[16] Some 'drugs' are nutritionally sound.

Neurotransmitters require exogenous nutrients to be synthesised in our brains; some require up to 36 amino acids and several enzymes (each of which needs to be synthesised first) to be completed.[17,18] Tryptamines (LSD, psilocybin, DMT, etc.) are variants on serotonin[19] and the phenethylamines (mescaline, MDMA, etc.) are variants on dopamine.[20] Consuming these complete, or nearly so, neurotransmitters saves on our nutritional and energetic requirements. Further, while they are acting in our brains, we temporarily don't need our own, giving those who use them an evolutionary advantage in nutrition.[21]

By approaching psychedelics as 'medicinal foods' instead of 'drugs' we can better understand how they are related to the interleaving of disease and illness over evolutionary time. For example, any ape out there who ate a few psilocybin-containing mushrooms would know their effects, and its body would know what that felt like. Stress depletes neurotransmitters. When the neurotransmitters drop below a certain point, bodily harm can occur.[16] Much like the cravings for sugar and fats,[16] the depletion of neurotransmitters would lead to a craving for them in the diet. Though stress effects appear to be illness, their relationship to neurotransmitters implies a disease process, and thus psychedelics can be said to be addressing a disease as well. The taking of psychedelics may produce a buffer zone to help us deal with stress in both illness and disease aspects.

In this vein, Timothy Leary, in 1965, did an experiment with giving psilocybin to incarcerated criminals to see if it reduced their recidivism rates.[22] The six-month follow-up showed the rates to be significantly lower than that of the regular prison population. But by the 34-year follow-up it looks like there was no real change in the rates. It has been suggested that the data were poor due to the relative shortness of the study (or perhaps their interpretation was overzealous). However, using nutrition as a model, the effects may not have been a psychological restructuring but, exactly as it appears, something that faded over time. This looks a lot like nutritional supplementation that gets used by the body and then needs to be re-consumed. In fact, the results are similar to a study where violent criminals were given essential fatty acid (EFAs) supplements. They calmed down just because they had a better diet. This led to the idea that criminality may be related to nutritional deficiencies.[23] The effect faded over time because they maintained the same nutritional deficiencies that led to criminal behaviour in the first place. Likewise, pigs supplemented with EFAs had more monoamines (dopamine and serotonin-like chemicals including tryptamines and phenethylamines) in the frontal cortex.[24] So having more EFAs in your diet creates more of these neurotransmitters. It may just be more nutritionally sound, in a crisis situation, to take the monoamines (most psychedelics) in the first place and then supplement with improved diet.

So there is this relationship between diet, neurotransmitters and psychedelics, which are involved in the way the body regulates and builds itself even though it just seems, on the surface, that psychedelics are working in a psychological way. Another good example of this interleaving is ibogaine addiction therapy. One gets a powerful psychedelic and introspective experience, it also blocks your biological craving for opiates and other drugs and on top of that it seems to allow near instantaneous habit formation or a brain reset.[25] Ibogaine seems to work on illness and disease simultaneously through introspective and chemical pathway effects.

Beyond the simple reductionism of chemistry and nutrition, a useful tool for looking at the interface between illness and disease is salutogenesis,[26,27] the causes of good health. Typically in biomedicine we focus on pathogenesis, the causes of poor health such as viruses, poor diet, bacteria, etc. A focus on pathogenesis leads to addressing biological problems at the expense of social, meaning rich aspects of being sick. The ultimate goal of the pathogenic model is to reverse the biological insult and then the job is done. However, it does not spend much effort and attention to bringing the person above the baseline of health. Salutogenic forces are those that will bring us above the baseline and therefore give us a buffer zone where we can withstand biological insults without getting sick. In short the focus of biomedicine is on avoiding sickness instead of enhancing health.

The key to salutogenesis is related to illness. Feeling as if one is part of a larger whole and that there is purpose to one's life appears to be related to lower incidence of heart attack, fewer sick days from work, and lower mortality in general.[28] This experience has been dubbed 'sense of coherence' and underlies the maintenance of good health just as pathogens, or agents of disease, are associated with poor health.[29,30]

If we look at the ayahuasca research I mentioned above,[12] salutogenesis is invoked and ayahuasca is described as a "generalized resistance resource" that addresses "psychosocial stressors."[12 p192] In fact, users of ayahuasca have been found to be more stable and resilient psychologically than controls in sustained psychological testing.[9] Psilocybin has also been found to have strong salutogenic qualities through its inducing classic mystical experiences.[31,32] A classic mystical experience includes, among other aspects, union with God, the source, everything, or a deep sense of being part of ecology that leaves individuals with a sense of purpose and belonging. The overlaps with 'sense of coherence' are obvious. Psychedelics, it would seem, increase 'sense of coherence' on top of enhancing neurotransmitters and thus reducing their nutritional costs, especially in poor diet and high stress situations.

'Sense of coherence' may be a strong force for combatting illness, but there are social forces related to psychedelic use that can subvert it. Schizmogenesis is the origin of rifts between members of the same community.[33] These rifts develop in a variety of ways, and in traditional tribal level societies they often lead to the splitting of a community into two. However in modern state-level society this is not possible, where do we locate Britain II? Because of the inability to create autonomous communities people get caught in a double bind, a damned if you do, damned if you don't situation. With regard to psychedelics, the schizmogenic forces take the form of information manipulation.

In the case of psychedelic medicines, biological citizenship is a schizmogenic force. Scientific research, as discussed above, shows that psychedelics are among the safest psychoactive substances a person can take.[34] Most users of these substances know this. However, in terms of being a member of the global community, these substances are anti-social (for example, see how the UN Single Convention on Narcotic Drugs as discussed in Feilding, this volume, has led to the prevention of access to medicines in the third world in order to stop the 'scourge' of psychoactive recreation). Media aligned with mainstream society (which is a large majority of available media) supports this political and moral stance; psychedelics are said to cause you to jump out of windows or go permanently insane. This information war leads those who are aware of the scientific material and who have personal experience to question the integrity of those in power who berate them with apocryphal or sensationalised stories of drug use. Those fully invested in mainstream society who never question the high levels of information saturation, or propaganda, of the media and thus think the drug community is irrational and falsely justifying their use, they are good citizens of a moralistic regime. This is classic schizmogenesis; both sides see the worst in, and can't trust *any* communications from the other, on this or any topic. The double bind that develops is that one must hide one's use from the mainstream and either quit that which one finds salutogenic to the detriment of one's health or live a life of criminality. These stressors, in turn, can cause negative health effects that subvert the salutogenic potentials of these substances. The fact that people find strong healing effects in such unsupported environments seems to me a minor miracle. This may also explain why it is in shamanic contexts that psychedelic healing is most dramatic; the negative schizmogenic forces are simply not of the same force in the jungles of Peru.

By looking at multiple threads of information a programme of study emerges. The biological effects of psychedelics, with regards to health, are woefully understudied. If it is true that we have evolved in relation to psychedelics and that our bodies have learned to use them productively over millennia, the nutritional possibilities of psychedelics should be better understood. Perhaps psychedelics could be incorporated as a tonic to quickly bring one's monoamine health to a functioning level, which can then be supplemented by improved diet. With a sophisticated understanding of illness and disease as well as salutogenesis, a series of studies could be made with psychedelics to assess the specifics of the articulations of these two different threads of poor health. These insights could hold the secret for bringing public health above a level where the most basic of health insults makes us sick. Finally, the nature of political and moral aspects of self-medication are thrown into stark contrast with psychedelics. Biological citizenship gives us the perspective from which to address the human rights aspects of banning potential medicines on moral grounds. The political need to legislate against substances that for the length of human existence have provided healing, spiritual insight and, yes, even recreation, leads to conflicts in society that need not be. Understanding the schizmogenic forces surrounding as politically charged a topic as the sin of psychedelics will help us understand more subtle sources of social rifts and may even be a catalyst for broader community healing.

1. Strassman RJ. 'Adverse reactions to psychedelic drugs: A review of the literature.' *The Journal of Nervous and Mental Disease.* 1984;172(10):577–95.
2. 'Road casualty britain: 11 years of deaths and injuries mapped and visualised' | news | *guardian.co.uk*; Available from: http://www.guardian.co.uk/news/datablog /interactive/2011/nov/18/road-casualty-uk-map. Accessed 19 March 2012.
3. Nonfatal bathroom injuries among persons aged ≥15 years --- united states, 2008; Available from: http://www.cdc.gov/mmwr/preview/mmwrhtml/mm6022a1.htm?s_cid= mm6022a1_e&source=govdelivery. Accessed 19 March 2012.
4. Rose N, Novas C. *Biological citizenship.* In: Ong A, Collier SJ, editors. *Global Assemblages: Technology, Politics, and Ethics as Anthropological Problems.* Oxford: Blackwell Publishing Inc; 2004. p. 439–63.
5. Available from: http://www.cancer.gov/cancertopics/factsheet/Therapy/preventive-mastectomy. Accessed 19 March 2012.
6. Pennsylvania anti-abortion bill would mandate transvaginal ultrasound | addicting info; Available from: http://www.addictinginfo.org/2012/03/12/pennsylvania-anti-abortion -bill-would-mandate-transvaginal-ultrasound/. Accessed 19 March 2012.
7. Gable RS. 'Toward a comparative overview of dependence potential and acute toxicity of psychoactive substances used nonmedically.' *American Journal of Drug and Alcohol Abuse.* 1993;19(3):263–81.
8. Bergman RL. 'Navajo peyote use: Its apparent safety.' *The American Journal of Psychiatry.* 1971;128(6):695–9.
9. Grob CS, McKenna DJ, Callaway JC, Brito GS, Neves ES, Oberlaender G, et al. 'Human psychopharmacology of hoasca, a plant hallucinogen used in ritual context in Brazil.' *Journal of Nervous and Mental Disease.* 1996;184(2):86–94.
10. Halpern JH, Sherwood AR, Hudson JI, Yurgelun-Todd D, Pope HG. 'Psychological and cognitive effects of long-term peyote use among native Americans.' *Biological Psychiatry.* 2005;58(8):624–31.
11. Gable RS. 'Toward a comparative overview of dependence potential and acute toxicity of psychoactive substances used nonmedically.' *American Journal of Drug and Alcohol Abuse.* 1993;19(3):263–81.
12. Schmid JT, Jungaberle H, Verres R. 'Subjective Theories About (Self-)Treatment with Ayahuasca.' *Anthropology of Consciousness.* 2010;21(2):188–204.
13. Available from: http://www.maps.org/research/. Accessed 21 February 2012.
14. Helman CG. 'Disease versus illness in general practice.' *The Journal of the Royal College of General Practitioners.* 1981;31(230):548–52.
15. Grob CS, Danforth AL, Chopra GS, Hagerty M, McKay CR, Halberstadt A0L, Greer GR. 'Pilot study of psilocybin treatment for anxiety in patients with advanced-stage cancer.' *Archives of General Psychiatry.* 2011;68(1):71–8.
16. Sullivan RJ, Hagen EH. 'Psychotropic substance-seeking: Evolutionary pathology or adaptation?' *Addiction.* 2002;97(4):389–400.

17. Available from: http://web.williams.edu/imput/synapse/pages/I.html. Accessed 3 April 2012.
18. Available from: http://www.ncbi.nlm.nih.gov/books/NBK11110/. Accessed 3 April 2012.
19. Shulgin A, Shulgin A. *TIHKAL: The continuation.* Transform Press; 1997.
20. Shulgin A, Shulgin A. *PIHKAL: A chemical love story.* Transform Press; 1991.
21. Sullivan RJ, Hagen EH. 'Psychotropic substance-seeking: Evolutionary pathology or adaptation?' *Addiction.* 2002;97(4):389–400.
22. Doblin R. Dr. Leary' s concord prison experiment: A 34 year follow-up study. *The Bulletin of the Multidisciplinary Association for Psychedelic Studies* MAPS. 1999;9(4):10–8.
23. Gesch CB, Hammond SM, Hampson SE, Eves A, Crowder MJ. Influence of supplementary vitamins, minerals and essential fatty acids on the antisocial behaviour of young adult prisoners. Randomised, placebo-controlled trial. *British Journal of Psychiatry.* 2002;181:22–8.
24. de la Presa Owens S, Innis SM. Docosahexaenoic and arachidonic acid prevent a decrease in dopaminergic and serotoninergic neurotransmitters in frontal cortex caused by a linoleic and alpha-linolenic acid deficient diet in formula-fed piglets. *Journal of Nutrition.* 1999;129(11):2088–93.
25. Alper KR, Lotsof HS, Kaplan CD. 'The ibogaine medical subculture.' *Journal of Ethnopharmacology.* 2008;115(1):9–24.
26. Antonovsky A. *Health, Stress, and Coping.* San Francisco: Jossey-Bass; 1979.
27. Lindström B, Eriksson M. Salutogenesis. *Journal of Epidemiology and Community Health.* 2005;59(6):440–2.
28. Suominen S, Gould R, Ahvenainen J, Vahtera J, Uutela A, Koskenvuo M. Sense of coherence and disability pensions. A nationwide, register based prospective population study of 2196 adult Finns. *Journal of Epidemiology and Community Health.* 2005;59(6):455–9.
29. Becker CM, Glascoff MA, Felts WM. Salutogenesis 30 years later: Where do we go from here? *International Electronic Journal of Health Education.* 2010;13:25–32.
30. Suominen S, Gould R, Ahvenainen J, Vahtera J, Uutela A, Koskenvuo M. Sense of coherence and disability pensions. A nationwide, register based prospective population study of 2196 adult Finns. *Journal of Epidemiology and Community Health.* 2005;59(6):455–9.
31. Griffiths RR, Johnson MW, Richards WA, Richards BD, McCann U, Jesse R. 'Psilocybin occasioned mystical-type experiences: Immediate and persisting dose-related effects.' *Psychopharmacology* (Berl). 2011;218(4):649–65.
32. Griffiths RR, Richards WA, McCann U, Jesse R. 'Psilocybin can occasion mystical-type experiences having substantial and sustained personal meaning and spiritual significance.' *Psychopharmacology* (Berl). 2006;187(3):268–83.
33. Bateson G. *Culture Contact and Schizmogenesis.* In: *Steps to an Ecology of Mind: Collected Essays in Anthropology, Psychiatry, Evolution, and Epistemology.* Northvale, New Jersey: Jason Aronson, Inc.; 1987.
34. Nutt DJ, King LA, Phillips LD. 'Drug harms in the UK: A multicriteria decision analysis.' *The Lancet.* 2010;376(9752):1558–65.

A DECLARATION OF PSYCHEDELIC STUDIES

NEŞE DEVENOT

The scientific research community is in the midst of a 'psychedelic renaissance,' but sanctioned platforms for mainstream discussion are heavily weighted in the direction of objective scientific research. In light of these recent advances, it is an opportune time to address the question of psychedelics and their continuing impact on culture from a critical perspective—and to confront the issues that have impeded this conversation. It is time for psychedelic research to expand from the artificial disciplinary confines of medicine and anthropology to include philosophy and other humanistic avenues of inquiry.

While psychedelic science has tenuously reemerged as a legitimate academic focus, the cultural and philosophical issues surrounding psychedelic experiences remain largely unacknowledged and taboo within the academy. In light of this impediment to open dialogue, it is important to establish as precedents academic conversations that are already accepted as legitimate. At this inertial juncture in history, I propose that queer studies can provide one such precedent for the inauguration of psychedelic studies as an interdisciplinary academic field.

ESTABLISHING PRECEDENTS:
THE QUEERING OF CONSCIOUSNESS

While irreducible, a psychedelic critical theory would have sub-stantial overlap with queer theory's concerns, and pushing queer theory to its limits necessitates taking things like non-normative states of consciousness and identity seriously. Halperin defines 'queer' as that which differs from the norm; "Queer is... *whatever is at odds with the normal, the legitimate, the dominant. There is nothing in particular to which it necessarily refers.*"[1 p62] With this definition in mind, psychedelia is—properly speaking—queer; as a multiplicity of social groups, interests, and worldviews, psyche-delia is a 'queer' deviation from dominant cultural norms.

Recently, the proximity of queer and psychedelic studies sur-faced in reference to the Horizons Psychedelics Conference in New York City. An undergraduate administrator at the University of Pennsylvania, responding to my request to bring my students to the conference on a field trip, wrote:

> *I'm afraid I have to decline to provide funding for this activ-ity.* What I had imagined was an academic conference on hallucinogens or on the psychedelic movement *seems from the website to be* more advocacy than critical reflection [...] *Although I do not want to impede the critical work you want to lead your students to undertake on a fraught subject, it's not evident to me how the conference supports it. (personal com-munication, October 2011, emphasis added)*

The specific rationale of this response took me by surprise. When I attended Horizons the previous year, its hallmark was a focus on legitimate, academic discourse, which was invoked as of primary significance. Pondering the disjuncture, it occurred to me that the author might have responded the same way—"advocacy rather than critical reflection"—if he were out of touch with queer studies and received an analogous request; a queer studies conference focusing on the legitimacy of the field, rather than featuring speakers that questioned its right to exist, would not thereby be 'advocating' a queer lifestyle.

When I made this connection public, one respondent's protest echoed many of the detractions I have heard before:

> *a queer studies conference would have a strong focus on state and social repression and the specific oppression suffered by queer people, which is hardly glorifying, and queer identity is not a lifestyle by choice in the same way that psychedelics are.*

But this common reaction embarks on a slippery slope. To essentialise a queer identity or culture as of somehow primary importance to a psychedelic identity or culture, especially grounded in the tenuous concept of free will, undermines the very rights that queer theorists and activists promote:

> *A liberation movement demands an expansion of our moral horizons and an extension or reinterpretation of the basic moral principle of equality [...] If we wish to avoid being numbered amongst the oppressors, we must be prepared to re-think even our most fundamental attitudes. We need to consider them from the point of view of those most disadvantaged by our attitudes, and the practices that follow.* [2 p116]

It is counterproductive to argue that some forms of oppression are more egregious than others. How, for instance, is there not strong state and social repression against the use of or interest in psychedelics? How can one be certain that a psychedelic lifestyle is less of an identity issue than a queer lifestyle? Many view their psychedelic identities, interests, or religious views as inherent to who they are. Since queer studies is largely about the 'queering' of identity and consciousness relative to the normative, we could work collectively to support the validity of all forms of performative identification.

The parallels do not end there. Although I now publicly study psychedelic philosophy and visionary art at the University of Pennsylvania, this was not always the case. When I was a freshman undergraduate at Bard College in 2006, I had an experience that transformed my life; due in part to lack of information and improper set and setting, I was temporarily kicked out of school after I was introduced to LSD. Graciously, I was granted amnesty in exchange for a research paper and a righting of my ways. Although the event receded into the past, it was impossible to forget one of the most enlightening, awe-inspiring experiences of my life. As Narby explains in *The Spirit Molecule* documentary:

> *there is a growing number of [...] intellectuals, scientists, artists, movers and shakers, filmmakers [...] who realise that this stuff is all too interesting [...] to go on keeping it swept under the rug [...] At this point there is no good reason, apart from bad habit, to keep up these barriers.*[3]

But due to the pervasive cultural and legal taboos, I thought my intellectual interests had to remain implicit, unspoken. I applied to graduate school with a paper reading the philosophies of Hegel and Lacan through the lens of fractal mathematics, with a personal statement directed at mystical and visionary poetry. The ideas were there, but my rationale was absent. It was only after I found out about the scientific psychedelic renaissance—via a *New York Times* article[4] on the MAPS conference, 'Psychedelic Science in the 21st Century'—and after I attended Horizons for the first time that I realised there was a community of scholars working openly on these subjects. I decided to plug in, and come out of the closet, a common experience among those who, for the first time, find a community where they can speak openly about their interests.

DISSOLVING DISCIPLINARY BOUNDARIES

Precedents and rationales aside, the time is ripe for a genuinely interdisciplinary field on psychedelics and their attendant societal repercussions to come to fruition. At the fourth annual Horizons psychedelics conference in New York City in September 2011, data surfaced from a 2006 psilocybin study[5] at Johns Hopkins University demonstrating that roughly two-thirds of study participants had a mystical experience. Reacting to this cross-circuiting of secular and mystical discourses, author Erik Davis responded by asserting, flatly: "We already knew that."[6] The study, he claimed, was a secularisation and materialisation of a spiritual experience rather than a discovery of genuinely novel content. Davis continued, "The research model is not sufficient [...] Neurology is on a collision course with the full-on [psychedelic] experience."[6] While serving a distinct and timely purpose, scientific discourse is by nature unable to exhaust the psychedelic question.

That same weekend, at Alex and Allyson Grey's Chapel of Sacred Mirrors, Strassman participated in a panel discussion for the premier screening of *The Spirit Molecule*, where he remarked:

How to explicate the full meaning [...] of the psychedelic experience in this current wave of interest in studying these drugs again? [...] I don't think that we can solely depend on psychiatry to be the leader in discussing how these drugs work and their effect and their application to everyday life. I think it has to be as multidisciplinary a pursuit as possible, because the full psychedelic experience impacts on everything—it impacts on art, anthropology, music, religion, cosmology, physics, psychology, cognitive sciences, chemistry, everything [...] We don't want to overextend one discipline at the expense of the other[s][7]

As Alex Grey expressed during the same event, "Now with the gifts of science and scientific research, serious interest is again making it legally possible to discuss these matters,"[7] but this fortuitous resurgence of activity and attention demands a chorus of new voices, new models and approaches. Clearly, it is finally an appropriate time to address the question of psychedelics and their continuing impact on culture from multiple critical, academic perspectives—and to confront the issues that have impeded these conversations during the past century.

There is a growing community of younger scholars who are actively focusing their academic work on this field. In mid-January, MAPS announced to attendees of their recent 'Catalysts' conference that they would be sponsoring a new listserv for graduate students actively working or writing on some aspect of 'psychedelic culture, use, practice, or theory.' Professor Jim Fadiman, PhD, co-founder of the Institute for Transpersonal Psychology, wrote—in response to students like myself, who found it difficult to locate support and mentorship for psychedelic research—"It's time to build [an international] graduate student research support network." (from personal communication, 20 January 2011). This event is significant both for psychedelic studies—since every major academic subject has networks of a similar kind—and for academia at large, which aspires to but frequently falls short of realising genuinely interdisciplinary work.

My personal contribution to this movement lies at the cross-sections of literature, philosophy, comparative religion, and art history, and I cite psychedelic philosopher Terence McKenna as my immediate forebear.

IN DEFENCE OF THOUGHT EXPERIMENTS

In April 2011, I presented a paper at the American Comparative Literature Association's annual conference in Vancouver, Canada on the concept of 'hyperspace' in the context of dimethyltryptamine (DMT). I explained that since the DMT experience is notoriously difficult to integrate into the terms of consensus reality, the concept of hyperspace has emerged as a framing mechanism that enables participants in this field to articulate and co-create an alternative worldview. My thesis was that even if we leave the ontological status of hyperspace suspended, it functions as a Kantian 'as-if' that pertains to a communicable, phenomenological experience. By examining how ideas operate within concrete social contexts, we can begin to develop a genealogical understanding of what these ideas do and how they function in particular communities over time, without necessitating a justification of hyperspace entities in any absolute terms.

The etymology of 'hyperspace' is multi-faceted and complex, the result of a rich history with definite relevance to the fields of literature and art history. While the concept of fourth dimensionality extends back to Pythagoras, hyperspace began its heyday in the late nineteenth century, when the concept circled extensively among *avant-garde* and spiritualist circles. The term 'hyperspace' proper emerged out of the specialised context of mid-nineteenth-century analytic geometry, satisfying the need for a new word to designate a space of more than three dimensions.[8] But as Chernosky, working on literature and hyperspace philosophy, explains:

> *A change in geometrical theory which carried with it such important philosophical ramifications...gave writers and thinkers a new metaphor [... H]yperspace mediates between realms of discourse that otherwise would not communicate.*[9]

Consequently, Henderson[10] pointed out the tremendous impact of hyperspace philosophy on art history. Paradigm shifts propagate indiscriminately across multiple domains, and the impact of hyperspace on culture and its means of representation has been both tangible and under-scrutinised.

In the humanities, establishing a historical canon of hyperspatial, interdimensional artists and philosophers creates a concrete discursive context for further investigations. It establishes an aesthetic tradition within which one can include artists ranging from William Blake to the cubists to the interdimensional and visionary painters of the modern day.

This is just one example of the manifold ways that psychedelic discourse pertains and responds to questions of philosophy, creativity, imagination, religion, culture and language. The crucial step now is to bring these conversations into the open.

One necessary component of this involves developing critical rationales and precedents for investigating issues like hyperspace entities within a mainstream academic conversation. Thought experiments, acknowledged as such, should be encouraged rather than taboo. Strassman writes:

> *The only explanatory model that held itself out as the most intuitively satisfying, yet the most theoretically treacherous, involved assigning a parallel level of reality to these experiences. In other words, I engaged in a thought experiment [...] I had to accept their reports as descriptions of things that were "real." I allowed myself, at least theoretically, to accept that under the influence of DMT, these things do happen—in reality, although not in a reality we usually inhabit.*[11 p75]

If we are able to remain unattached to the particularities of such thought experiments, they can help us to overcome the anachronistic privileging of the seen over the unseen. In the words of Terence McKenna, "I would prefer a kind of intellectual anarchy where whatever was pragmatically applicable was brought to bear on any situation; where belief was understood as a self-limiting function."[12 p39]

Literary studies can make a significant contribution to psychedelic studies by providing the infrastructure for creative explorations within this domain. As an extension of the absurdist philosophy known as 'pataphysics, 'pataphor is a term referring to a metaphor gone cataclysmic, seeking to "describe a new [and] separate world, in which an idea or aspect has taken on a life of its own."[13] Using the concept of 'pataphor, we can explore the internal potentials for a concept like hyperspace without committing ourselves to limiting beliefs. Similarly, 'psychotic knowledge' is described as the result of "ripping apart the fabric of consensual reality."[14] It is only psychotic "from the perspective of the hegemonic paradigm that cannot permit multiple realities," [14] encouraging the retention of sanity while remaining open to new horizons of possibility. Thus, alien intelligence, vine spirits, and eschatologies are ideas that can be played with, in ways that don't depend on absolute truth values for intellectual significance.

THE RISE OF VISIONARY CULTURE

In addition to what literary and cultural studies can do for psychedelia, the latter needs to be accounted for by the former in any comprehensive description of modernity. The term 'visionary culture' references a network of interrelated movements that are growing exponentially beyond the purview of academia and the mainstream media. Considering their scope—hundreds of thousands of people around the world are actively involved—and the intellectual, aesthetic, and political significance of these movements in relation to many of the most pressing issues of our time, they have received extraordinarily limited scholarly attention.

The rise of visionary culture is a landmark event within the history of aesthetics and philosophy. At the most fundamental level, it offers an alternative to the postmodern discourse that still preoccupies many scholars of the humanities across disciplines, despite a search for new alternatives. Notably, a Google Books search for 'after postmodernism' produces over 8,500 results at the time of this writing. Although a definition of postmodernism is difficult to pin down, due in part to an emphasis on difference and the rejection of its label by many of its most influential thinkers, it is often predicated on an absence of perspectival view and an emphasis on irony.

According to the editors of *After Postmodernism: An Introduction to Critical Realism*:[15]

> *A buzzword which began as an emerging, radical critique became, by the 20th Century's end, a buzzword for fracture, eclecticism, political apathy and intellectual exhaustion... [A] new and different intellectual direction must come after postmodernism... because [it] is inadequate as an intellectual response to the times we live in. The realization of this has been growing for some time now without it yet being clear just what this new perspective will be.*[15 p4]

My work at the university has involved developing an alternative to the outdated notion of a secular, ironic postmodernism within which the academy is still entrenched. I have expanded Eshelman's definition of 'performatism'[16] to include: although heterogeneous, performatism is antithetical to the ironic conception of postmodernism described here. Performative works create their own temporalities and perspectives. They create worlds and ways of seeing, performances in and of context. As an important instance, visionary art and culture is a performative approach to the conscious construction of a sustainable, aesthetically inspired worldview. In opposition to secular irony, the visionary art of Alex Grey, Amanda Sage, Michael Divine, Adam Scott Miller and others is spiritual, optimistic, and performative—which is to say it aims to do something, to introduce new symbolic frames and create ritualistic spaces wherein personal and collective identities can be consciously shaped and refashioned.

Finally, there is a long list of 'buzzwords' associated with psychedelic discourse that leads to immediate disqualification from being taken seriously in an academic setting, including 'spirit,' 'destiny,' 'prophecy,' 'psychic,' 'aliens,' 'channels,' et cetera. This is a large reason Terence McKenna, possibly the greatest psychedelic philosopher of our time, is virtually absent from university syllabi, where he definitely belongs. The ideas that he champions have consequences reaching far beyond the psychedelic community, which has ultimately been his sole audience. The media philosopher Marshall McLuhan, whom McKenna greatly admired and who championed very similar ideas, has nearly been relegated to the same fate.

RESET YOUR OPERATING SYSTEM

McLuhan[17] highlighted the radical character of the epochal shift facing humanity, arguing that the transition from the 'mechanical' to the 'electric age' requires a corresponding transformation in the nature and function of the humanities. He writes:

[T]he discovery of the twentieth century [is...] the discovery of the process of insight itself, the technique of avoiding the automatic closure of involuntary fixing of attitudes that so easily results from any given cultural situation. The technique of open field perception [...] is a method of organized ignorance [...] the means of abstracting oneself from the bias and consequences of one's own culture [...T]he technique of the suspended judgment [...] means, not the willingness to admit other points of view, but the technique of how not to have a point of view.[17 p8-11]

McLuhan, who saw the university's potential to promote and explore this capacity, is explaining a notion similar to McKenna's description of 'resetting your operating system,' a function that McKenna associates with psychedelic use. These two figures—along with Derrida,[18] who is also disparaged but highly regarded within the academy—are aware of the inability of existing constructions to account for future developments or even contemporaneous alternatives, and they are interested in how the knowledge of ideological contingency influences existing ideological structures.

There is much to be learned from a conversation blending absolute alterity with boundless creativity, and the future of the humanities depends on the uninhibited cooperation of these different strands of thought. Queer theory in particular can contribute to a nascent psychedelic theory in recognising the limitations of established cultural norms. Just as gender and sexuality can be understood as a spectrum, so can consciousness be investigated beyond the binaries of conscious and unconscious, normal and deviant. It is only by acknowledging—without passing judgment on—the full scope of possible conscious states that we can advance our understanding of human psychology and extend hospitality to the as-yet unencountered and unknown.

Strassman writes:

> *Within traditional Western academic settings, anthropology is the field that has focused attention on psychedelic plant use and the role of these plants in the societies that use them. More than any other field, it has maintained the flame of interest in these plants and drugs over several hundred years of Western suppression of all information about them. Within the last sixty to seventy years, however, it has been within the medical-scientific framework, primarily psychiatry, psychology, and the neurosciences, that our culture has viewed and understood psychedelic drugs.*[11 p13]

It is now time for the false iron curtain to fall. I hereby inaugurate psychedelic studies as a post-disciplinary field. Let the games begin.

1. This work was supported by the Benjamin Franklin Fellowship.
2. Halperin DM. *Saint Foucault: Towards a Gay Hagiography*. Oxford: Oxford University Press; 1997.
3. Singer P. *All animals are equal*. In: LaFollette H, editor. *Ethics in Practice: an Anthology*. Cambridge, MA: Blackwell Philosophy Anthologies; 1997. p. 107–16.
4. Shultz M, director. *DMT: The Spirit Molecule* [DVD]. San Antonio, TX: DMT Production LP/Warner Brothers Studio; 2010. Available from http://www.thespiritmolecule.com.
5. Tierney J. 'Hallucinogens have scientists tuning in again.' *New York Times*. New York, NY; 2010 April 12;A1. Available from: http://www.nytimes.com/2010/04/12/science/12psychedelics.html.
6. Griffiths RR, Richards WA, McCarn U, Jesse R. Psilocybin can occasion mystical-type experiences having substantial and sustained personal meaning and spiritual significance. *Journal of Psychopharmacology*. 2006;187(3):268–83.
7. Traveler JM. Psychedelics and human destiny: Notes from the Horizons Conference; *Reality Sandwich*. Available from http://www.realitysandwich.com/node/69500. Accessed 14 October 2011.
8. Grove R, director. *DMT: The Spirit Molecule* – CoSM premiere [Video file]; Available from http://www.youtube.com/watch?v=eMOC44vby9g. Accessed 14 October 2011.
9. Pike, FB. *The Politics of the Miraculous in Peru: Haya de la Torre and the Spiritualist Tradition*. Lincoln, NE: University of Nebraska Press; 1986.
10. Pacchioli D. Deflating hyperspace. University Park, PA: Research/Penn State; 1995;16(4). Available from http://www.rps.psu.edu/dec95/hyper.html.
11. Henderson LD. *The Fourth Dimension and Non-Euclidean Geometry in Modern Art*. Princeton University Press; 1983.
12. Strassman RW, Slawek W, Luna LE, Frecska E, editors. *Inner Paths to Outer Space: Journeys to Alien Worlds Through Psychedelics and Other Spiritual Technologies*. Rochester, VT: Park Street; 2008.
13. McKenna T. *Psychedelic society*. In: Grob, CS, editor. *Hallucinogens: a Reader*. New York, NY: Jeremy P. Tarcher/Putnam; 2002. p. 38–46.
14. 'Pataphysics; Available from http://en.wikipedia.org/wiki/'Pataphysics. Accessed 14 October 2011.
15. Shunyamurti. The ascendance of psychotic knowledge; *Reality Sandwich*. Available from http://www.realitysandwich.com/node/78438. Accessed 14 October 2011.
16. López J, Potter G. *After postmodernism: the new millennium*. In: López J, Potter G, editors. *After Postmodernism: an Introduction to Critical Realism*. London: Athlone Press; 2001. p.1–18.
17. Eshelman R. *Performatism, or The End of Postmodernism*. Aurora, Colorado: The Davies Group, Publishers; 2008.
18. McLuhan M, Gordon TE, Nevitt B, Innis HA, editors. *Marshall McLuhan Unbound: the Humanities in the Electronic Age* (Vol 7). Corte Madera, CA: Ginko Press; 2005.
19. Derrida J. *Points...: Interviews, 1974–1994*. Weber E, editor. Palo Alto, CA: Stanford University Press; 1995.

BIOPHENOMENOLOGY OF ALTERED STATES

VÍT POKORNÝ

My first experiences with hallucinogens have resulted in haunting questions about the philosophical meaning of hallucinatory experiences and all similar extraordinary states: How are such experiences possible? What is their nature, i.e., are they functional anomalies or something else? What is their epistemological value, i.e., what kind of conscious processes may we relate to them? What is their ontological value, i.e., what part of reality do they constitute? And last but not least, what is the proper theoretical context for their explanation?

These extraordinary states, including dreams, certain mental disorders, near-death experiences, meditation, religious experiences and especially the states induced by psychoactive substances, fall within the scope of anthropology of consciousness. Different terms and concepts are circulating among academics and the non-academic public to describe these states such as, 'extraordinary,'[1] 'altered,'[2] 'unusual,' 'hallucination,' 'trance' or 'ecstasis,' but no consensus has yet been established.[3] Psychonauts, literary authors and occasional drug users talk about 'trips,' shamanic practitioners about 'journeying,' the expression 'spiritual' or 'mystical experience' may be used in religious contexts while psychiatrists try to understand 'dissociative states.'[4] But, in spite of such variety, there are certain features common to all of the aforementioned states; special induction techniques[5] are required and different modes of alteration of both inner and outer experience are induced.

Therefore I have decided to use the term altered states (AS). The reason is, as I am convinced, that the 'alteration' involves not only cognitive processes but corporeal as well, and that even the entire existential situation undergoes a transformation.

As the term itself suggests, any interpretation of these states assumes that they differ from a common or normal state of consciousness. I believe that the conventional concept of consciousness is based on alertness, or, "behaviorally, intrinsic alertness represents the internal (cognitive) control of wakefulness and arousal."[6 p797] To be alert means to be "fully aware and attentive, wide-awake"[7]; it is characterised by states of vigilance and absence of sleep. To alert someone means to "warn to prepare for action" or "to advise... to be on guard."[7] To be conscious of something means, from the alertness perspective, to be aware of it with a degree of certainty. And to be certain means to be able to testify what one knows, i.e., to know that one knows it (self-reflection).

Such a concept of alertness implies the idea that any state of consciousness lacking direct self-control constituted in self-reflection is irrelevant. From this standpoint, modes of consciousness exceeding these hunter-like principles, actually rooted in a stress reaction,[8] are referred to as unconscious. And as states lacking basic qualities of alertness, they are dismissed as mere fancies. Such a concept of consciousness, at least in the context of everyday experience and scientific rationality, can therefore be termed 'egocentric,' since it allocates all epistemologically valid and ontologically relevant experiences to the alert self-reflecting ego. We may call this perspective a "singlestate fallacy: the erroneous assumption that all worthwhile abilities reside in our normal, awake mindbody state."[9 p49,10]

To avoid the single-state fallacy and consequently the dismissal of AS as mere anomalies of experience, I will adopt a multistate paradigm of consciousness.[9] From this perspective, a model of consciousness cannot be built around the central state of alert self-reflection. In order to better understand AS, it is more appropriate to model consciousness as a multilayer continuum of structurally different, but epistemologically and ontologically equivalent modes. Thus it could be possible to show that consciousness is not a self relying, autonomous process, but a biological activity deeply rooted in an organism and its environment.

PERSPECTIVES

Once we reject the self-thinking ego as the primary centre of conscious behaviour, we need to replace it with another model that is able to bridge the mind-body gap and allows for the rehabilitation of the cognitive value of AS. Drawing from two different but interconnected traditions that bridge the dualism of scientific thinking towards a 'new synthesis'[11,12]—the phenomenology of perception and corporeality on one hand[13] and biosemiotics[14] on the other—we may define consciousness as *a continuum of modes of a self-referential,*[15] *situated presence of an organism in its environment.*

Using this combination of phenomenology and biosemiotics I have created an interpretational framework that could elucidate the conditions of AS in general. I understand phenomenology as a philosophical discipline dealing with the structure and conditions of experience, whose primary aim is to explain how any kind of reality is constituted in our experience. And, in order to do that, it must also address how any experience is possible at all, i.e., what is the source of sense-making in consciousness. Biosemiotics is a set of biological theories that view life in general as cognition[15] (or knowing[16]). It allows us to trace self-referential processes on all levels of the incarnate mind (i.e., the conscious body) and model them as a multilayer continuum of different levels of self-referential behaviour.

Since various conceptions of phenomenology may be found in the literature,[17] here I use inscriptional phenomenology of perception and corporeality. Phenomenology of perception is based on the idea of 'primacy of perception,'[18,19] meaning that the primal and original mode of our living presence in the world is centred around the perceiving body. Inscriptional phenomenology may be characterised with Merleau-Ponty's statement that, "Being is the 'place' where the 'modes of consciousness' are inscribed as structurations of Being."[20 p253] Nitsche interprets this as follows:

> *Merleau-Ponty explains description more as an inscription. Thus, he completely overturns the usual way of interpreting conscious-ness: natural attempts of our consciousness to capture what is perceived within firm boundaries of meaningful contours and to inscribe it, thus captured, into our mind are not directed to our consciousness, but as a structuration into the visible world.*[21 p54]

Thus, consciousness is not understood as registration and structuration of external stimuli inside our brains, but rather as an active and bodily based transformation of perceptual fields.

In biosemiotics, we can call this set of inscriptive fields an 'um-welt';[22,23] an organism's environment growing up from its modes of bodily and perceptual actions. It is, therefore, not appropriate to view an organism as a unity of two parts (body/mind) separated by a mystical gap. Rather, the term 'living system' should be used to denote wholeness of an organism, with mind and body as two abstractive views of a single unit.

We need to focus on a kind of phenomenon that is already beyond this gap. Life or living being is precisely this kind of phenomenon. For biology, living being is living organisms; for phenomenology, it is living subjectivity. Where these two meet is in what phenomenologists call the lived body. What we need, and what the neurophenomenology aims for, is an account of the lived body that integrates biology and phenomenology, and so goes be-yond the gap.[24 p384]

UMWELTS

AS provide a possibility to transcend the narrow boundaries of self-reflecting ego consciousness. They entail a direct experience of conscious activity that is not a mere reflection and registration of the outer world affecting our sensory organs and thus producing data that our neural networks mysteriously transform into conscious images inside our minds. Instead, a careful phenomenological analysis of AS may reveal that something different is the case, a living organism organises its lived world by its integral behavioural activity and that this activity itself is possible only as a situated presence of a living organism in the world.

The key questions here are: What are the ways living beings inhabit the world? And what kind of world do we have in mind? Here, we may refer to the concept of 'umwelt,' that translates as the world around and can be explained as a subjective world:[25]

> *Modern biology employs the objective term 'ecological niche,' that is to say, the set of conditions—in the form of living space, food, temperature, etc.—under which a given species lives. One might say that the* umwelt *is the ecological niche as the animal itself apprehends it. (emphasis in original)*[26 p6]

So, from both phenomenological and biosemiotical perspectives, there is not a single common world as a conglomerate of outer objects and conditions, but rather a plurality of subjective worlds originating in the behavioural structures of individual species and even individual organisms. The worlds of cats, sea anemones or humans differ essentially from each other, because of different ways in which these organisms inhabit and constitute their worlds.

The semiotic niche[26] is organised according to what is relevant for a certain species or individual organism. The measure of relevance is what the organism experiences as relevant or meaningful. Relevance of a world is not firmly set in the structure of the external environment; it is constituted as an interplay of needs, sensory fields and the mobility of an organism and its environment.

Every organism tries to stay alive and for this purpose it must be able to maintain its inner equilibrium. It does so by communicative metabolisation of the surrounding world—it communicates with individuals of the same species, it consumes food and tries to avoid all things hostile and threatening. This constant activity is carried out by means of continuous exchange of substances and information within the environment. Each and every organism must therefore keep itself open to remain closed. Or, to put it reversely, in order to stay closed, stable and alive, an organism must be open to the ongoing exchange of matter and information that constitutes its umwelt. But the environment speaks; it is accessible and relevant to an organism only to the extent to which the organism is open. Each organism has a limited set of possibilities of how to move, interpret and transform its surroundings. These possibilities determine what is harmful or beneficial, what poses danger and what keeps alive, what is to be accepted or to be avoided. This 'knowledge' guides the behaviour of an organism, and thus constitutes its world.

PATTERNS

Each organism shares its individual world not only with beings of the same species, but also with those of many other species, based on the similarity of their bodily organisation and patterns of experience. For example, while food differs for different organisms, some food is always needed to survive. Therefore, various organisms share similar patterns of experience (lack or sufficiency) and activity. They experience similar 'stories,' with a story being "a little knot or complex of that species of connectedness which we call relevance."[27 p13] Also:

> *whatever the story means in the story which I told you, the fact*
> *of thinking in terms of stories does not isolate human beings*

as something separate from the starfish and the sea anemones, the coconut palms and the primroses. Rather, if the world be connected, if I am at all fundamentally right in what I am saying, then thinking in terms of stories must be shared by all mind or minds, whether ours or those of red wood forests and sea anemones.[27 p13]

But what kind of connectedness is Bateson actually referring to? Or, what is the "pattern of all patterns"[27 p11] he speaks about that connects all the living beings and reveals the necessary unity of mind and body?

Let us again consider the two ways one could address these issues. The first takes place in the realm of inscriptive phenomenology and may be called chiasmatic. Chiasm[20] is Merleau-Ponty's concept of the reversible unity of dual opposites, such as body and mind, inner and outer environments, self and the world, etc., any of which is impossible without its opposite. They create unity, but do not represent the same perspective on it. We are beings of the world; we are present in it as its parts. We grow within our world in a similar way fungi grow out of their mycelial web; the world precedes us. Who we are, how we decide and act, and what we want is given to us along with our conscious bodies and shared stories. What is meaningful or relevant to us is determined by the structure of openness of our species, our tribe and our family. But at the same time, we transform and influence our world in its physical as well as narrative appearance. The structure of the world depends on our personal and/or collective qualities, abilities and decisions.

Singular worlds of individual beings may thus merge to co-create shared worlds of whole communities. Different communities of organisms compete and choose various modes of coexistence—symbiotic, parasitic or antagonistic. Communicational macro-communities of different kinds of organisms and niches gradually emerge, such as forests, lakes, meadows or cities. All the inhabitable environments may thus be understood as a multiplicity of stories, as a bio-semi-osphere or a multilayered planetary web of life.

The second path begins with the idea of the entire bio-semiosphere, traditionally referred to as 'nature.' Microorganisms, fungi, plants or animals may appear, develop and prosper under certain favourable conditions. The sum of all inhabitable environments may be called planet Earth. The Earth as a cosmic body provides a nutritious matrix suitable for the emergence and evolution of living organisms in its atmosphere, geosphere and hydrosphere. Individual organisms and their communities grow out of this matrix in constant cycles of appearance and disappearance. Singular forms ascend from their concealment in the multiverse of possibilities only to die again and submit their dead bodies to the new generation of individual forms. Thus, every living organism is preceded by the evolution of life on Earth as its condition of possibility, becomes its active co-creator for a given time and place, and finally dies and dissolves in its nurturing and devouring complexity.

RHIZOMATIC MODEL

This brings us to the question: How can we employ this idea of an incorporated organism, a result of the overall conditions of planetary life and simultaneously a co-creator of these conditions, to explain altered states?

Regardless of the way AS are induced, the notion of 'altered' states suggests the existence of an unaltered state in relation to which other states are evaluated. I have said before that the unaltered or normal state consists of alertness as its main quality. At the core of this alertness, and hence the centre of the unaltered consciousness, resides the self-reflecting ego. Ego is the 'I' that is in conscious control of its own actions, may relate to them in reflection and describe them as its own. This concept of the ego as a self-inspecting, self-mirroring and constantly self-present entity—known as the subjectivity of modern science and philosophy—remains the measure of veracity and plausibility of any experience to this day despite being massively criticised by philosophy. We tend to consider any experiences that are not egocentric in this way to be mere anomalies; in only exceptional circumstances do we acknowledge them to be of any informative value.

From this perspective, all of the intriguing and mysterious experiences, such as separation from one's own body,[28] hallucinatory transformation into another being[29] or empathic fusion with another's psyche[30] are perceived as disorders. They represent a disruption of the normal egocentric order as AS experiences cannot be directly controlled. When you are 'on a trip' you can't simply leave, which is how you cease to be the sole author of the contents of your mind. The subject of such experiences is neither the empirical person with its fluctuating alertness, nor a pure transcendental ego independent of anything physical and empirical. That is, AS are inseparable from changes in biochemical processes taking place in the brain and the entire body.

Therefore, I make two suggestions. A) it is not precise to speak about altered states of *consciousness*, because in altered states, not only cognitive but also emotional and corporeal functions are transformed. We should possibly, to be precise, speak about altered states of the situated and integral presence of an organism's behaviour in its environment. B) a model of consciousness should be proposed that avoids the 'single state fallacy' of the egocentric model. Instead, consciousness could be interpreted as a multidimensional continuum of communicative states of organic presence in the world—from vegetative states to transcendental ones. In accordance with Deleuze, I propose to call the model 'rhizomatic.'[31] The model makes it possible to perceive consciousness as a multiplicity and is based on following principles:

• Consciousness (in any state) is a process of communication between an organism and its environment or 'umwelt.'

I understand 'communication' in the broadest sense as "to commune, to share, to participate in; to join, and unite,"[32] and thus to inhabit our environment. It is necessary to stress that the environment is not an inert space of objects, but a web of living exchange of matter and meaning.

• Communication is an integral part of the bodily activity of living organisms and of external physical processes. Every form of consciousness, including out-of-body or transpersonal experiences, is bound to an organic and/or physical medium. That is, AS are neither purely psychic or mental nor solely neural activities, but the transformation of your situation.

• The assumption that incarnation is a necessary condition of consciousness allows us to model consciousness using a biologic scale. It begins with elementary forms of cellular communication, continuing from various types of signal and neural systems to simple sign systems, and culminating in complex symbolic systems.

From this point of view, the conventional alert consciousness becomes but a part of another scale. Its centre is represented by everyday alertness. To the left from the centre, the extent of alertness and authorial self-control decreases, ranging from impulsive behaviour within alert states to daydreaming, sleep, unconsciousness and clinical coma, and finally to the non-reflective processes of bodily regulation. To the right from the centre of the scale, alertness intensifies from common and deep concentration to abstract and symbolic thought, contemplation, meditative states and finally to mystical experiences.

While consciousness is necessarily incarnate and impossible without physical and chemical processes taking place within living tissues, it cannot be reduced to these processes. Consciousness cannot be localised to any part of the body, and the meaning of any such localisation is merely a metaphorical one. Indeed, I believe that the communicative and therefore transitive nature of consciousness implies that it is never present to itself or other conscious entities as anything other than certain behaviours that it generates and from which it is inseparable. From this point of view, the existence of consciousness assumes not only the wholeness of a living organism, but also the connection to its living environment as a medium of its appearance.

CONCLUSION

My intention has been to uncover the possibilities of a bio-phenomenological interpretation of AS. I have tried to open a perspective on consciousness as an integral part of the corporeal situatedness of an organism in the world of communication. In the home state, an organism is under the control of automatic feedback control and habits. But during altered states, one's home base is transformed. The sensory and neural networks change their biochemistry and consequently also the manner of communication with themselves and the outside environment. This allows us to break out of our usual patterns and enter the continuum of life from which we have to separate ourselves in order to be unique, but, paradoxically, from which we are also inseparable, because it represents the necessary conditions of our existence.

1. Ludwig AM. *Altered States of Consciousness.* Archives of General Psychiatry. 1966;15:225–34.
2. Cardeña E, Winkelman M, editors. *Altering Consciousness: Multidisciplinary Perspectives.* Santa Barbara: Praeger; 2011.
3. Rock AJ, Krippner S. 'Does the concept of "Altered States of Consciousness" rest on mistake?' *The International Journal of Transpersonal Studies.* 2007;26:33–40.
4. Bremner JD, Krystal JH, Putnam FW, Southwick, SM, Marmar C, Charney DS, Mazure CM. 'Measurement of dissociative states with the clinician-administered dissociative states scale (CADSS).' *Journal of Traumatic Stress.* 1998;11(1):125–36.
5. Lewis-Williams D. *The Mind in the Cave: Consciousness and the Origins of Art.* London: Thames & Hudson; 2002.
6. Sturm W, de Simone A, Krause BJ, Specht K, Hesselmann V, Radermacher I, et al. *Functional anatomy of intrinsic alertness: evidence for a fronto-parietal-thalamic-brainstem network in the right hemisphere.* Neuropsychologia. 1999;37(7):797–805.
7. Dictionary.com; Available from: http://dictionary.reference.com/browse/alert. Accessed 15 December 2011.
8. Bracha HS, Ralston TC, Matsukawa JM, Williams AE, Bracha AS. *Does "Fight or flight" need Updating?*, Psychosomatics 2004;45(5):448–9.
9. Schroll ME, Greenwood S. *Worldviews in collision/worldviews in metamorphosis: towards a multistate paradigm; Anthropology of Consciousness.* 2011;22(1):44–60.
10. Roberts TB, *Psychedelic Horizons.* Exeter, UK: Imprint-Academic.com; 2006.
11. Prigogine I, Stengers I. *Order Out of Chaos: Man's New Dialogue With Nature.* New York: Bentam; 1984.
12. Sanders TI. *Strategic Thinking and the New Science: Planning in the Midst of Chaos, Complexity and Change.* New York: The Free Press; 1998.
13. Novotný K, Hammer TS, Gléonec A, Špecían P, editors. *Thinking in Dialogue with Humanities: Paths Into the Phenomenology of Merleau-Ponty.* Zeta Books; 2011.
14. 14. Barbieri M. *What is biosemiotics?* Biosemiotics. 2008;1:1–3.
15. Varela F, Thompson E, Rosch E. *Cognitive Science and Human Experience.* Cambridge: MIT Press; 1991.
16. Narby J. *Intelligence in Nature: an Inquiry Into Knowledge.* Penguin; 2005.
17. Petříček M. *Die Bedeutung der Phänomenologie.* in: Waldenfels B, Tengelyi L, Richir M, editors. *Mesotes: Das Phänomen und die Sprache.* Turia und Kant: Wien; 1998. p.62–8.
18. Merleau-Ponty M, *The Primacy of Perception and Other Essays on Phenomenological Psychology, the Philosophy of Art, History and Politics.* Edie JE, editor. Evanston: Northwestern University Press; 1964.
19. Gendlin ET. *The primacy of the body, not the primacy of perception: how the body knows the situation and philosophy.* Man and World. 1992;25(3–4):341–53.
20. Merleau-Ponty M. *The Visible and the Invisible.* Lafort C, editor. Evanston: Northwestern University Press; 1968.
21. Nitsche M. *Topological space as a model of being in the late working notes of Maurice Merleau-Ponty.* Filosofický asopis. 2010;58(1):49–56.
22. Witzany G. *From umwelt to mitwelt: natural laws versus golden rule-governed sign-mediated interactions (rsi's).* Semiotica. 2006;1(4):1–14.
23. Witzany G. *From biosphere to semiosphere to social lifeworlds: biology as an understanding social science,* TripleC. 2005;1(1):51–74.
24. Thompson E. *Life and mind: from autopoiesis to neurophenomenology: a tribute to Francisco Varela.* Phenomenology and Cognitive Sciences. 2004;3:381–98.
25. Von Uexküll J. *Theoretische Biologie.* 2nd ed. Berlin: Julius Springer; 1928.
26. Hoffmeyer J. 'The Semiotic Niche.' *Journal of Mediterranean Ecology.* 2009;9:5–30.
27. Bateson G. *Mind and Nature: A Necessary Unity.* New York: E. P. Dutton; 1979.
28. Twemlow SW, Gabbard GO, Jones FC. 'The out of body experience: A phenomenological typology based on questionnaire responses.' *American Journal of Psychiatry.* 1982;139(4):450–5.
29. Winkelman M. 'Shamanism as neurotheology and evolutionary psychology.' *American Behavioral Scientist.* 2002;45(12):1873–85.

30. Larøi F. 'The phenomenological diversity of hallucinations: some theoretical and clinical implications.' *Psychologica Belgica*. 2006;46(1/2):163–83.
31. Deleuze G, Guattari F. *A Thousand Plateaus: Capitalism and Schizophrenia*. Minneapolis: University of Minnesota Press; 1987.
32. Available from: http://dictionary.reference.com/browse/communication.

COGNITIVE PHENOMENOLOGY OF MIND MANIFESTATION

JOSEPH BICKNELL

Psychedelic experiences typically involve intense temporary alterations in perception, and commonly lead to radical and permanent transformations in belief. The LSD experience was described by Watts as: "revelations of the secret workings of the brain, of the associative and patterning processes, the ordering systems which carry out all our sensing and thinking."[1 p44] Similarly Grof described the LSD experience as:

> *complex revelatory insights into the nature of existence [...]*
> *typically accompanied by a sense of certainty that this knowl*
> *edge is ultimately more relevant and "real" than the perceptions*
> *and beliefs we share in everyday life.*[2 p38]

In this essay I will be examining the themes that are contained in descriptions of psychedelic tripping such as these. I will present a generalised phenomenological model which relates psychedelic experience to the brain's associative and patterning process, by examining the most standard and prominent features of such experiences and inferring general principles from them. These standard features of tripping are the alterations in visual perception, and the strong tendency for transformation/reformation of core belief structures ('life-changing' experiences) during the course of psychedelic exploration. My aim is to examine these features of psychedelic phenomenology (that is, the subjective mental content of psychedelic trip experiences) for the purposes of highlighting the underlying alterations in cognitive processing that are responsible for the psychedelic effect, and thereby to capture the original insight behind the label 'psychedelic' (or 'mind revealing').

A major theme in what follows is the phenomenological comparison of the ordinary (non-intoxicated) state of consciousness with the non-ordinary psychedelic state of consciousness, for the purposes of highlighting the specific peculiarities of the latter. During a psychedelic trip session, the mind (or at least, certain major aspects of the mind) becomes explicitly manifested such that it is made available for conscious inspection; by implication then, the mind is not manifested in ordinary, sober consciousness. The question arises, therefore, of what exactly is meant by the 'mind' in this specific context, and what it means to say that the mind becomes temporarily 'manifested' in the psychedelic state of consciousness; what exactly is the thing that can be clearly perceived during intense psychedelic tripping, which is hidden during ordinary experience. In what follows I will offer a substantive answer to this question.

This essay is intended as a basic conceptual model of psychedelic experiencing, using the general approach of phenomenology (the study of conscious appearances). It should be interpreted first and foremost as an approximation for the phenomenological content of experience: any metaphysical assertions are secondary to this main aim. There are a few books dealing explicitly with the phenomenology of drug-induced altered states, these include Huxley's *Doors of Perception*[3] and Shanon's *Antipodes of the Mind*.[4] Also, the literature in psychiatric phenomenology provides some useful concepts which can be applied to the drug-induced experiences, especially the writing of Sass[5,6] and Stanghellini.[7]

ANALOGY AND THE DESCRIPTION OF EXPERIENCE

Analogy is a very useful tool for understanding the cognitive dynamics of psychedelic tripping; likening mental phenomena to physical situations and occurrences elucidates the structure of the perceptual alteration. I will now briefly run through several of the most pertinent analogies and explain how they can be applied to psychedelic altered-state phenomenology. Plato's[8] famous 'cave allegory' likens ordinary perception to staring at shadows on the back wall of a cave, a perspective that most people are fully immersed in most of the time. It is only the philosopher who is privileged to get a glimpse of reality from the higher-dimensional perspective, when he turns his head around to see the light at the mouth of the cave and discovers that the shadows are actually flat lower-dimensional projections of a deeper, hidden actual reality. Plato's suggestion is that a person who had never seen beyond the shadows would come to believe that the mere shadows constitute actual reality itself (as opposed to a lower-dimensional projection of actual reality): the altered perspective experienced by the philosopher presents a radical challenge to that belief.

In a similar vein, ordinary perception can be likened to staring at reflections in the surface of a perfectly still pool of water (the mind) where the surface of the pool is invisible. The reflections remain perfectly solid and convincing/realistic so long as the surface of the water/mind is undisturbed, the psychedelic trip-effect is like causing a splash in the water so that the surface is distorted and becomes visible; the reflections then ripple, undulate and fragment, and reveal themselves to be mere reflections as opposed to being the actual things that they reflect. Albert Hofmann, the discoverer of LSD, described how during his bicycle ride home after his first deliberate LSD self-administration: "Everything in my field of vision wavered and was distorted as if seen in a curved mirror."[9] The same as in Plato's example, a person who had only ever seen the reflections, and who had never experienced the surface-manifesting psychedelic 'splash' effect, would believe in the concrete reality of the reflections, and in the illusion of direct perceptual access to concrete reality.

Jackson[10] has written about the psychological effect of radically new experience; he constructs a thought-experiment involving a character 'Fred' who possesses the ability to perceive one additional colour (a subdivision of red) that nobody else can see. This serves as an analogy for psychedelic tripping, because the discovery of the psychedelic perspective provides new information that is not available in the ordinary state of consciousness. Jackson suggests that Fred would be unable to communicate his experience to anyone who had not seen the extra colour. In much the same way, a tripper cannot communicate meaningfully about his psychedelic experiences to someone who had never had the experience; trip-reports cannot fully convey what it is like to trip for to truly know the experience a person has to have it him- or herself. It could be argued from a behaviouristic point of view that what one learns on discovering psychedelic tripping is simply an ability to recall and describe the experiences; a person who had never had the experience, will be unable to recall and describe it. Hoffman[11] has similarly likened the discovery of psychedelic tripping to an adolescent's discovery of the experience of sexual climax.

Whether psychedelics cleanse the doors of perception or ripple the surface of consciousness, the value of these analogies lies in the overall picture they provide of how the psychedelic effect works to reveal the operational structures of the mind. Analogies such as these serve to model and reflect the two core effects of psychedelic tripping; the temporary alteration in perception, and the permanent transformation of belief structures.

FROM ANALOGY TO COGNITIVE PHENOMENOLOGY

The various structural analogies can be translated into the language of philosophy of mind. According to Marr's[12] theory of visual perception, the two-dimensional array of coloured light information on the surface of the eyes is translated by the mind into a complex, multi-levelled mental representation of the three-dimensional physical environment. Our external environment is illuminated by light which is reflected off the surfaces of physical objects; some of the reflected light hits the surface of our eyes, and this two-dimensional pattern of light of the surface of the eyes is processed and translated into a three-dimensional mental image of the surrounding environment. Fodor[13] makes a similar claim in his theory on mental modularity, according to which the brain contains dedicated modules for processing the information that is received as input from the body's sensory organs; the output of these modules is the detailed mental image of the physical environment. It is the mental image which is directly revealed to consciousness, so our ordinary conscious perception is inherently representational, we perceive three-dimensional physical reality indirectly via mental symbols. Hofmann[14] uses the terms 'explicit representationalism' and 'dissociated cognition' to describe the psychedelic perceptual/cognitive mode; perception is representational at all times, but in the ordinary perceptual modality the mental representations behave so predictably and consistently (they are so tangibly *realistic*) that they are tacitly conflated (or *associated*) with the mind-independent realities that they represent.

Hoffman[14] suggests that during a psychedelic trip the mind adopts the *metaperceptive* point of view. From this vantage point the distinction between the subjective mental representations and objective physical reality is explicitly revealed to the mind; physical objects look less solid and realistic during a trip, they cease to appear as mind-independent objective entities and take on a cartoon-like character. A psychedelic trip is induced by altering the brain's endogenous chemistry via externally introduced chemicals, yet the altered visual effects are perceived as actual *qualities* of external objects (along with their shape, colour, etc.). Huxley conveyed this idea in his description of his first mescaline trip, by describing how his trousers appeared to him in his altered state as follows:

> *Those folds in the trousers—what a labyrinth of endlessly significant complexity! And the texture of the grey flannel—how*

rich, how deeply, mysteriously sumptuous! [...] the folds of my grey flannels were charged with 'is-ness.' [15 p12]

Note how Huxley directly attributes these fantastic qualities to his actual trousers, and not to his own perception of his trousers.

The physical surfaces of solid objects are commonly observed to flow, undulate and ripple like the surface of a liquid when psychedelic chemicals are introduced into the brain; it follows logically from this that what the mind normally holds to be external, mind-independent concrete existence, is actually a deceptively detailed mental appearance. There is no alternative way to account for the observation that an alteration of brain chemistry causes alterations in external reality other than by postulating that what we refer to as 'external reality' is in fact internal/mental in origin; psychedelic visual alterations combined with basic reasoning conclusively demonstrate the principle of representationalism. During a psychedelic trip, each person can observe for him- or herself that an alteration of internal neurochemistry results in a tangible alteration in the perceptual qualities of the external world, this naturally leads an inquiring mind to question the origin of perceptual phenomena, and the metaphysical status of the subject/object distinction. This is why the temporary perceptual alteration can result in a permanent transformation of the mind's conceptual framework; the psychedelic effect challenges our most basic assumptions about the nature of perception.

The phenomenologist Husserl[16] held that the ordinary (natural, habitual) manner in which the mind perceives reality is shaped by implicit background assumptions that give a coherent structure to our experience (this idea is much in line with the general Kantian philosophical framework), when these assumptions are made explicit and bracketed off by a process of private philosophical reflection which he called the *phenomenological epoche*, the mind's 'sphere of ownness' is revealed, the raw subjective datastream prior to the mind's conceptualising activity. The psychiatrist Depraz[17] has likened Husserl's phenomenological epoche to the process of psychotic mental dis-integration in schizophrenic patients, suggesting that such experiences constitute a 'phenomenological exploration of consciousness,' and that schizophrenia consists essentially in an 'enhanced aptitude to perform the epoche.'

Freud[18] anticipated the comparison of psychosis and mind-manifestation when he compared the mind to a crystal, and used this comparison to suggest that observation of psychotic/schizoid mental processes can shed light on the structure of the sane mind. According to Freud's analogy a whole, undamaged crystal contains a complex internal structure which remains invisible so long as the crystal remains whole and undamaged. However when a crystal shatters, the shape of the resulting shards of broken crystal reveal this (previously hidden) internal structure. Similarly, the internal structure of the mind is invisible so long as it retains its wholeness and integrity; the mental shattering/fragmentation which occurs during periods of psychosis reveals its underlying structure in the 'lines of cleavage' along which it falls apart. According to Freud, the madman possesses a somewhat privileged perspective compared to a sane man because of his ability to perceive the hidden mental structures which are hidden to the sane man's perspective. This analogy of Freud's is readily applicable to the phenomenological model of drug-induced mind manifestation that I am outlining here.

The psychiatrist Osmond,[19] who was one of the earliest scientific investigators of LSD, and who is responsible for creating the word 'psychedelic,' observed that the mental dynamics involved in schizophrenic psychosis have crucial similarities to psychedelic tripping. It was for this reason that LSD was first labelled as 'psychotomimetic' (psychosis mimicking), and only later relabelled 'psychedelic.' So Depraz's[17] insight about the comparison of Husserl's epoche to schizophrenic mental dis-integration can be extended to shed light on psychedelic mental alteration. The heightened perspective of transcendental subjectivity, which is a new field of awareness that is revealed after exercising the epoche (and, if Depraz's comparison is valid, also during periods of schizophrenic psychosis) is equivalent to the perspective of explicit representationalism that is revealed in a psychedelic trip; the core implicit assumption that is made explicit and bracketed off is the assumption that consciousness is directly in contact with external objects, or equivalently, the assumption of straightforward identity between mental representations and their referents.

Sass[6] and Stanghellini[7] both employ the term 'hyperreflexivity' to describe the core peculiarity of the schizophrenic patient's subjective experiences during periods of psychosis, and this term can be used equivalently to describe the temporary cognitive alteration of the psychedelic trip experience. For Sass, cognitive hyperreflexivity contrasts with ordinary cognition because of its intensely inward-pointing orientation, such that, "the ego disengages from normal forms of involvement with nature and society, often taking itself, or its own experiences, as its own object."[6 p37] Similarly Stanghellini suggests that in the hyperreflexive mind, "the 'I' breaks down into an experiencing I-subject contemplating an experienced I-object" such that, "the act of perception itself turns out to be an explicit intelligible object."[7 p165] Again here we see a clear indication of the general idea that altered state experience involves a specific kind of dissociation in the mind between symbol and referent, a cognitive process of representation which normally operates silently in the background is brought intensely into the foreground of awareness.

With this model of psychedelic experiencing in mind, it is worth pointing out that the word 'hallucinogen' which is sometimes used to denote psychedelic drugs is misleading, insofar as it implies that the effect of the drug is to *induce* hallucinations that are not present in the ordinary state of consciousness. What is actually happening in a psychedelic trip is that a certain hallucinatory (or illusory, mistaken) aspect of our ordinary experience (our tacit conflation of the mind-dependent internal perceptual image with the mind-independent external world) becomes explicitly apparent, which is merely implicit (and therefore typically taken for granted and not noticed) during ordinary experience. In his exhaustive compendium of phenomenological alterations that are observed in ayahuasca sessions, Shanon includes "the assessment, very common with ayahuasca, that what is seen and thought during the course of intoxication defines the real, whereas the world that is ordinarily perceived is actually an illusion."[4 p205]

Similarly Watts likens psychedelia to the transformations of consciousness that are undertaken in Taoism and Zen, which he says is:

> *more like the correction of faulty perception or the curing of a disease... not an acquisitive process of learning more and more facts or greater and greater skills, but rather an unlearning of wrong habits and opinions.*[1 p15]

Psychedelic drugs are often referred to as 'teachers' (particularly the plant-based drugs such as ayahuasca and psilocybin mushrooms), so this can be understood as the core lesson that they teach—they reveal the fundamental cognitive operation of fusing together representation and referent, this is the sense in which 'mind' becomes 'manifested' during a trip.

Hoffman[20] states that the representational nature of mind is obscured in our ordinary perceptual modality by the high degree of stability and consistency in the way that mental representations behave (for example, solid objects remain firmly solid). This creates the strong impression that mental phenomena are concretely existing (and therefore non-mental) entities, and that consciousness *directly* perceives mind-independent reality so that perception is not mediated by mental representations; this is the real meaning of a 'hallucination' insofar as it applies to hallucinogenic drugs. The hallucinatory aspect of perception is exposed by the psychedelic trip-effect because the ordinary stability and consistency of the representations is noticeably diminished during a trip, solid objects appear much less solid, physical reality takes on a fluid appearance.

MIND MANIFESTATION AND TRANSFORMATION OF BELIEF NETWORKS

In addition to the temporary perceptual alterations observed during psychedelic trip sessions, another important aspect of psychedelic phenomenology is a kind of radical psychological restructuring. An intense trip can be a life-transforming experience which leads to a major overhaul of a person's internal framework of beliefs (Hoffman[21] calls this framework the *mental worldmodel).* Thagard[22] has comprehensively modelled the process of psychological paradigm transformation; when new information comes to light that cannot be accounted for or explained by an established belief network; the entire network must undergo revision in order to accommodate the new information. For example, someone who had lived his or her entire life in a black-and-white environment would believe implicitly that there are no other colours since he or she has no way of perceiving them. Such a person would experience a drastic disproof of that implicit belief, if suddenly exposed to the world of colour for the first time (like Jackson's[10] thought-experiment character 'Mary,' who is suddenly shown a red rose after spending a lifetime in black-and-white). This is comparable to the mental transformation that is undergone when a person becomes acquainted with psychedelia; the central difference between the pre- and post-psychedelic belief configurations, is that the new configuration accommodates the possibility of psychedelic experience (it accommodates the perceptual dissociation between symbol and referent).

The epistemological dynamics that occur during the process of waking up from a vivid dream provide a close analogy for psychedelic mental transformation; when fully immersed in a dream world one is not aware that one is dreaming, so the contents of dream-consciousness are taken to be simply real, the subject is not aware that his surrounding environment is mentally projected and imaginary. After waking up, when reflecting back on the dream, the mental contents are immediately re-interpreted as unreal, imaginary mental projections in light of the new experience of waking consciousness ("it was just a dream"). Similarly, upon perceiving directly the symbol/referent distinction in the psychedelic state of consciousness, the phenomenal content of ordinary consciousness is reinterpreted in the light of the new information that is provided by the heightened psychedelic perspective. Every psychedelic trip lasts for a certain duration then ends as the chemicals are metabolised by the body, so the psychedelic perspective which reveals manifest phenomena as projected mental representations is only experienced on a temporary basis. But if a person is able to fully grasp and remember the psychedelic insights after the trip ends (and become generally acquainted with the intense altered experiential modality), then the mind is permanently transformed.

The psychedelic belief revision is held in place by the *memory* of the transformative psychedelic experience. This memory provides a constant reminder which prevents the old pre-psychedelic set of beliefs/assumptions from re-establishing itself. The existence of the altered-state modality of dissociated/hyperreflexive cognition presents a fundamental overrider to pre-established belief networks, which forces an overhaul of those networks. The axiomatic basis of the pre-psychedelic, experientially naïve mental worldmodel (essentially, the belief in straightforward identity between mental representations and their referents) is critically undermined by transformative psychedelic experience. Per Thagard[22] this undermining of a metaphysical model necessitates a systematic restructuring of the model, adding crucial qualifiers to foundational assumptions; in this case the qualifiers concern the existence of an experience which seems to disprove the assumed identity of representation and referent.

1. Watts A. *The Joyous Cosmology; Adventures in the Chemistry of Consciousness*. New York: Pantheon Books; 1962.
2. Grof S. *The Holotropic Mind; The Three Levels of Human Consciousness and How They Shape our Lives*. San Francisco: San Francisco Harper; 1993.
3. Huxley A. *The Doors of Perception: And Heaven and Hell*. London: Thinking Ink; 2003.
4. Shanon B. *The Antipodes of the Mind: Charting the Phenomenology of the Ayahuasca Experience*. Oxford: Oxford University Press; 2003.
5. Sass L. *The Paradoxes of Delusion; Wittgenstein, Schreber and the Schizophrenic Mind*. New York: Cornell University Press; 1994.
6. Sass L. *Madness and Modernism*. New York: Basic Books; 1992.
7. Stanghellini G. *Disembodied Spirits and Deanimated Bodies; the Psychopathology of Common Sense*. Oxford: Oxford University Press; 2004.
8. Plato. *The Complete Works*. Cooper J editor. Indianapolis: Hackett publishing. 1997.
9. Albert Hofmann, inventor of LSD, dies at 102. *The Guardian*. 1 May 2008. Available from: http://www.guardian.co.uk/world/2008/may/01/medicalresearch.
10. Jackson F. 'Epiphenomenal Qualia.' *The Philosophical Quarterly*. 1982;32(127):127–36.
11. Hofmann M. *Determinism as Enlightenment*. *1985–2007*. Available from: www.egodeath .com/DeterminismEnlightenment.htm.
12. Marr A. *Vision: A Computational Investigation into the Human Representation and Processing of Visual Information*. San Francisco: W. H. Freeman & Company; 1983.
13. Fodor J. *The Modularity of Mind*. Cambridge: MIT Press; 1983.
14. Hoffman M. *The Entheogen Theory of Religion and Ego Death.1985–2007*. Available from http://www.egodeath.com/mobile.htm.
15. Huxley A. *The Doors of Perception*. London: Flamingo; 1977.
16. Husserl E. *Cartesian Meditations*. Dordrecht: Kluwer Academic Publishers; 1999.
17. Depraz N. *Putting the epoché into practice: schizophrenic experience as illustrating the phenomenological exploration of consciousness*. In: Fulford B, Morris K, Sadler J, Stanghellini G editors. *Nature and Narrative, an Introduction to the Philosophy of Psychiatry*. Oxford: Oxford University Press; 2003. P. 187–98.
18. Freud S. *New Introductory Lectures on Psychoanalysis*. London: Penguin, 1988.
19. Obituary; Doctor Humphry Osmond. *The Telegraph*. 2004 16 Feb. Available from: http://www.telegraph.co.uk/news/obituaries/1454436/Dr-Humphry-Osmond.html.
20. Hofmann M. *Mental Construct Processing*. 1985–2007. available from http://www .egodeath.com/mcp.htm.
21. Hofmann M. *The Egoic and Transcendent Mental Worldmodels*. 1985–2007. Available from: http://www.egodeath.com/egoictranscendentmentalmodels.htm.
22. Thagard P. *Conceptual Revolutions*. New Jersey: Princeton University Press; 1992.

PSYCHEDELICS, PARAPSYCHOLOGY AND EXCEPTIONAL HUMAN EXPERIENCES[A]

DAVID LUKE

At the beginning of the 1950s the developed world began in earnest its psychedelic research era. Since then these profoundly mind-altering substances have been inextricably associated with paranormal experiences—such as telepathy, clairvoyance, precognition and out-of-body experiences—by many of the researchers who have studied their effects. Currently however, virtually no research is being conducted in this area despite the recent revival of research into the potential therapeutic benefit of psychedelics in humans. This paper briefly discusses some of the author's research to date in this field: a review of the literature on parapsychology (the psychological study of apparently paranormal processes) and psychedelics,[1] a survey of paranormal experiences associated with different psychoactive substances,[2] and correlation of self-reports of the number of consumed psychedelics with performance on a precognition task.[3]

The word psychedelic, meaning 'mind-manifesting,' was created by Dr. Humphry Osmond in correspondence with Aldous Huxley in 1956. Four years earlier Osmond had published an article in the *Hibbert Journal* with his colleague John Smythies[4] in which they proposed that a new theory of mind was needed that could account for both mescaline experiences and what they considered to be the scientifically-proven fact of extra-sensory perception (ESP). Huxley read this article and requested that Osmond, who like Huxley hailed from Surrey in England but lived in North America, should visit Huxley and give him mescaline.[5]

Huxley then catalysed the popularisation of psychedelics with the publication of *The Doors of Perception* in 1954.[6] In the book, not only did Huxley eloquently describe his experience of mescaline, disappearing beautifully into the mystical folds in his trousers, but he also proposed a nascent neurochemical model of ESP. He suggested that the French philosopher Henri Bergson was right to propose that the brain's primary function was to filter out all the excess sensory data that we do not attend to. Otherwise, this information would overwhelm the conscious mind with a mass of information that was ordinarily irrelevant for the organism's survival.

However, building on Bergson's notion, Huxley added that substances such as mescaline serve to override the brain's 'reducing valve' that filters out this sensory data. Under such psychedelic disinhibition of the brain's inhibiting function, the mind is thereby capable of potentially remembering anything it has ever experienced and sensing everything within its immediate environment. Furthermore, it is also able to access the entirety of information available in the universe, even forwards and backwards in time. Such mystical or paranormal feats are known as clairvoyance, precognition and telepathy, and are collectively termed extra-sensory perception (ESP), or, more recently, 'psi.' To illustrate this psychic psychedelic process, Huxley took the title of his book from a quote by the English mystic, William Blake—"If the doors of perception were cleansed everything would appear to man as it is, infinite."

Elsewhere in the USA, just prior to the publication of the *Doors of Perception* in 1954, Gordon Wasson was recently back from his first trip to Mexico where he discovered both an active mushroom cult and the identity of their sacrament as *Psilocybe mexicana*. The Mazatec shaman, Don Aurelio, (who Wasson worked with before meeting the more famous Maria Sabina) held a mushroom ceremony for him and told him two important facts about his son in the US that neither of them could otherwise have known. Both were ultimately true, although one was still yet to happen, thereby demonstrating Don Aurelio's accurate clairvoyance *and* precognition under the influence of psilocybin. Yet, as far as scientific evidence goes, this is far from conclusive.[7]

Similarly, it was in the mid-1950's that LSD began doing the rounds. About 10 years earlier Albert Hofmann had discovered the exceptional psychological effects of LSD and had the first-ever LSD-induced out-of-body experience when he found himself hovering above his body and assumed that he had died.[8] But these two tales of exceptional human experience from our foremost psychedelic pioneers are just the opening of the rabbit hole.

Anthropology, particularly from the New World, has long informed us that the people who traditionally use psychedelic plants and potions do so specifically for 'magical' purposes, such as ESP, psychic diagnosis and healing.[9,10] More compelling yet, there is an abundance of stories of anthropologists either witnessing or experiencing first-hand the occurrence of apparently paranormal phenomena with the use of psychoactive plants and fungi: peyote among the Huichol indians, psilocybin-containing mushrooms with the Mazatec, fly agaric mushrooms with the Ojibwa, datura in India, pituri in Australia, and practically all known psychedelic plants in all regions of the world.[1]

Of particular importance in this equation is ayahuasca, which is so often accompanied by reports of psychic ability that when one of its psychoactive constituents, harmine, was isolated at the beginning of the 20th century it was named 'telepathine.' It is also interesting to note that, conversely, there is a serious lack of similar paranormal reports with the non-visionary psychoactive plants that have also been in use for centuries, such as coffee, coca, and cacao.[11]

These numerous reports collected by anthropologists and from the early psychedelic explorers soon began surfacing among psychotherapists as well once these substances started seeping out of the labs and into the clinics. As just one example, Stan Grof, who we can probably credit as being the leading expert on psychedelic psychotherapy, reported observing past-life recall, out-of-body experiences, and ESP on a daily basis.[12,13]

Thinking there might be something magical about these medicines that has been largely overlooked I conducted a comparison of spontaneous ESP phenomena occurring, with good supporting evidence in the therapy room, either with or without psychedelics. Reports of spontaneous ESP occurring within ordinary psychotherapy were fairly rare, although definitely evident, but they were seemingly more frequently reported by *psychedelic* psychotherapists during the 1960s.[11]

Substantiating these anecdotal reports a number of surveys have been conducted that have consistently found a positive relationship between the reporting of having had a paranormal experience and the use of psychedelics, with heavier users having more experiences.[2] What the surveys also show is that between 18–83% (depending on the type of experience) of those using cannabis and/or psychedelics also reported ESP experiences occurring whilst actually under the influence. There is very good reason to believe that these substances can induce paranormal experiences, regardless of whether these experiences are genuine or not.

A survey conducted by myself and my colleague, Dr. Marios Kittenis, extended this research and explored the taxonomy of these phenomena to try and identify which drugs related to which experiences in particular. While psychedelics in general were associated with a range of phenomena, we found that particular substances were more readily associated with certain experiences than others. For instance, entity encounter experiences were very common under DMT, telepathy was common under cannabis and DXM, out-of-body experiences typified ketamine, and plant spirit encounters occurred particularly with psilocybin but also with a host of other psychedelic flora.[2]

Since the prohibition of psychedelics in the late 1960s most of this field of research, which I like to call 'parapsychopharmacology,' has been conducted through surveys. Yet these provide very little evidential value for the genuine occurrence of psi. Fortunately, the notion of using psychedelics to investigate parapsychology was considered a viable method just prior to prohibition and about a dozen or more controlled experiments were conducted. Walter Pahnke, for instance, who conducted the original Good Friday experiment some 50 years ago and published his findings in the *International Journal of Parapsychology*, also conducted an ESP experiment with LSD.[12] The results of this experiment were not significant overall. However, Stanislav Grof was one of the participants and had a string of increasingly improbable direct hits on the target symbol, determining a randomly selected target beyond the expectation of chance probability. Grof, explained that:

> *When I got the third correct answer in a row, the feelings [of a universe where no laws of time and space exist] were so powerful that I could not continue. The reason for discontinuation of the ESP experiment was a strange mixture of a conviction that it was absurd to test the obvious and, on the other hand, a metaphysical fear of confusion that would follow if I had to give up the usual concept of time and space and with it all the related reference points we feel so secure with.*[15 p3]

Overall, the catalogue of 'pharma-psi' experiments from the sixties had some promising findings, which were in direct proportion to the sophistication of the methodology. Studies that used boring experimental procedures (such as massively iterative card-guessing tasks, sometimes for hours on end) and psychedelically-inexperienced participants returned poor results, while those that used engaging tasks and experienced trippers got the best outcomes. However, most of these experiments lacked the stringent degree of control expected by today's standards and so also have limited evidential value (for a detailed review see[1]).

What is needed is a series of well-controlled and methodologically-advanced experiments to more fully explore the capability of psychedelics to induce psi. I suggest that this research is now both timely, given the growing renaissance in psychedelic research, and extremely worthwhile.[16] For instance, my own research into precognition,[3] using a methodologically-rigorous design with 100 participants, found that precognitive ability correlated positively with the reported number of psychedelics consumed by the individuals in the sample ($r_S = .27$, $p = .008$, two-tailed). Although indirect, this adds further support for the notion of psi-inducing psychedelics.

Given the enormous difficulties still evident in attempting to get funding and approval to conduct research administrating psychedelics directly, let alone when parapsychology is involved, researchers in the past have considered various alternatives. One proposal is to conduct basic ESP research, inviting participants who have just partaken of mind-expanding substances, along with those who haven't, and testing their abilities. The parapsychologist Charles Tart[17] proposed conducting such 'drop-out drop-in' experiments shortly after prohibition to circumvent the difficulties in getting legal and ethical approval for such work. Such research techniques are now evident in non-parapsychological psychedelic research,[18] but have yet to be used in parapsychology.

Alternatively, it would be preferable to conduct direct psi experimentation through the administration of psychedelic substances, although probably with those substances which are still legal and have been reported to induce ESP, such as dextromethorphine.[2] Yet there still remain many obstacles to such work. Perhaps the greatest opportunity to conduct research at the present time would be to hitch an ESP experiment on the back of an existing psychedelic research program. We would be very happy to hear from any researcher interested in collaborating on this. As another alternative the use of hypnosis to re-induce psychedelic states[19] could offer a novel drug-free methodology.

Psychedelic researchers since the time of Huxley and Osmond have been fascinated by exploring the apparently parapsychological affects of these drugs. Rightly so, because the implications of such research for understanding our capabilities as a species and for understanding reality itself are deeply profound. Huxley's nascent notion of psychic abilities becoming available through the psychedelic inhibition of the brain's reducing valve, which opens up awareness to an infinite field of information, is now quietly gaining some credibility. Recent human experiments show that the serotonergic effect of psychedelic tryptamines can inhibit the 'sensory gating' function of the brain thereby opening up the flood gates of information to the mind and expanding one's sensory awareness.[11] Parapsychopharmacological research of this nature could tell us a great deal about the neurochemistry of apparently psychic abilities, the experience of which has probably been observed with these substances for millennia.

It is an exceptional shame that since prohibition psychedelic researchers have veered away from parapsychological research and, *vice versa*, parapsychologists have shied away from psychedelic research. Most likely this is because of the position of both of these fields at the fringes of mainstream science and the fear of jeopardising one's insecure but legitimate positions by dabbling in an even more taboo field of research to one's own. Given the widening acceptance of parapsychology within mainstream academia, in the UK at least, and with the new renaissance dawning in psychedelic research globally, such an interest shouldn't have to be considered as double career suicide anymore. Rather, the kind of ontological questions being asked through the research of parapsychopharmacology appear to be fundamental to our very sense of reality and should deserve special attention. And if philosophical prejudice appears to be in danger of keeping us from investigating such a topic it would seem wise to remember the words of Haldane, "my own suspicion is that the universe is not only queerer than we suppose, but queerer than we *can* suppose."[20 p286]

A. Gratitude is expressed to my colleague Dr. Marios Kittenis for his help in preparing the original talk on which this manuscript is based, and to Dr. Anna Waldstein and Dr. Cameron Adams for feedback on drafts of this manuscript.

1. Luke DP. 'Psychedelic substances and paranormal phenomena: A review of the research.' *Journal of Parapsychology.* 2008;72:77–107.

2. Luke DP, Kittenis M. 'A preliminary survey of paranormal experiences with psychoactive drugs.' *Journal of Parapsychology.* 2005;69(2):305–27.

3. Luke DP. Invited Lecture: Sacramental plants and their role in understanding the possible neurochemistry of psi [Abstract]. Proceedings of presented papers of the 4th Psi Meeting: Parapsychology and Psychology, Curitiba, Brazil. 2008; 188.

4. Osmond H, Smythies J. 'Schizophrenia: A new approach.' *Journal of Mental Science* 1952;98(411):309–15

5. Stevens J. *Storming heaven: LSD and the American dream.* William Heinemann; 1988.

6. Huxley A. *The doors of perception.* London: Flamingo; 1977.

7. Wasson RG, Wasson VP. *Mushrooms, Russsia, and history* (2 vols.). Pantheon; 1957.

8. Luke DP. A tribute to Albert Hofmann on his 100th birthday: The mysterious discovery of LSD and the impact of psychedelics on parapsychology. Paranormal Review. 2006;37:3–8.

9. Dobkin de Rios, M. *Hallucinogens: Cross-cultural perspectives.* Prism; 1990.

10. Schultes RE, Hofmann A. *Plants of the gods: Their sacred, healing, and hallucinogenic powers.* Healing Arts Press; 1992.

11. Luke D, Friedman H. The neurochemistry of psi reports and associated experiences. In Krippner S, Friedman H, editors. Mysterious minds: The neurobiology of psychics, mediums and other extraordinary people. Greenwood / Praeger; 2009. p.163–85.

12. Grof S. *Realms of the human unconscious: Observations from LSD research.* Viking Press; 1975.

13. Grof S. *LSD psychotherapy.* Hunter House; 1980.

14. Pahnke WN. 'The use of psychedelic drugs in parapsychological research.' *Parapsychology Review.* 1971;2(4);5–6 & 12–4.

15. Grof S. Subjective experiences during the LSD training session; 1970. Unpublished manuscript, available at http://www.maps.org/research/cluster/psilo-lsd/grof1970.pdf

16. Luke D. 'Connecting, diverging and reconnecting: Putting the psi back into psychedelic research.' *Journal of Parapsychology.* 2010;74:219–34.

17. Tart CT. Drug-induced states of consciousness. In Wolman B, editor. *Handbook of Parapsychology.* Van Nostrand Reinhold; 1977. p.500–25.

18. Curran HV, Morgan C. 'Cognitive, dissociative and psychotogenic effects of ketamine in recreational users on the night of drug use and 3 days later.' *Addiction* 2000;95:575–90.

19. Hastings A, Berk I, Cougar M, Ferguson E, Giles S, Steinbach-Humphrey S, et al. 'An extended non-drug MDMA-like experience evoked through hypnotic suggestion.' *Bulletin of the Multidisciplinary Association for Psychedelic Studies.* 2000;10(1):10.

20. Haldane, JBS. *Possible worlds and other essays.* London: Chatto and Windus; [1927] 1932.

THE ANAESTHETIC REVELATION: PSYCHEDELIA AND MYSTICISM

WILLIAM ROWLANDSON

"Drugs appear to induce religious experiences; it is less evident that they can produce religious lives."

Huston Smith

Borges wrote: "There is no classification of the Universe that is not arbitrary and conjectural. The reason for this is very simple: we do not know what the universe is."[1 p231] The debate concerning mysticism and psychedelic consciousness is equally arbitrary and conjectural: we do not know what mysticism and consciousness are. Notwithstanding these divergent, often conflicting terms, scholars of religion and of the psychedelic experience have engaged in a timeworn debate concerning whether authentic religious or mystical states can be achieved by ingesting psychoactive substances. Here, I provide a brief overview of the key moments and figures in this discussion, and synthesise the various emergent patterns. I then assess whether psychedelia and mysticism are indeed two names for a similar epistemological enterprise.

The relationship between religious practice and psychoactive plants is ancient and cross-cultural. There is extensive research into shamanism across the world and its association with hundreds of different psychoactive plants. For example, it has been proposed that the ancient Vedic intoxicant *Soma* may have been the fly agaric mushroom (*Amanita muscaria*),[2] the ceremonial drink *kykeon* of the Eleusinian Mysteries and the Old Testament *manna* contained psychoactive alkaloids from ergot *(Claviceps purpurea)*.[3,4]

A new chapter in this relationship began with the industrial age and the isolation and synthesis of psychoactive compounds. The widespread consumption of these drugs in the nineteenth century began with Humphry Davy and the Pneumatic Society's experimentation with nitrous oxide.[5] Opium (and its derivatives laudanum, morphine and heroin), cannabis, ether, cocaine and mescaline also impact on nineteenth century society. Though the question of mystical revelation or religious experience inspired by these drugs is not explicit, the reported experiences of many of the figures naturally approach this issue, making this a pivotal moment owing to the secular and yet mystically revelatory quality of the experiences. The question was of great concern to William James,[6,7] the grandfather of psychedelic research, whose experiences with nitrous oxide and ether led him to consider the relationship between spontaneous mystical states and induced ones:

> *Nitrous oxide and ether [...] stimulate the mystical consciousness in an extraordinary degree. [...] I know more than one person who is persuaded that in the nitrous oxide trance we have a genuine metaphysical revelation.*[7 p387]

James concluded his musings on 'anaesthetic revelation' with the well-known comparison between intoxicated and mystical states:

> *our normal waking consciousness, rational consciousness as we call it, is but one special type of consciousness, while all about it, parted from it by the filmiest of screens, there lie potential forms of consciousness entirely different. [...] No account of the universe in its totality can be final which leaves these other forms of consciousness quite disregarded. [...] to me the living sense of its reality only comes in the artificial mystic state of mind.*[7 p387-9]

Despite these considerations, his chapter on mysticism asserts that the true mystical state is 'passive.' The legacy of James's investigations into these artificial states of mind is vast, and has influenced countless researchers in their evaluation of such experiences.

Mescaline was first isolated in 1897 by Heffter and synthesised by Späth in 1919. While many cultural figures reported their experiences with mescaline, it was Huxley[8-10] who proposed a phenomenological connection between mystical states and experiences of mescaline, although he was careful not to make the association so close as to make the two states wholly equivalent:

> *I am not so foolish as to equate what happens under the influence of mescalin or of any other drug, prepared or in the future preparable, with the realization of the end and ultimate purpose of human life [... but] to be shaken out of the ruts of ordinary perception, to be shown for a few timeless hours the outer and the inner world, not as they appear to an animal obsessed with survival or to a human being obsessed with words and notions, but as they are apprehended, directly and unconditionally, by Mind at Large—this is an experience of inestimable value to everyone and especially to the intellectual.*[8 p59-60]

Huxley's works were hugely influential, and were critiqued by scholars of religion and mysticism.[11] Importantly, *The Doors of Perception* was read by Carl Jung, whose participation in this debate is curiously sparse. He comments only briefly about Hofmann's isolation of LSD-25 at the Sandoz labs in Basel in 1938, Hofmann's first experiences of the drug in 1942, and his isolation of psilocybin and psilocin in 1958. I am grateful to my colleague Leon Schlamm for referring me to Jung's correspondence wherein he expresses his misgivings about the use of psychoactives not solely in psychoanalysis, but also in recreation:

> *[Mescalin] has indeed very curious effects—vide Aldous Huxley!—of which I know far too little. I don't know either what*

its psychotherapeutic value with neurotic or psychotic patients is. I only know there is no point in wishing to know more of the collective unconscious than one gets through dreams and intuition [...] I am profoundly mistrustful of the "pure gifts of the Gods." You pay very dearly for them. [...] That is the mistake Aldous Huxley makes: he does not know that he is in the role of the "Zauberlehrling," [sorcerer's apprentice] who learned from his master how to call the ghosts but did not know how to get rid of them again.[12 p172-3]

Jung's language is striking here as, despite a slight ironic edge, he acknowledged mescaline's deep power and the numinosity of the experience. He clearly did not question whether the mystical state is *achievable* through mescaline, but whether it is *advisable*. More outspoken was Jung's associate von Franz, discussing the need to maintain 'the storm-lantern' of the ego and not to permit its engulfment in the dark seas of the unconscious. She transposed this storm-lantern image onto the psychedelic culture whose heyday had only just passed, following Jung's critique of Nietzsche as a man whose ego-inflation led him to delusion:

When the ego, however, identifies to that degree with the greater inner presence, No.2, the result is a "puffed-up ego and a deflated self." History is full of examples of such figures: Sabbati Sevi, Hitler, Manson, Leary and all the other pathological demagogues and religious pseudo-prophets. They have inflicted infinite damage on the world because they have transformed normal inner experiences of the unconscious into morbid poison through inflated identification with them.[13 p42]

Jung was mistrustful of drugs prescribed by psychiatrists to treat patients, preferring to develop his own rich methods of pursuing each personal narrative, allowing unconscious content to inform and direct the consciousness. The method was never to abandon ego consciousness. This is visible in his mistrust of European adulation of eastern spiritual practices that he assumed advocated ego abandonment,[14] and his own fear of ego-loss when in Africa. So close was von Franz to Jung, and so versed in his views, one can assume that such a strong opinion about psychedelics would likely represent Jung's thoughts, though one can only speculate whether Jung would have placed Leary on the same list as Hitler.

Leary, Metzner and Alpert acknowledge Jung's voluminous research into the psychology of religious experience and esoteric texts such as the *Bardo Thodol*,[15] though they recognise Jung's perspective *vis-à-vis* ego-loss, an attribute they consider essential to the psychedelic experience. They propose that Jung's reservation on this matter prevented his fuller understanding both of the *Bardo* and of psychedelics. Likewise, many analysts and therapists— Grof, Shulgin, Stolaroff, Metzner—employ Jung's models of the self, unconscious, archetypes and complexes within psychedelic therapy. So too, Campbell, who like Jung was wary of psychedelics, nevertheless recognised that the Hero Journey provided a guide for those experiencing psychedelics.

> *That was the era of inward discovery in its LSD phase. Suddenly,* The Hero with a Thousand Faces *became a kind of triptych for the inward journey, and people were finding something in that book that could help them interpret their own experience. [...] Anyone going on a journey inward or outward to find values will be on a journey that has been described many times in the myths of mankind, and I simply put them all together in that book.*[16]

Zaehner, refuting Huxley's mystical claims, suggested that ego-loss is, indeed, a fundamental attribute of the mystical and religious state and that the intoxicated state provides only a *temporary* release from ego, not a lasting and constructive one.[11] Criticising Huxley's use of Catholic and Hindu terms, he argued that these bold declarations about 'gratuitous grace,' 'Beatic state' or 'one-ness' are matters of spiritual practice within established traditions of faith. The mescaline experience, he argued, aside from specific traditions, lies outside established traditions of faith. Zaehner's outlook was so coloured by his religious faith[17] that he made naïve comments, such as suggesting that the feeling of communion of god through drugs is "merely a vulgar error shared by many primitive communities and certain ecstatic sects."[11 p24] Clearly, Zaehner argued not from a phenomenological position— whether a mystical state is *possible*—but a theological one—is it *permissible*. At the core of Zaehner's critique was his disquiet of psychedelic explorers' attempts to bypass years of spiritual devotion and God's grace.

Theory and practice were married in 1962 in Pahnke's Good Friday Experiment.[18] The objective of the experiment was to evaluate whether psilocybin, in a double-blind experiment, could occasion mystical experience in religiously-predisposed subjects. Pahnke, using Stace's nine categories of mysticism to evaluate the experiences of the subjects, found that provided with a suitably reverent context, psilocybin can induce states of consciousness equivalent to mystical states. In particular 'Persisting Positive Changes in Attitude and Behavior' (Stace's ninth category) was observed. Zaehner[19] critiqued Pahnke, as he had Huxley, again arguing theologically: can the experience be considered religious if, given the Christian context, there is no experience of Christ?

Following the widespread popularity of psychedelics as championed by Kesey and the Pranksters, and Leary, the question of religiosity became public. Indian guru Meher Baba presented the perceived dangers of attempting to gain enlightenment through psychedelics. "If God can be found through the medium of any drug, God is not worthy of being God."[20 p7] Like Zaehner, Baba was concerned with 'short cuts' to the divine:

No drug, whatever its great promise, can help one to attain the spiritual goal. There is no short-cut to the goal except through the grace of the Perfect Master, and drugs, LSD more than others, give only a semblance of "spiritual experience," a glimpse of a false Reality.[20 p8-9]

Baba's message was taken up by vocal supporters and led to a profusion of publications and public debates about the spiritual dangers of the psychedelic experience.

Masters and Houston reviewed the debate and its most important spokespeople and set out its precise problem: "One of the most important questions raised by the psychedelic drugs is whether authentic religious and mystical experiences occur among the drug subjects."[21 p187] Most notable in their list of scholars is Watts, who argued that the substances are a tool and not an end, and that the non-enlightened person will be no closer to the divine for all the mescaline in Mexico.[22] Watts addressed the affinity between the "vague" terms, 'religious experience,' 'mystical experience,' 'cosmic consciousness,' and "such states of consciousness induced by psychedelic drugs, although they are virtually indistinguishable from genuine mystical experience,"[23 p1] arguing for the judicious and sacramental use of psychoactive substances in order to *prepare the path towards* the states of awareness that religious practices so often failed to achieve. His debt to William James is clear in his delineating four salient characteristics of the psychedelic experience: 1) slowing down time, 2) awareness of polarity, 3) awareness of relativity and 4) awareness of eternal energy.

Watts reflected Jung's concern with the dangers of sudden and deep immersion in the unconscious, describing his first experiences with LSD:

I qualified as an expert insofar as I had also a considerable intellectual knowledge of the psychology and philosophy of religion: a knowledge that subsequently protected me from the more dangerous aspects of this adventure, giving me a compass and something of a map for this wild territory.[24 p323]

He was dismayed at the "stupidity of the federal governments by passing unenforceable laws against LSD [which] not only drove it underground but prevented proper research" which led to "the injudicious use of LSD [which] has afflicted uncounted young people with paranoid, megalomaniac, and schizoid symptoms."[24 p326] Despite suggesting that Jungians themselves are scared of the unconscious, Watts resembled more the studious and cautious Jung than the gregarious and populist Leary or Kesey. This is best reflected in Watts's misgivings at Leary's rising messianic status, which he describes in pure Jungian terms:

> *Nevertheless, I myself began to be concerned, if mildly, at the direction of Timothy's enthusiasm, for to his own circle of friends and students he had become a charismatic religious leader who, well trained as he was in psychology, knew very little about religion and mysticism and their pitfalls. The uninstructed adventurer with psychedelics, as with Zen or yoga or any other mystical discipline, is an easy victim of what Jung calls "inflation," of the messianic megalomania that comes from misunderstanding the experience of union with God [...] He was moving to a head-on collision with the established religions of biblical theocracy and scientific mechanism, and simply asking for martyrdom.*[24 p331]

Watts's most concise conclusion to the relationship between psychedelics and mystical states is his declaration that they are the *medicine* not the *diet*, and that once the state has been experienced, it can be cultivated through traditional psycho-spiritual practices:

> *psychedelic experience is only a glimpse of genuine mystical insight, but a glimpse which can be matured and deepened by the various ways of meditation in which drugs are no longer necessary or useful. When you get the message, hang up the phone. For psychedelic drugs are simply instruments, like microscopes, telescopes, and telephones. The biologist does not sit*

*with eye permanently glued to the microscope; he goes away
and works on what he has seen.*[22 p25]

In the wake of severe government legislation of psychedelic drugs
and the passing of a certain aesthetic era, the debate lost mo-
mentum from the early 1970s. While Leary continued his vocal
support of psychedelics, his star had fallen since many vilified
him as being the chief catalyst of this government clampdown.
However, McKenna, a friend and supporter of Leary, became
a popular fringe figure in the 1980s and 90s with his animating
philosophies of psychedelics, shamanism, ecology, hermeticism
and ethnobotany. McKenna articulated his vision of a psychedelic
society in which he avers that not only do psychedelics lead to a
state of mystical encounter with the Otherworld, they surpass all
other practices at achieving these states.[25] McKenna shared much
with Watts, most notably in his affirmations that the criminalisation of these substances arises not from health concerns but from
authoritarian fear of the insights that are gained. Yet, while Watts
equated psychedelics with scientific instruments, McKenna's shamanistic perspective saw the plants themselves as conscious, the
mushrooms as intelligent, instructive, conscious entities, living
in synergy with humans. In this sense, McKenna's contribution
to the ancient debate of psychedelic plants and mystical states is
perhaps the most radical of all the aforementioned theorists, as
it rests on a position of plant-consciousness. While the scientific
and academic communities may tolerate Watts equating psychedelics and telephones, McKenna's talking mushrooms constitute
a greater epistemological challenge.

The debate continues to this day in numerous contexts and
discourses, and critical approaches to this wide and nebulous field
have reclaimed respectability. This is principally due to the resurgence of the role of psychotropic substances in therapy and
medicine. Current studies are focusing on psychedelic treatments
for a wide range of disorders and addictions. Figures such as Grof,

Strassman, Doblin, Goldsmith, Griffiths, Stolaroff, the Shulgins and Krupitsky have deepened the field of research into psychedelics and medical and psychotherapeutic practice that was silenced at the end of the 60s. Griffiths, in particular, has refocused on the question addressed by Pahnke, and reported that "58% [of subjects receiving high doses of psilocybin] met criteria for having had a 'complete' mystical experience."[26 p621]

It is significant that the resurgence of scholarly research into psychedelics should be principally in the field of medicine and therapy, not in the wider popular cultural arena as in the 1960s. This is firstly because, in contrast to the religious fervour accompanying psychedelics in the past, the medical avenue is respectable. Secondly, it concerns treating the sick and the dying, and is thus contained within a defined social demographic. Therefore the attention that such substances generate proposes no immediate threat to established moral, ethical or social order, aside from within strictly defined medical and psychoanalytical communities.

Medicine and therapy also provide a structure to accommodate the transformative and potentially unnerving aspects of psychedelics. For this reason Grof and others have successfully guided patients through trauma towards wholeness within a safe and nurturing environment. Grof, for example, incorporates them gradually and methodically within the treatment, considering them powerful tools in a toolbox that includes holotropic breathing and meditation. Schlamm[14 p40] argues that had Jung visited Ramana Maharshi on his trip to India in 1938, he may have understood that the individuation process was far closer to the yogic traditions than he had supposed. Likewise, had Jung met Grof or Metzner, he may have understood that controlled use of psychedelics can be incorporated within analysis more cohesively than he had imagined.

One might suggest that the question that concerned Huxley, Watts, Smith and Pahnke about the religious dimension of these substances has been deprioritised. The medics and therapists are not surrogate priests, and no figure has emerged demonstrating the same religious fervour as Leary. Nevertheless, scholarly endeavours have not lost sight of this old debate concerning mystical or religious states of consciousness and psychedelics. Grof's numerous publications focus on this issue, and are encapsulated as this ancient relationship between the 'holotropic states of consciousness' and religion:

> *Mystics have encountered very difficult challenges in organized religions, even though direct experiences of numinous dimensions of reality in holotropic states of consciousness have provided inspiration for all great religious movements. Such experiences, moreover, are essential to preserving the vitality and relevance of religious creeds.*[27 p60]

Smith, however, is still particularly interested in the question of the religious dimension of the psychedelics, observing that "The goal (it cannot be stressed too often) is not religious experiences, but the religious life."[17 p80] The substance can facilitate the experience, he argues, but certainly not guarantee the religious life, as once the trip is over, the subject must incorporate the experiences into established religious or spiritual systems. Here, though, we must be careful not to align too closely 'religious' with 'mystical.' While no 'church of psychedelics' has emerged to provide spiritual structure for individual experience, this does not in all cases infer a desacralisation either of the plants or the experience. Set and setting are, as always, important, and where such reverence is not observed, such as slapstick salvia trips posted on YouTube, the perceived dangers of the plant are amplified in the eyes of prohibitionists. Ayahuasca, whether drunk in Iquitos, Europe or the US, is commonly treated with respect and solemnity, and as such those advocating its use have been better able to present coherent and reasoned arguments to the legislature.

It is important to stress that when approaching the term 'psychedelic' we are in the same non-consensual area that we are with the term 'mystical' and as such no clear empirical definition can be adequately reached:

> *The narratives of psychedelic drug trips are as luxuriant and varied as myths, dreams, and psychoanalytical revelations. In a sense there is no 'psychedelic effect' or 'psychedelic state;' to say that someone has taken LSD tells little more about the content and import of his experience than to say that he has had a dream.*[28 p13]

The whole debate is not about the phenomena of 'psychedelics' and 'mysticism' but of the language describing phenomena. Mystical states are like 'peak experiences' that we are all (to a greater or lesser extent) familiar with.[29] While one may demur from describing a psychedelic experience as mystical, one may find it hard to define, for example, one of McKenna's 'heroic doses' of psilocybin, LSD or DMT as anything *other* than a peak experience. Watts intuitively suggested as much when acknowledging that for all his desire "to delineate the basic principles of psychedelic awareness," he must recognise "that I can speak only for myself. The quality of these experiences depends considerably upon one's prior orientation and attitude to life."[23 p76] Both James and Stace include 'ineffability' as one of the definitions of the mystical state; accordingly the description of the experience will necessarily be arbitrary. Therefore the debate is between linguistic systems rather than a perceived consensual experience. Much ink has been spilled on this nebulous debate, and we are no nearer consensus. Can one encounter the divine with psychedelics? It depends on your moral, ethical and theological assumptions, and on your understanding of the divine and of psychedelics. And thus the debate continues.

1. Borges JL. *The Total Library: Non-fiction, 1922–1986.* Allen Lane: The Penguin Press; 1999.
2. Wasson RG. *Soma: Divine Mushroom of Immortality.* New York: Harcourt Brace; 1967.
3. Wasson RG, Hofmann A, Ruck CP. *The Road to Eleusis: Unveiling the Secret of the Mysteries.* New York: Harcourt Brace; 1968.
4. Merkur D. *The Psychedelic Sacrament.* Vermont: Inner Traditions; 2001.
5. Jay M. *Emperors of Dreams: Drugs in the Nineteenth Century.* Cambridgeshire: Dedalus; 2000.
6. James W. 'Consciousness under Nitrous Oxide.' *Psychological Review.* 1898;2:194–6.
7. James W. *Varieties of Religious Experience.* London: Longmans, Green & Co; 1913.
8. Huxley A. *The Doors of Perception.* Chatto and Windus; 1954.
9. Huxley A. *Heaven and Hell.* Chatto and Windus; 1956.
10. Huxley A. 'Drugs that shape men's minds.' *Saturday Evening Post.* 1958;231:16–28.
11. Zaehner RC. *Mysticism: Sacred and Profane. An inquiry into some Varieties of Praeternatural Experience.* Oxford University Press; 1957.
12. Jung, CG. *Letters, Volume 2: 1951–1961.* Princeton University Press; 1954.
13. Von Franz M-L. *C.G. Jung: his Myth in our time.* New York: Putnam; 1971.
14. Schlamm L. 'Revisiting Jung's dialogue with yoga: observations from transpersonal psychology.' *International Journal of Jungian Studies.* 2010;2(1):32–44.
15. Leary T, Metzner R, Alpert R. *The Psychedelic Experience: A Manual Based on the Tibetan Book of the Dead.* Citadel; 1964.
16. Kisly L. *Living Myths: A Conversation with Joseph Campbell.* Parabola. 1976;1(2):70–81.
17. Smith H. *Cleansing the Doors of Perception: the religious significance of entheogenic plants and chemicals.* Sentient Publications; 2000.
18. Pahnke W. 'Drugs and Mysticism.' *The International Journal of Parapsychology.* 1966;8(2):295–313.
19. Zaehner RC. *Zen, drugs and mysticism.* New York: Vintage Books; 1972.
20. Baba M. *God in a Pill?* California: Sufism Reoriented; 1966.
21. Masters REL, Houston J. *Varieties of Psychedelic Experience.* New York: Holt, Rinehart and Winston; 1966.
22. Watts A. *Joyous Cosmology.* Vintage Books; 1962.
23. Watts A. 'Psychedelics and Religious Experience.' *California Law Review.* 1968;56(1):74–85.
24. Watts A. *In my own way: an autobiography.* California Novato: New World Library; 2007.
25. McKenna T. *Psychedelic Society.* In: Forte R, editor. *Entheogens and the Future of Religion.* San Francisco: Council on Spiritual Practices; 1997. p.57–67.
26. Griffiths RR, Johnson MW, Richards WA, McCann U, Richards BD. 'Mystical-type experiences occasioned by psilocybin mediate the attribution of personal meaning and spiritual significance: 14 months later.' *Journal of Psychopharmacology.* 2008;22(6):621–32.
27. Grof S. *The Ultimate Journey: Consciousness and the Mystery of Death.* Florida: MAPS The Multidisciplinary Association for Psychedelic Studies; 2006.
28. Grinspoon L, Bakalar JB, editors. *Psychedelic Reflections.* New York: Human Sciences Press; 1983.
29. Wilson C. *Beyond the Occult.* Bantam Press; 1988.

DECEPTIVE CADENCES: A HERMENEUTIC APPROACH TO THE PROBLEM OF MEANING AND PSYCHEDELIC EXPERIENCE

ANDY LETCHER

Once, on a hill in Wiltshire, my wife and I took a heavy dose of Liberty Caps, the indigenous British psilocybin mushroom. At one point she gasped for she saw lines of rainbow light rising up from the grass all the way to the stars. The lines connected everything, a giant network of light with glittering intersections. We too were plugged into this extraordinary, ever-changing web. Later she said how moving it was, for while the sense of connection endured there was no fear of death.

Some months afterwards I stumbled across the Indian myth of 'Indra's Net.' This story, from third century Mahayana Buddhism but based on a much older Vedic source, has Indra, god of thunder and rain, throwing a net across the universe. Tied to every inter-section is a jewel that reflects the light of all the others, and all the reflections too, and so in Buddhism the story is used to illustrate the interconnectivity of all things. When I told it to my wife her eyes went wide. "That's it! That's what I saw! I saw Indra's Net!"

The hermeneutic question of how psychedelic experiences come to be meaningful is rarely asked. Rather, debate remains focused on their ontological and epistemological validity, with opinion sharply divided. On the one hand there are those who regard psychedelic experiences as meaningless, as a pathological impairment of normal cognitive functioning with potentially long-lasting health consequences. For these adherents of what I call the pathological discourse,[1] a vision of Indra's Net is easily explained away. It is a perceptual aberration to which we willingly but mistakenly ascribe meaning.

On the other hand there are those for whom psychedelics have undoubted psychotherapeutic potential (the psychological discourse), or are portals to mystical or shamanistic realms (the mystical and shamanistic discourses). Such enthusiasts would argue that psychedelic visions, of Indra's Net or whatever, are glimpses of the hidden facets of reality and therefore have genuine ontological validity. The fact that Indra's Net can be perceived through Buddhist meditation *or* psychedelics lends credence to the notion that it really is 'out there.' In other words, psychedelics reveal to the hard-headed Westerner what the Eastern spiritual adept has always known.[1]

For many, therefore, psychedelics are the last refuge of mystery in a secular age. If, as Max Weber contended, science, modernity and rationalism have disenchanted the world and swept it clean of gods, spirits and magic (or, at least, problematised believing in them),[2,3] then psychedelics offer a potential way out of the ensuing existential impasse. Unlike many religions, they offer re-enchantment *within* a scientific paradigm, for, whatever it is they do, they do it through neurochemistry. No wonder the stakes are so high. Prohibition has only served to raise them further.

Consequently the two positions have become somewhat entrenched. Strength of feeling is such that any attempt to investigate the question of psychedelics and meaning risks antagonising both, to be branded at once an apologist *and* anti-psychedelic. Nevertheless, a critical approach to the subject demands that we do.[A]

In this chapter I avoid siding with either camp, suggesting both are problematic, and come at the question of meaning from different angles. Bracketing off the matter of whether Indra's Net *actually* exists as anything more than a striking metaphor, I want to ask how it is that psychedelic experiences become meaningful *at all* (especially as there are other, equivalent, non-ordinary experiences that seem not to acquire the same cultural resonance: fever-dreams or the haunted borderlands of anaesthesia, for example). What is it about psychedelic experiences that invite so much interpretation? To answer this question I begin by introducing a debate about the nature of mystical experience from the Study of Religion. While hoary, the debate is not widely known, and it has important implications for the critical study of psychedelics.

TWO THEORIES OF MYSTICISM

Theologians have long been interested in the nature and provenance of mystical experience. Given that individuals professing to have had some direct, numinous encounter with the divine are found in many cultures, the apparent similarities between their reported experiences might suggest a common core to all religions that transcends local theological particularities. If mystical experience is *sui generis* then it provides a sure foundation upon which the truth claims of religion can be established.

Until the 1970s the predominant view among scholars was just this, that a 'common core' lay behind particular descriptions of mystical experience, one that could be pieced together using careful textual and comparative analysis. In this so-called 'perennialist tradition' (of which Aldous Huxley was perhaps the most famous champion) all religions are, to use a familiar trope, 'different paths up the same spiritual mountain.' The Christian mystic recalling absorption by God, or the Hindu union with Brahman, are actually talking about the same thing, albeit using different concepts to do so.

Two scholars in particular refined this hypothesis. Stace concluded that all mystical experience is of unity, but nevertheless distinguished *extrovertive* from *introvertive* mysticism.[4] Extrovertive mysticism occurs as the experience of the unity of all things. "This unity is not linked to any one perceptual object; instead all objects are unified into a perception of totality or oneness."[5 p332] By contrast, introvertive mysticism "is an experience of unity devoid of perceptual objects. It is literally an experience of 'no-thingness'"[5 p332] and is sometimes, therefore, called "pure conscious experience."[6] Stace thought extrovertive mysticism less developed than, or preparatory to, introvertive but following William James made no distinction between classically-occurring and drug-induced mysticism.[7,8]

The Oxford scholar Zaehner, however, found the psychedelic experience altogether lacking when compared to classic accounts of mysticism, a position reached after a somewhat dismal mescaline trip undertaken in response to Huxley's *The Doors of Perception*.[9,10] Zaehner distinguished three types of mysticism—theistic, monistic and natural—and while reluctantly including psychedelic experiences in the latter and the Buddhist experience of unity in the second, he privileged theistic mysticism because, he argued, it arose as a gift from God.

Critics have accused the Catholic Zaehner of letting faith cloud his judgment,[5,11,12] which is perhaps why Stace's work has proved the more influential upon the (largely American) empirical study of mysticism. In 1975 the psychologist of religion Ralph Hood used Stace's typology to develop a 32-point scale—the so-called Mysticism or M-Scale—to measure statistically whether someone has had a mystical experience and the degree to which they interpret that experience religiously.[13] This, and other related scales, provided the basis for recent experiments at Johns Hopkins University which found that psilocybin was statistically more likely to occasion mystical experiences than a control drug when administered to willing volunteers in a double-blind experiment.[14–16]

The common core hypothesis has therefore had a profound impact on our subject, an impact that masks the extent to which it has been contested. In 1978 a collection of essays edited by Katz laid out a trenchant philosophical critique of the common core hypothesis and put forward an alternative constructivist position. In his own essay, Katz began from the position that "there are no pure (i.e., unmediated) experiences."[11 p26] There can be no common core to mystical experiences because "the experience itself as well as the form in which it is reported is shaped by concepts which the mystic brings to, and which shape, his experience."[11 p26] In other words, the kind of experience a Christian mystic has depends entirely on her Christian presuppositions, which is why she "experiences the mystic reality in terms of Jesus, the Trinity, or a personal God, etc., rather than in terms of the non-personal, non-everything, to be precise, Buddhist doctrine of nirvana."[11 p27]

Persuasive as the constructivist position might appear to be, especially the point that there is no unmediated experience, it, too, has been challenged in another collection of essays.[6] While conceding that extrovertive mysticism may indeed be shaped by a priori concepts, Forman argues that it is difficult to see how presuppositions can have any bearing on introvertive mysticism, which is content-less.[6] Accordingly for Forman, 'pure conscious experience' is a universal, but one that is subsequently rendered using culturally specific language.

While these debates rumble on in the pages of academic journals, space limitations preclude me from expanding further. However, their relevance to psychedelic experience is obvious. Adherents of the pathological discourse (that psychedelics impair normal perception) and psychological discourse (that psychedelics rearrange the contents of the psyche in novel but meaningful ways) are constructivists. There is no meaning 'out there'; rather meaning arises from what the subject brings to the experience. Meanwhile, enthusiasts who think psychedelics afford access to some essential or transpersonal experience (the mystical and shamanistic discourses) hold more closely to a common core hypothesis.

TWO ANTHROPOLOGICAL STUDIES

As I suggested earlier, it is not my aim to side with either position: indeed, both have their weaknesses. The pathological discourse seems unsustainable as certain psychedelic drugs, for example psilocybin and DMT, have been licensed as safe for medical research in Europe and the US.[14-18] Furthermore, a slew of first hand trip-reports, on the Internet and elsewhere, show that people find psychedelic experiences anything but meaningless. At the same time, the sheer variety of psychedelic experiences suggests that enthusiasts' tendency towards common core thinking is premature: an essentialist position is neither supported by history nor cross-cultural analysis. In the earliest Western accounts of psilocybin mushroom consumption, from the eighteenth century, the people concerned thought they had been poisoned: a psychedelic discourse only emerged much later in the light of the discovery of mescaline and LSD.[1,2]

Similarly, consider cross-cultural experiences of the African psychedelic, iboga (the root bark of *Tabernanthe iboga*). Increasing numbers of Western 'entheotourists' are travelling to Gabon in West Africa to take part in the *akwia nlô* ('breaking open the head') initiation ceremony of the local, syncretic Bwiti religion, during which large, sub-lethal, doses of iboga are consumed.

Western participants often emphasise the psychological and empathetic aspects of iboga: a typical experience is the reliving of one's past misdemeanours but from the perspective of those affected by them. Uncomfortable as this moral interrogation is, it seems to offer absolution.[19 p259] Yet this kind of experience does not appear in Fernandez's exhaustive ethnography of Bwiti. What is always stressed by *indigenous* initiates is that they have been propelled by iboga out of their bodies, along the correct 'path' to the land of the ancestors.[20]

What these lines of evidence seem to suggest (and as the old adage of 'set and setting' hinted) is that the trip is not isolable from the culture in which it occurs. Any theory of psychedelic meaning must therefore take into account that these agents work on *encultured psyches.*

But while such observations might seem to support constructivism, both constructivism and the common core hypothesis rely on the same problematic hermeneutic assumption: namely that *accounts* of mystical experiences are somehow commensurable with the experiences themselves. Even constructivists "assume that since the historical, social, and linguistic processes that give rise to the narrative representation are identical with those that give rise to the experience, the former, which are amenable to scholarly analysis, provide a transparent window to the latter."[21 p113] But the grounds for making such an assumption are shaky as the following example about dreams illustrates.

Originally it was hoped that the anthropological study of dreams might allow us to prove or disprove Western, Freudian, theories of dream symbolism.[22] However a philosophical critique by Malcolm[23] turned scholarly attention away from the content of dreams, which, being private, are inaccessible to the scholar, to the way in which dreams are told. For Malcolm "the dream report is indeed the only criterion for the dream, and thus to report that one has dreamed *is* to have dreamed; there is simply no other criterion for the dream's existence."[21 p113] The dream only 'exists' once it has been reported, and it is therefore the *reporting* of dreams that forms the legitimate anthropological study, not the manifest content of the dreams themselves.[22] The resonances for critical psychedelic studies are obvious.

Experience is something *private*, irrespective of whether we be dreaming, tripping or communing with the divine.[21] Scholars have reached their respective positions—common-core and constructivist—on the basis of *accounts* of other people's experiences, not the experiences themselves, to which they have no access. But an account of an experience (be that textual, visual or musical) is always a *representation*, an *interpretation*, and therefore both a reduction and something that is, by necessity, culturally bound. Neither common-core theorists nor constructivists would contest this last point but both overreach themselves in making judgments about experiences from which they are distanciated and about which, therefore, it is not possible to speak.

Here my thinking is shaped not just by hermeneutics but also by the philosophy of Bergson, somewhat neglected of late, despite his lasting influence on psychedelic thought via James and Huxley. Bergson, railing against the psychometric testing of his day, thought experience to be pure *quality*, not something that can be measured or quantified.[24] Just as the prow of a ship continually cuts through waves, so experience is something that continuously unfolds in duration. Any attempt to represent experience is forced, therefore, to do violence to its very nature, rendering that which unfolds in duration as something static, and fixed in space.

We talk of a psychedelic trip—an excellent metaphor which conveys the sense of an unfolding journey. But however artfully conceived, an account cannot convey the trip's qualitative complexity—or to use a Bergsonism, its 'confused multiplicity'—nor can it, in its fixity and linear structure, faithfully render the way that complexity emerged. Perhaps that is why, quite aside from the purple prose and clichés, trip reports are so often tedious and distanciating, leaving the reader further from the very thing he or she attempts to bring near. Language seems an inadequate tool for representing psychedelic experience.

As with the study of mysticism, psychedelic research has tended therefore to make the mistake of confusing representation for experience. That is why scales like the aforementioned Hood Mysticism Scale, as employed in the recent Johns Hopkins University psilocybin experiments, cannot provide the objective measure of 'mysticality' they purport to do. Rather, they force informants to interpret the confused multiplicity of their experiences through a culturally agreed and limited set of signifiers (in the case of the M-Scale, just 32 items). But being culturally agreed, those signifiers are familiar—the link between psychedelics and mysticism is firmly established in the popular imagination—so it is perhaps unsurprising that the predominantly white, educated, religiously sympathetic volunteers of the Johns Hopkins experiment instinctively reached for them to render their psilocybin experiences. Following Malcolm, I maintain that the only criterion for establishing if a volunteer had a mystical experience is whether or not *the volunteer* says he or she had one—it is not something that can be measured or quantified.[B] All *we* can legitimately conclude is that in this particular experimental setting, volunteers found taking psilocybin a more meaningful experience than taking Ritalin, even when they did not know in advance which drug they were getting: a less than shattering conclusion.

DECEPTIVE CADENCES

The rendering of private psychedelic experience for public consumption therefore requires a hermeneutic act, an act of interpretation, which is necessarily an act of reduction and distanciation. But meaning isn't simply made at this post hoc, narratological stage. Even the psychedelically-naïve, eighteenth century mushroom-eaters 'knew,' as the experience occurred, that they had been *poisoned*. Psychedelic experiences are made meaningful in real time. We cannot say anything about the manifest content of psychedelic experiences but perhaps it is possible to say something about the hermeneutic process by which that content is made meaningful.

Though it might not sit well with the philosophy of consciousness[25] the most commonly reported phenomenological experience of taking an indole alkaloid (DMT, psilocybin, LSD, iboga etc.) is that of the Cartesian theatre: some normal, observing, rationally-engaged part of the self remains unperturbed by the drug, and, watching, is able to interpret.[26,27] To address the question of how it does so I want to borrow a theory put forward by Meyer to explain meaning in music.[28] Music seems an apposite metaphor for the psychedelic experience. Both unfold in duration; both are profoundly affectual and difficult to convey in words; and both only make sense in the light of cultural expectation.

Meyer's theory, influenced by Gestalt psychology, can be simply put: "[e]motion or affect is aroused when a tendency to respond is arrested or inhibited."[28 p14] From Bach to the Beatles, Western musicians have always played with the musical conventions and expectations of their time. Both creators and listeners are habituated by the music to which they have been culturally exposed to expect certain musical cues to result in particular musical outcomes. The pleasure from a 12-bar blues comes from knowing that the V chord will always resolve back to the I again. However, by playing with expectations and setting up what is called a 'deceptive cadence'—modulating to some other unexpected key centre—composers create tension and arrest that tendency to respond. It is in the resulting gap that meaning and emotion emerge.

What unfolds during a psychedelic experience is a unique product of a particular pharmacology working on an encultured psyche. Trips are therefore always bounded (if never quite the same),[29] but continually throw up deceptive cadences in the ordinary flow of experience. Then, exactly as Meyer says occurs in music, meaning and emotion emerge in the inhibition of tendencies to respond.

While the theory brackets the question of where the phantasmagoria actually come from, and will therefore not satisfy all psychedelic enthusiasts—we cannot extend the metaphor to include a 'composer' or even a 'score'—it has the merit of including cultural expectation. Whatever the actual provenance of a trip, the psyche or something transcendent, culture and expectation will determine the aspects of it to which we attend.

Irrespective of how well this stands up as a theory,[c] I nevertheless think such a hermeneutic approach has much to offer critical
psychedelic studies, in particular by drawing attention to the importance of metaphor. For here's the rub. What makes psychedelics
so interesting is that the experiences they occasion aren't really
like anything else; and yet because those experiences are private,
metaphor remains the only means we have of grasping them. In
the post-war period, writers have used a variety of metaphors,
taken from religion ('mysticism,' 'hierophany,' 'ecstasy,' 'entheogen');[1] psychology ('ego loss,' 'mind expansion,' 'consciousness');
anthropology ('spirits,' 'shamanism'); and increasingly science and
technology ('cognition,' 'fractals,' 'information,' 'download'). The
risk is that by forgetting we have no choice but to use metaphor,
we confuse the metaphor, the representation, for the thing itself.
It therefore behoves all of us—writers, artists, scholars, enthusiasts and naysayers alike—to avoid cliché, to think more carefully
about the metaphors we use, and thereby to render the psychedelic
mysterium in ever more nuanced and exacting ways.

A   I maintain that psychedelic studies (to the extent that it can actually be called a
     discipline) remains problematically wedded to modernism and has yet to undergo the
     revolution of critical thinking that has transformed the humanities. All my writings on
     psychedelics can be considered work towards a critical psychedelic studies.
B   However useful they are in persuading politicians of the merits of psychedelics (and in
     that sense, the Johns Hopkins experiments were impeccably done), studies of this kind
     privilege the scientific observer, who has not had the experience, over the subject who
     has. In making this critique I seek to restore a voice to the silenced trip subject.
C   Ironically, the theory is at its weakest when applied to music, for Meyer's Western,
     Classical bias prevents him from appreciating repetition, a staple ingredient of dance
     music the world over, and the power of fulfilled expectations.
1.   Letcher A. *Mad Thoughts on Mushrooms: Discourse and Power in the Study of Psychedelic
     Consciousness*. Anthropology of Consciousness. 2007;18(2):74–97.
2.   Weber M. *Science as a Vocation*. In: Gerth HH, Wright Mills C, editors. *From Max Weber:
     Essays in Sociology*. London: Routledge; p.129–58.
3.   Letcher A. *Shroom: A Cultural History of the Magic Mushroom*. London: Faber &
     Faber; 2005.
4.   Stace WT. *Mysticism and Philosophy*. London: Macmillan; 1961.
5.   Hood RW Jr, Hill PC, Spilka B. *The Psychology of Religion. An Empirical Approach*. 4th

Edition. New York: The Guilford Press; 2009.

6. Forman RKC, editor. *The Problem of Pure Consciousness: Mysticism and Philosophy.* Oxford: Oxford University Press; 1990.

7. James W. *The Varieties of Religious Experience: a Study in Human Nature.* Centenary edition. London: Routledge; 2002 [1902].

8. Smith H. *Cleansing the Doors of Perception. The Religious Significance of Entheogenic Plants and Chemicals.* Boulder, CO: Sentient Publications; 2003.

9. Huxley A. *The Doors of Perception and Heaven and Hell.* London: Flamingo; 1994 [1954].

10. Zaenher RC. *Mysticism: Sacred and Profane.* Oxford: Oxford University Press; 1961.

11. Katz ST. *Language, Epistemology and Mysticism.* In: Katz ST, editor. *Mysticism and Philosophical Analysis.* New York: Oxford University Press; 1978.

12. Partridge C. Sacred *Chemicals: Psychedelic Drugs and Mystical Experience.* In: Partridge C, Gabriel T, editors. *Mysticism East and West: Studies in Mystical Experience.* Carlisle: Paternoster Press; p.96–131.

13. Hood RW Jr. 'The Construction and Preliminary Validation of a Measure of Reported Mystical Experience.' *Journal for the Scientific Study of Religion.* 1975;14:29–41.

14. Griffiths RR, Richards WA, McCann U, Jesse R. 'Psilocybin can Occasion Mystical-Type Experiences Having Substantial and Sustained Personal Meaning and Spiritual Significance.' *Psychopharmacology.* 2006;187:268–83.

15. Griffiths RR, Richards WA, Johnson MW, McCann UD, Jesse R. 'Mystical-Type Experiences Occasioned by Psilocybin Mediate the Attribution of Personal Meaning and Spiritual Significance 14 Months Later.' *Journal of Psychopharmacology.* 2008;22(6):621–32.

16. Griffiths RR, Johnson MW, Richards WA, Richards BD, McCann U, Jesse R. 'Psilocybin Occasioned Mystical-Type Experiences: Immediate and Persisting Dose-Related Effects.' *Psychopharmacology.* 2011;218(4):649–65.

17. Vollenweider FX, Leenders KL, Scharfetter C, Maguire P, Stadelmann O, Angst J. 'Positron Emission Tomography and Flourodeoxyglucose Studies of Metabolic Hyperfrontality and Psychopathology in the Psilocybin Model of Psychosis.' *Neuropsychopharmacology.* 1997;16(5):357–72.

18. Strassman R. *DMT: The Spirit Molecule.* Rochester, Vermont: Park Street Press; 2001.

19. Pinchbeck D. *2012: The Return of Quetzalcoatl.* New York: Jeremy Tarcher/Penguin; 2006.

20. Fernandez JW. *Bwiti: An Ethnography of the Religious Imagination in Africa.* Princeton: Princeton University Press; 1982.

21. Sharf RH. *Experience.* In: Taylor MC, editor. *Critical Terms for Religious Studies.* Chicago: University of Chicago Press; 1999. p.94–116.

22. Tedlock B. *Dreaming: Anthropological and Psychological Interpretations.* Santa Fe, New Mexico: School of American Research Press; 1992.

23. Malcolm N. 'Dreaming and Skepticism.' *Philosophical Review.* 1956;65:14–37.

24. Guerlac S. *Thinking in Time: An Introduction to Henri Bergson.* Ithaca and London: Cornell University Press; 2006.

25. Dennett DC. *Consciousness Explained.* London: Penguin Books; 1993.

26. McKenna T. *The Archaic Revival: Speculations on Psychedelic Mushrooms, the Amazon, Virtual Reality, UFOs, Evolution, Shamanism, the Rebirth of the Goddess, and the End of History.* San Francisco: HarperSanFrancisco; 1991.

27. Pinchbeck D. *Breaking Open the Head: A Psychedelic Journey into the Heart of Contemporary Shamanism.* New York: Broadway Books; 2003.

28. Meyer LB. *Emotion and Meaning in Music.* Chicago: University of Chicago Press; 1956.

29. Shanon B. *The Antipodes of the Mind: Charting the Phenomenology of the Ayahuasca Experience.* Oxford: Oxford University Press; 2002.

A MATTER OF SPIRIT:
AN IMAGINAL PERSPECTIVE
ON THE PARANORMAL

ANGELA VOSS

It is encouraging to see the current academic interest in therapeutic properties and usages of psychedelics and psycho-active plants.
Sociological methods of quantitative data analysis and scientific
investigation into the physiology of altered states of consciousness
(ASC) are challenging negative and prohibitive attitudes and contributing to a general re-evaluation of legal constraints regarding
their use. However, despite the undoubted importance of such
research, there is one aspect of the ASCs which arise from hallucinogenic ingestion which remains outside the epistemological
framework of conventional approaches, namely the evaluation of
the *ontological reality* of the visionary experiences.

It is this dimension which interests me, for when a scientific-
materialist paradigm is dominant, the question of the numinous
and revelatory content of non-rational states of consciousness is inevitably marginalised or even ignored. This is to a large extent due
to the polarity between rational and metaphysical epistemologies
which has become intrinsic to post-enlightenment thinking and
the resulting hegemony of the critical and analytical model of etic
research. Often, the only thing that can be said of overwhelming
visionary experiences is that they are personal, mystical, transcendent, or transformative. Individuals may relate their visions with
vivid narrative, describing enhanced colours, strange beings and

situations perceived in ways that are impossible to articulate. But for those firmly anchored in the sense-perceptible reality of this world, it is easier to focus on 'how' such visions are achieved in physiological, neurological or mechanical terms than on 'what' is being revealed, and why.

This is not to deny the value of phenomenological approaches by researchers who are open to the possibilities of autonomous beings existing on multiple levels of consciousness[1-5] but often their accounts are presented with a pragmatism which belies the ontological chasm between this world and the 'other.' Unless we acknowledge that our normal ways of knowing may be inadequate for shedding light on these dimensions there is always the danger of the *reductio ad absurdum*—for example the identification of the other-than-human as the all-too-familiar alien or UFO from outer (physical) space. More often, the attempt to explain other-worldly events results in their dismissal as either hoaxes or hallucinations.

I would like to suggest a way of redeeming the authenticity of visionary experience from both the scepticism of a literalist, physicalist mentality and the 'infra-subjective reductionism' which is characteristic of modernist approaches to 'personal' spiritual experience.[6] Another mode of speaking is required to illuminate realms that lie beyond scientific discourse and to do justice to the lived experience of encounters with other worlds, one that does not attempt to explain or subsume them into its own preconceptions, but which engages with their ontological ground on its own terms. To illustrate such a mode, I will draw on the observations of the Sufi mystic Muhyiddin Ibn 'Arabi (1165–1240), who speaks from a tradition of Islamic mysticism deeply infused with neoplatonism.

Neoplatonic epistemology arises out of a unitive yet hierarchical vision in which human consciousness partakes of both cosmic and divine intelligence in a variegated whole characterised by degrees of quality of *being*, all emanating from a primordial energy source termed the One. Most importantly, it differentiates between various subtle conditions of 'knowing' which link the human soul with corresponding realms or dimensions of existence, from the most material and earthy to the most rarefied and 'spiritual.'

Each condition of being has a mode of perception appropriate to it, and humans are simply the most material manifestations of a panoply of intelligences which include elemental, aetherial and angelic spirits. The cognitive faculty which enables humans to apprehend these 'higher' planes of existence is termed, by Plato, the intellect. This is not intellect as disembodied rationality, but rather an intuitive *connection* of understanding, a resonance of the deepest stratum of the mind with its original ground of being. As such, it transcends the possibilities of rational thinking.[7] For the neoplatonist Plotinus the imagination came to play a distinctive mediating role between sense perception and intellectual understanding. Such an imagination is not to be confused with 'fantasy' or mere distortions of sense-impressions of 'this' world, but is a faculty which produces mirror images of archetypal or spiritual realities.[8 vol. IV,9]

I suggest that the study of visionary and paranormal phenomena would greatly benefit from a metaphysical perspective that acknowledges the role of this 'higher' imagination in revealing knowledge of another order entirely from sense-perception or reason. Such a perspective would provide an integrative model for both mystical and rational epistemologies. Reinstating the imagination as the mode of perception which mediates between the two will facilitate insight into the nature of visions whose origin is non-sensible. One could argue that this is also a function of the visual arts, in which images may open up layers of meaning inaccessible to the rational mind. Indeed it is precisely this power of the symbolic which needs to be evoked in any methodology harnessed to the deeper understanding of 'paranormal' visionary experience. I hope the reasons for this will become clear.

Let us now approach the question of the ontology of 'altered states' with Ibn 'Arabi. In his *Meccan Illuminations (Al-Futuhat al-Makkiyya*) he describes and theorises about his own encounters with spirits or jinn:

> *One embodied himself to me in the earth,*
> *another in the air:*
> *One embodied himself wherever I was,*
> *Another embodied himself in heaven.*
> *They gave knowledge to me, and I to them,*
> *Though we were not equal,*
> *For I was unchanging in my entity,*
> *But they were not able to keep still.*
> *They assume the form of every shape,*
> *Like water taking on the colour of the cup.*[11 p83]

These spiritual intelligences are mobile, changeable entities which may appear as embodied in both outer 'objective' reality and 'internal' visions, but whose autonomous existence is unquestioned. The cosmology within which Ibn 'Arabi locates these beings is threefold, following the fundamental Platonic distinction between the material and spiritual worlds and placing a middle realm, corresponding to the visible cosmos, which links heaven and earth. Here we are presented with a symbolic image that reflects 'one world' in which the tripartite, harmonious structure is mirrored in the human soul as a microcosm. Each realm can be known via its corresponding cognitive faculty; the material world is known through sense perception, the intermediate world—the world where sense-perception and spiritual reality meet—through the imagination, and the spiritual world is 'unveiled' to the intuitive intellect. This is what leads Ibn 'Arabi to place emphasis on the idea that the soul has two eyes: the eye of reason, which deals with 'human' affairs and empirical/rational knowledge, and the eye of revelation which sees into the divine world through its images, giving us access to it via visible forms. This metaphor suggests a parallel with left and right brain hemisphere functions.[12]

Post-enlightenment epistemology has firmly separated these two forms of vision, exalting the former to the status of indisputable truth and relegating the latter to mere 'subjectivity' or 'belief.' Yet, in neoplatonic thinking revelation precedes and informs both sense-perception and reason. It is primary, disclosing truthfulness and meaning which is then subjected to interpretation:

> *Revelation is a meaning. When God wants meaning to descend to sense-perception, it has to pass through the Presence of Imagination before it reaches sense-perception. The reality of imagination demands that it gives sensory form to everything that becomes actualised within it [...] If the [revelation] arrives at the time of wakefulness, it is called 'imaginalisation' [...] that is why revelation begins with imagination.*[11 p75]

The imagination, then, is able to conceive immaterial meaning through clothing it with an image: "the degree of imagination embraces that of sense perception and meaning. Hence it subtilises the sensory object and densifies meaning."[13 p115] Perhaps the nearest most people come to experiencing this is through the kind of dream where people and objects manifest as fully embodied and tangible and is startling in its sense of heightened reality. Ibn 'Arabi suggests that such visions do indeed partake of two realities, as Chittick explains:

> *[Imagination] brings spiritual entities into relationship with corporeal entities [...] By giving incorporeal realities the attributes of corporeal things [...] imagination allows unseen realities to be described as possessing attributes that pertain to the visible world [...] Unseen things actually take on visible form in the imaginal realms.*[11 p73]

These 'unseen things' are discarnate intelligences, which may exist at many levels of non-material being. The earth is inhabited by human beings whose essence is complex and material, the spiritual world by angels whose essence is simple and luminous, and the intermediate world by the spirits or Jinn whose essence is paradoxically both simple and compound. In this medial place, spirits may appear as embodied and bodies as spiritualised as in dreams and apparitions. Ibn 'Arabi also uses the metaphor of a mirror-image to describe the ambiguity of the imaginal realm, for material things seen in a mirror are paradoxically both fully real yet fully unreal at the same time.[11] However, it is important to remember that although spiritual presences may appear to have 'broken through' into sense-perceptible reality, they, in fact, inhabit a fundamentally different ontological reality and are therefore immune to the laws which govern our material world.

Ibn 'Arabi explains that these imaginal beings can be seen through two different 'eyes'; the wakeful eye of sense-perception, and the eye of the imagination which, in most people, sees only during sleep and other ASCs. However, it appears that certain individuals may also see with the imaginal eye during wakefulness and then the veil between the two worlds falls away: "the person who undergoes unveiling sees while he is awake what the dreamer sees while he is asleep."[11 p84] Such refined souls will be able to distinguish between embodied spirits and humans by a 'mark' of identification, on which Ibn 'Arabi does not elaborate further. Presumably such a mark would be obvious to those able to discern it, but as Chittick points out, "the Shaykh could live joyfully in the knowledge that he recognised the mark of every apparition. The rest of us, lacking in marks, had best be careful."[13 p95]

The ability to distinguish more advanced spirits from those still attached to the material world is of utmost importance. Often the 'lower' jinn will play tricks or deceive with illicitly obtained knowledge from higher realms. Thus the sitter is advised to be on his guard.[11] How seriously are we to take this advice? It is relatively easy to deliberately create situations in which autonomous beings may be encountered, whether through psychedelics, mediumship, hypnosis or meditation. But we have lost a sense of what medieval scholastics called *adaequatio*: that the intellect of the knower must be adequate to the thing known to perceive its truth.[14] Spirit phenomena will reveal themselves through sympathetic resonance with the participant's own desire, intention and 'psychic' capacity. The more earth-bound the consciousness, so the spirit. This explains the importance of spiritual training and specific ritual contexts to cultivate a purity and refinement of soul that attracts higher beings. Such was the central aim of neoplatonic theurgy, whose rites culminated in the 'divinisation' of the human soul as it fully realised its identity as an embodied deity.[15]

Chittick proposes four constituents of spiritual vision: the consciousness of the observing subject, the reality-status of the observed, the form it takes, and the location of its actualisation. Firstly, the observer may be either awake or in an ASC. If awake, the 'eye of imagination' may see an apparition, invisible to anyone else, possessing full material form to the observer. But this is not a hallucination in the pejorative sense, rather, to the neoplatonic understanding the observer is seeing into a dimension whose ontological status as 'real' supersedes our notions of reality. This 'ontological inversion'[16] is impossible for the physicalist to grasp, and exposes the inadequacy of conventional empirical research methods. Despite the apparent concreteness and tangibility of these visions, they belong to a different modality of matter. Without a three-world metaphysics providing a foundation for the ontological reality of non-material being, it is difficult to locate the direct encounter with it in terms of its significance and transformative effect.

Ibn 'Arabi describes two kinds of ASC in which spiritual encounters take place: in dreams, or in a state of 'absence' of the soul (or 'annihilation' of the self/ego), where it is experienced as leaving the body and abandoning the world of the senses. Angels, jinn and humans may all undergo 'imaginalisation,' or manifest themselves in their subtle bodies, for in neoplatonic pneumatology, the imagination is both an attribute of the subtle or astral body and the means by which it is perceived.[17,18] Humans who manifest in this way may be either alive or dead, for the highest part of the soul-energy of the embodied human is retained in the spiritual world and rejoined after death. Thus it is possible to 'see' as real someone hundreds of miles away, or who has died. The imaginalised entity may be fully sense perceptible—but again one must emphasise that this does not mean it belongs in our world or is subject to its laws. Thus it may instantly vanish, or appear as non-human, angelic, or even monstrous and alien. Similarly, the apparition's location will depend on which 'eye' is seeing it:

> *The imaginal being perceived by the eye of sense-perception would be located 'out there' in the world of discontiguous imagination, while the being perceived by the eye of imagination would be 'in here' in the world of contiguous imagination.*[11 p89]

This suggests that it is not the spiritual beings who change location, but rather it is a matter of *how* they are seen, which 'eye' is looking. They can be perceived as either external or internal to the subject. In fact it is impossible to apply temporal-spatial concepts to this ambiguous and paradoxical realm, for 'inner' and 'outer' have no meaning in non-spatial dimensions. In practice, the *daimonic* or spiritual intelligence (particularly in channelling and mediumship) confounds attempts to define it as either a psychological condition or an autonomous being.[19] As the fifteenth century Platonist Marsilio Ficino reminds the reader, "our daemon and genius is not only, as is thought, our intellect, but [also] a numinous being *(numen)*."[20 p515]

It is very easy to confuse the discontiguous imagination with the material world if the eye of revelation is not active. Corbin relates an anecdote by Ibn 'Arabi of the Prophet Muhammed seeing the Angel Gabriel in the form of a beautiful Arab youth, whereas his companions saw only the youth.[21] Some imaginal embodiments apparently have the power to leave a concrete impression or even object in our world, but according to Ibn 'Arabi this can only be achieved if the human medium is an enlightened sage. The common sorcerer may be able to conjure objects that are not fully and concretely embodied, and they would soon disappear.[11] One is reminded here of the apports and ectoplasmic materialisations in contemporary mediumship, which attain various degrees of objectivity and physicality.[A]

Ibn 'Arabi's own encounters with spirits fall into three categories: when he alone could see the apparition, when it could possibly be seen by others and when it was definitely seen by others. For example, in 1202 he encountered the spirit of a holy man, Ahman al-Sabit, who had died 400 years previously. Ahman appeared as a beautiful man who seemed to pass through the bodies of other walkers as Ibn 'Arabi was circumambulating the Kabbah:

> *My mind was turned toward him and my eyes were upon him, lest he slip away [...] when he had completed his seven turns and wanted to leave, I seized hold of him and greeted him. He returned the greeting and smiled at me. All this time I did not take my gaze off him fearing that he would slip away from me. For I had no doubt that he was an embodied spirit, and I knew that eyesight kept him fixed.*[11 p94]

The idea of 'fixing' the spirit through the quality and direction of perception implies that the human gaze allows a spirit to take form, although Ibn 'Arabi emphasises that there is no disjunction between the outer form and the spiritual essence of the apparition "even if it is found in a thousand places, or in all places, and is diverse in shape."[11 p94] Once the gaze is released and the spirit moves, it may instantly disappear.

The 'imaginalisations' which appear in our world are therefore anomalous, ambiguous and paradoxical. As Ibn 'Arabi points out, they are "neither entirely existent or non-existent, neither entirely known or unknowable, neither entirely affirmed or denied."[22 p4] Yet they inhabit a very real dimension, and "It is to something like this reality that each human being goes in their sleep and after their death" where the observer "sees [moral and spiritual] qualities and characteristics as self-subsistent forms that speak to him and with which he converses, as being [human] bodies without any doubt."[22 p4] Corbin calls this realm the *mundus imaginalis*, "a precise order of reality, corresponding to a precise mode of perception... a world as ontologically real as the world of the senses."[23 p1,9] This world's cognitive faculty is the active imagination, which, Corbin warns, must not be confused with "the imagination that modern man identifies with 'fantasy,' and that, according to him, produces only the 'imaginary.'"[23 p9]

As we are unfamiliar with the neoplatonic premise that visibility of spiritual phenomena is entirely dependent on the observer's *quality of perception*, we can conclude that not everyone will have opened their eye of revelation. This raises the problematic question of empirical evidence and its assessment. With modern technology it is possible to obtain a permanent, apparently 'objective' record of spirit activity. I would suggest, however, that such 'evidence' (whether as photographs, film or recordings) is highly problematic because (fraud aside) it presents phenomena as objectively 'real'; of the same ontological status as tables and chairs. It is then very easy for 'the eye of reason' to insist on a rational explanation or fall prey to Kant's 'surreptitious concept' whereby numinous revelations are subjected to the same 'positive thought' as material objects.[B] Unless the limitations of sense perception and rational thought in relation to spiritual events are acknowledged, their truth will remain in the realm of speculation or subjective opinion, their manifestation baffling and therefore ignored or explained away. Objective proof belongs in the world of empiricism and is therefore an impossible criterion for the realm of spirit to fulfil.

To sum up, it is vitally important that research methodology acknowledges the interdependence of the researcher's mode of perception with what he or she sees and how it is evaluated. A framework for paradigms of knowledge beyond the rational should be established. Psychical research should become open to metaphysics, spiritual hermeneutics and the power of imaginal perception in order to gain access to a dimension beyond social context or objective analysis. Ambiguity and paradox accompany manifestations of the 'imaginal' in this world, and the right approach may not be 'either or' but rather 'both and.' Phenomena would be subjected to a multi-levelled investigation that recognises the differing discourses of sensory, rational and imaginal perspectives, and how they mutually inform each other. I conclude with the neoplatonist Proclus, who explains that whenever a faculty of knowledge is used to judge something beyond its remit, it will render itself ineffectual: "all knowledge when conjoined with an object of knowledge which does not at all pertain to it, loses its power."[25] Thus if rational thinking is applied to mystical or visionary experience, it will simply negate its own integrity. This is why I suggest that the human sciences can never be adequate for examining the reality of ineffable visions, and why researchers into the ontology of ASCs might benefit from recognising the authority of 'super-rational' modes of cognition.

A. The 'psychic' explanation given for apports is that spirit energy can change the vibration of matter so it can pass through other matter, and then re-solidify.[10]
B. For a discussion of Kant's epistemological stance with relation to the paranormal, see[24].
1. Fontana D. *Life beyond Death*. London: Watkins; 2009.
2. Hancock G. *Supernatural*. London: Random House; 2005.
3. Harpur P. *Daimonic Reality*. Ravensdale: Idyll Arbor; 2003.
4. Wilson C. *Poltergeist*. London: New English Library; 1981.
5. Wilson C. *Supernatural*. London: Watkins; 2011.
6. Ferrer JN. *Revisioning Transpersonal Theory*. New York: State University of New York Press; 2002.
7. Plato. *Republic*. Shorey P, translator. In Cairns H, Hamilton E, editors. *Plato, Complete Works*. Princeton, New Jersey: Princeton University Press; 1961. p.575–844.
8. Armstrong AH, editor. *Plotinus, Enneads. 7 vols*. Cambridge MA: Harvard University Press; 1966–88.
9. Dillon J. *Plotinus and the Transcendental Imagination*. In Mackey J, editor. *Religious Imagination*. Edinburgh: Edinburgh University Press; 1986.
10. Barnes Jefts L. *The Production of Apports, A Treatise on Physical Mediumship*. Available from www.psychicsoul.org.

11. Chittick W. *Imaginal Worlds: Ibn 'Arabi and the Problem of Religious Diversity.* New York: SUNY Press; 1994.
12. McGilchrist I. *The Master and his Emissary.* London: Yale University Press; 2010.
13. Chittick W. *The Sufi Path of Knowledge: Ibn 'Arabi's Metaphysics of Imagination.* New York: SUNY Press; 1989.
14. Aquinas T. *Summa theologiae 1.q.21.art.2 (veritas est adaequatio intellectus et rei: the truth is the adequation of the intellect and the thing).* Online edition at http://www.newadvent.org /summa/1021.htm.
15. Shaw G. *Theurgy and the Soul, the Neoplatonism of Iamblichus.* Pennsylvania: Pennsylvania State Press; 1995.
16. Milne J. *Providence, Time and Destiny.* Unpublished paper; 2002. At http://www .astrodivination.com/provid.pdf.
17. George L. *Iamblichus on the Esoteric Perception of Nature in Esotericism, Religion and Nature.* Fanger C. Irwin L. Phillips M. Versluis A, editors. Michigan: Association for the Study of Esotericism; 2010. p.73–88.
18. Shaw G. *The Role of Aesthesis in Theurgy.* Unpublished paper; 2010.
19. Klimo J. *Channeling: Investigations on Receiving Information From Paranormal Sources.* Berkeley, California: North Atlantic Books; 1998.
20. Ficino M. *Opera omnia. 2 vols.* Basle; 1576. Repr. Paris: Phénix Editions; 2000. p.515.
21. Corbin H. *Alone with the Alone: Creative Imagination in the Sufism of Ibn 'Arabi.* Princeton: Princeton University Press; 1969.
22. Morris J. *Spiritual Imagination and the Liminal World: Ibn 'Arabi on the Barzakh.* Postdata, Madrid. 1995; vol.15 (no.2): p.42–9, 104–9.
23. Corbin, H. *Mundus Imaginalis, or the Imaginary and the Imaginal.* In Fox L, translator. Swedenborg and Esoteric Islam. Pennsylvania: Swedenborg Foundation; 1999, pp1–33.
24. Cornelius G. *Field of Omens: A Study of Inductive Divination.* Unpublished thesis. University of Kent; 2009. Ch.1: Kant, Spirit and Divination.
25. Proclus. *Platonic Theology.* Taylor T. Translator. Online edition at http://www.archive.org/details/ProclusOnTheTheologyOfPlato-ElectronicEdition

COMMUNICATIONS FROM THE HERBS: A STEP-BY-STEP GUIDE TO INI CONSCIOUSNESS

HON. BINGHI CONGO-NYAH, REKA KOMAROMI, KIRKLAND MURRAY & ANNA WALDSTEIN

The Rastafari Way Of Life originated as individual, inborn seeds of Consciousness that grew into a global socio-political and spiritual movement. Initially, Rastafari seemed to be a response to exploitation and slavery that coalesced around the coronation of Ras Tafari Makonnen as Haile Selassie I, Emperor of Ethiopia in 1930. However fresh Rastafari of many races are being born with these seeds of Consciousness and express Self through the use of sacred Herbs, Roots and Mystical Drumming. Rastas use mixtures of Biblical, Kushite, Kamitic and/or other perspectives to explain and contextualise their unique *insperiences* (inner experiences) of higher consciousness.

Rastafari is well known for music and ritual smoking of (The) *Herbs* (*Cannabis spp.*) to reach higher states of unity and interconnection (*inity*) with other living and etheric beings. There are many books on the origins and history of Rastafari and libraries of material on *Cannabis* and its properties. However, the inner truth of this combination has not been explored fully by western science. We need to know what are the holistic mechanisms that link herbsmen and women to *Cannabis*. How are consciousness, healing, therapy and meditative practices involved in the mechanics of this ethnobotanical relationship?

The *Herbs* is the most sacred medicine in the Rastafari pharmacopoeia and is used in divination, *reasoning* and meditation.[1,2,3] Under the influence of *Herbs*, Rastafari establish ways of life based on intuited knowledge of the web of collective consciousness that connects all people, the ecosystem, inner-beings from etheric planes of existence and ultimately 'the Most High,' (Jah Rastafari; the first ancestor; the Source; the Creator). Through this genetic chord, Rastafari link through '*InI* consciousness' to the very beginning of creation. Rastas thereby assert their inalienable right to cultivate, trade and heal with *Herbs*. In so doing, they are breaking current social, cultural and legal conventions as well as conventionally held beliefs about the world's most popular illicit plant.

This chapter addresses the healing potential of exploring *InI* consciousness under the guidance of *Herbs*. *InI* consciousness is an intuited (right brain) experience/*insperience* of *inity*. This consciousness is a realistic awareness of the Universal Conscience (Divine Mind), which contains the body and the individual, interrelated mind. After describing our research process and providing more background on Rastafari and *InI* consciousness we will present a method of communication with *Herbs* (cultivation, breathing, smoking, meditation) that leads to holistic healing effects for individual, nation and planet.

RESEARCHING RASTAFARI

This chapter is inspired by the *Herbs* and based on Congo-Nyah's long-term study with/for Rastafari elders in Jamaica. This work was finalised during ten months of anthropological research with Komaromi, Waldstein and Murray in England, using Rastafari information-sharing techniques. Knowledge flows through Rasta networks via an intellectual teaching/reasoning process called *grounding*.[4] *Grounding* is a sacred rite of passage in which groups of people use *Herbs* (as incense and/or smoked) to create a direct connection to common sense (not to be mistaken with logic). At Breaking Convention 2011 the *Herbs* created a platform for a new and innovative research collaboration during a historic *grounding*.

Reasoning (discussion about important political, spiritual and social matters) is another essential part of *grounding*.[4] Although often inspired by *Herbs*, Rastafari *reasoning* is founded on knowledge of the interconnectedness of all things and can therefore be used for opening the gates of *InI* consciousness without smoking. Congo-Nyah is an expert in imparting the teachings of the elders via *reasoning*. *Reasoning* has also been identified by anthropologists as an effective way of collecting ethnographic data on Rastafari.[5] Likewise, Waldstein and Komaromi have found that *reasonings* with Congo-Nyah and Murray have been a fruitful source of knowledge and information on *Herbs* and *InI* consciousness.

Under Congo-Nyah's guidance, Komaromi and Waldstein are also learning and practicing Rastafari-inspired meditations, dietary habits and other daily rituals. Most of this participation in the Rastafari Way of Life has taken place privately, rather than in a social context as in conventional participant observation. However, the meditations require careful observation of the self, which leads to revelations about the underlying spiritual and practical logics of Rasta practices. Similar processes of sensorially engaged participant observation have been described by other anthropologists[6] as a way of complementing data collected through discourse-based techniques.

RASTAFARI AND INI CONSCIOUSNESS

As Rastafari has various expressions at different levels of cultivation/development of *InI* consciousness, it seems to lack a fully codified doctrine.[7] However there are several foundational characteristics that define Rastafari, such as taking words of Haile Selassie as *I-vine* (divine) truth, seeking African repatriation, drumming and burning *Herbs*. At some point all initiates make their own personal connections to (and embody) Haile Selassie I as the perfect exemplar of *InI* consciousness (God/Christ/Jah, etc.). A few general facets of Rasta linguistics, philosophy and ethics help explain *InI* consciousness further.

I is an important word/sound of power in RastafarI.[1,8,9] In Iyaric, the Rastafari language the pronoun *InI* (I and I) denotes the shared identity/source from which came all and is used to refer to 'I,' 'me,' 'we' and 'us' ('you,' is *the I*). The use of I in Iyaric emphasises the importance Rastafari places on identifying with and knowing the Self. Like the Sadhus, many Rastas experience a direct connection to the etheric double and find the Self's purpose in life through smoking *Herbs* and transcendental meditation. Rastas are united in and distinguished by knowing they are here to rebalance the earth by precipitating the collapse of global consumer capitalism (Babylon), returning descendants of African slaves to a motherland (Zion) that their ancestors were forcibly removed from[8] and cultivating sustainable agricultural systems.

In Iyaric *high* and *I* are conflated through sound symbolism and both words are likewise connected to 'eye'/vision.[5] By smoking *Herbs* and meditating Rastafari reach states of consciousness where they *insperience* the ability to communicate from the higher Self, via the *Herbs*, the ancestors, Haile Selassie/Empress Menen, etc. When Rastafari are high (I) these communications may be visual or verbal in nature. Most interesting is the *Herbs*' ability to impart even greater vision, in the sense of seeing connections between different global, historical and spiritual events that have shaped the African diaspora.

Central to Rasta ways of life (*livity*), is an ethic of harmonising with nature, peace and love. According to Rastafari *reasoning*, evidence of a blueprint of creation is empirically verified by looking at the womb or other mathematical patterns and ecological processes of nature. All forms of life on earth play a unique role/purpose in supporting its interconnection and interdependence. In Rastafari there is widespread respect for Life and the unique purpose/plan for each aspect of creation. Rastas who farm the land to provide the vegan food required of an *ital* diet are conscious of local ecological processes and use agricultural techniques that are similar to organic and biodynamic methods.[1,8] They cultivate the (v)ital force (spirit/vibrations/energy) from the earth, the air, the sun and the water through plants, which are consumed to build healthy bodies and worthy vessels to manifest 'Jah will on earth.'

The heart of Rastafari is a higher/wider awareness of being and existence and ultimately, re-connection with The Creator. Rastafari know that on earth, *InI* are all born of woman and that all beings possess a higher (divine) and an animal nature. In re-building connections with *InI* divinity, which is held in potential, Rastas eventually become aligned with The Source. This is associated with the realisation that we are consciousness and that the universe is an extension of the earthly body, which dwells in our mind. The earthly mind receives communications from greater universal cycles, energies and forces and can, in turn, create what we are inspired to manifest. This mystical *insperience* is similar to those that occur with the help of other psychedelic plant teachers or meditation techniques.

CULTIVATION OF HERBS

The ability of *Herbs* to lead Rastas to higher consciousness depends on how it is cultivated. Jamaican farmers usually grow strains of *Herbs* known to science as *Cannabis sativa* (as opposed to *C. indica* varieties). In Rastafari philosophy, wholesome existence depends upon truth, balance, order and justice. This is regulated by the Nyahbinghi order which states that the hungry must be fed, the naked clothed, the sick nourished, the infants cared for, the aged protected and the ignorant instructed. Thus, the Rastafari way of cultivating *Herbs* is concerned with balancing the order of the natural and spiritual worlds. From a Rasta perspective, hydroponic cultivation, use of artificial lighting and chemical fertilisers result in spiritually unbalanced *Herbs* that are tuned to a lower vibrational level and can create paranoia.

The Rasta herbsman holds a respectful relationship with the land on which he grows *Herbs*, recognising that everything is interrelated and interconnected by ecological and spiritual laws. The herbsman's thoughts while working are as crucial in the cultivation process as are the sun, earth, wind and water. He must be aware of the spiritual balance of seed, sun and sound and acknowledge the ancestors of the land. He observes the rules of *ital* farming, uses only organic manure (for best results bat manure) and chants/cares for the plants in his field on a daily basis. This dedicated care requires him to be in constant communication with the *Herbs*, the divinity of Haile Selassie and the reflection of his own divinity, expressing this through his creative work in the field. At harvest time, he retains all his creative energies for the crop and must refrain from sexual intercourse to be at the 'top of his game' because *Herbs* is known as a sensitive *hempress*.

SMOKING HERBS

Many Rastas smoke *Herbs* as and when they can, depending on the time, vibes (energetic and musical vibrations) and task at hand. In many parts of the world tobacco is rolled with *Herbs* into spliffs (cigarettes) and Rastas often follow this custom. However, to reach higher states of consciousness *Herbs* must be smoked ital (i.e., without tobacco), ideally from a chalice. A Rasta chalice is a water-pipe made from a plastic hose, a kutchie (bowl made of hardwood or clay) and a body (usually made from a coconut shell, bamboo or a glass bottle) (Figure 1). The water used to fill the body should be chlorine-free, ideally from a natural spring. The *Herbs* are loaded into the kutchie, lit (preferably without sulphur or gas) and the smoke is pulled through the water-filled shell and

FIGURE 1: Coconut shell chalice. Courtesy of Reka Komaromi.

hose into the lungs of the smoker via the mouth. Drawing a lung-ful of smoke from the chalice requires practice and coordination. Some Rastas blow the first puffs of smoke (without inhaling) into the air for the ancestors and for cleansing the face, hair and general environment.

During *reasonings* and other group meditations, the ritual prescription and general custom is three full pulls for each person in the session. This usually requires large quantities of *Herbs*, which can be difficult to find and/or afford in prohibitive societies that criminalise it, so experienced herbsmen and women must often make due with combinations of *Herbs*, tobacco and other admixtures (e.g., raspberry leaf). During private meditations, an experienced herbsman might use a *chalice* but higher states may still be reached using more economical means of smoking *ital Herbs* (i.e., in a 'pure' *spliff* or with a smaller pipe).

Smoking the *chalice* is a ceremonial activity based on balancing the elements and becoming aware of the connection between

FIGURE 2: The throne position. Courtesy of Anna Waldstein.

earthly and spiritual planes; every spirit must manifest in flesh. In order to calibrate participants to a receptive state, before lighting the *chalice* Rastas give thanks to the *Herbs*; the sun, air, earth and water that provided her nourishment; the herbsman who cared for her; and all the people involved in making it possible for *Herbs* to help the lower natures to find higher ones. This thanksgiving acknowledges the order within nature and the forces acting upon us that herbsmen are always mindful of. The blessing also serves as a reminder of the commodity chain that links producers, traffickers and consumers of this illicit sacrament and inspires action to correct the injustices of prohibition. Following a chant, the herbsman is ready to light.

Despite conventional proscriptions on holding smoke in the lungs, Rasta herbsmen teach *InI* to inhale deeply, hold the breath and exhale slowly through the nose when smoking *Herbs*. Rastas report that pure *Herbs*, which have been cultivated wisely and smoked in this way clear/burn out physical and spiritual debris that accumulates in human respiratory passages. *Herbs* is a known expectovrant[10] and does not appear to be a respiratory irritant/carcinogen.[11]

Deep breathing is facilitated by loose fitting clothing and good posture. Rastas are mindful of standing up straight or sitting in the throne position (Figure 2) when smoking, reasoning and meditating. The key to holding the body in these postures for any length of time is balancing the head on the top of the spine and the spine on the hips and pelvis, while relaxing all muscles, save for the few that must be flexed to maintain bodily balance. Thus, adopting the stance of the I-vine King and Queen, while deeply inhaling *Herbs* smoke has beneficial effects on the entire body. The final stage in smoking *Herbs* for higher consciousness is putting down the chalice and arranging the hands in the 'seal' mudra (Figure 3), a hand posture that helps tune the mind, focus the intellect and instruct the spirit during reasoning and meditation.

MEDITATION WITH HERBS

Rastas consider the form of ecstatic trance that can be reached by smoking *Herbs* (and coincidentally through sex) to be a particularly valuable meditative state. Ecstatic trance is the highly receptive midpoint between sleep and wakefulness, between the subjective/objective, conscious/unconscious, material/etheric, higher/lower self, etc. In ecstatic trance we can bridge the gap between the 'two worlds' and communicate with/from the higher Self and The Source. Trance states generally involve slowing/

FIGURE 3: The seal mudra. Courtesy of Reka Komaromi.

deepening patterns of breathing from 20 breaths of 250ml to 7.5 breaths of more than 500ml of air per minute, which the smoking techniques described above help achieve. *Herbs* meditation practice helps Rastafari to become conscious/aware of the oneness of all humans and our universal desires for joy, infallible guidance, inner peace and self reliance.

The higher Self and the individual (ego) unite in ecstatic trance, which (with practice) enables the Self to manifest higher states of being on earth. When the point of ecstatic trance is reached, messages and answers to questions are intuited from the space-beyond-thought in the form of visions, sounds and physical sensations. Using intuition can lead to better decisions than relying on human logic and/or emotions and unites *InI* with *Jah* to ensure that the forces of creation and destruction are balanced.

Many Rastas combine smoking with defined meditation techniques, while for others creating music is a form of meditation. Murray follows an informal practice of meditation that begins with prayer and praise of Haile Selassie, followed by a free flow of ideas and visions that he relates to his own perspective on life. Congo-Nyah has been instructing Waldstein and Komaromi in a more structured meditation technique that was developed by Ra Un Nefer Amen, an expert on ancient Egyptian philosophy and spiritual culture.[12] While the method was not necessarily intended to be done under the guidance of *Herbs*, it has been used in Rasta communities worldwide as it provides an effective means of navigating ecstatic and other forms of trance.

The guided meditations are based on the Paut Neteru (cake of the gods), also known as the Kamitic 'Tree of Life.' In the meditations there is a stilling and clearing of the mind, which happens through focusing on the breath and silently chanting relevant words of power. These *hekau* (mantras) are designed to enhance different faculties of human consciousness (talents) and the initiate learns which ones to access at will in meditation (e.g., to awaken latent talents). During this process, the mind is freed from/rises above negative thought patterns and conditioning. This allows Rastas to (re)programme with the image, life and times of Haile Selassie who embodies impeccability, integrity, courage and wisdom. One can also visualise desired outcomes of situations relating to oneself, other people and/or the world via the Life Force or Spirit, which is why Rastafari always hail life. Together, *Herbs* and meditation inspire change/transcendence, as well as specific inventions, research, ideas, etc.

HEALING WITH HERBS

Rasta conceptions of health integrate physical and spiritual aspects of wellbeing so in some sense, all encounters with *Herbs* may be considered healing. In Jamaica, *Herbs* is profoundly medicinal and many Jamaican men, women and children take *Herbs* in the form of *ganja* tea, either daily or as needed.[13] The tea contains many of the medicinal compounds of *Cannabis* and even THC may be extracted in water at a high enough temperature.[14] Among its many other healing qualities, *ganja* tea helps children grow and do better in school.[15,16] Like most Jamaican women, Rasta *Iyatas* prepare *Herbs* tea for themselves and their families. Congo-Nyah is living proof of the healing properties of a tonic made with *Herbs* that was administered to him by a local Rasta herbsman to cure his chronic asthma.

There is also evidence of medicinal benefits of smoked *Herbs* in Jamaica and elsewhere.[13,17,18] When practiced regularly, meditation with *Herbs* provides general therapeutic effects of the plant combined with regular benefits of meditation and there is also a synergistic effect as *Herbs* aid the process of meditation. One way that smoking *Herbs* enhances the Tree of Life meditations is by increasing sensitivity to physical and nutritional needs (e.g., urges to stretch, eat specific foods, etc.). In Rasta rituals *Herbs* as an incense is important for creating a healing atmosphere. The smoke may or may not be directly inhaled by all participants but in a small, enclosed shrine cannabinoids pass into the systems of all beings in the room. Rastas report that smoking *Herbs* takes the edge off of anger and helps people cope with stress more effectively. As spirits are heightened and a positive outlook is cultivated through *Herbs* and meditation, healing takes the form of relaxation, control over the emotions and knowledge of how to balance self-interests with the wellbeing of others.

REASONING AND CONCLUSIONS

The *insperiences* of ecstatic trance and *InI* consciousness that arise from meditation with *Herbs* share many characteristics with spiritual rituals that include other psychedelic sacraments. Komaromi has experienced *InI* consciousness as an emotionless state of stillness, embodied at a cellular level, through both Rasta meditations and in communal ayahuasca rituals.[19] Gradually, with the aid of music, chanting and concentration on the breath, this state of 'no-thought' may also be entered without sacrament. As this stillness is accessed by emptying the mind of all images, words and emotions it makes us receptive to intuitions from the higher Self. Initiates in Rasta meditations learn to ask questions and manifest *I-vine* will through balance, harmony and *inity*. As such, *Herbs* heals in a holistic way that links human health with that of other living and etheric beings in a web of ecological and spiritual processes.

However, *Herbs* can also inspire particular ways of approaching the world that are not compatible with global consumer capitalism, which helps explain why this healing sacrament continues to be criminalised. The prohibition of *Herbs* has supported global surveillance, border control and incarceration industries while removing a significant challenge to the monopoly pharmaceutical companies hold over human health. Whether they smoke *Herbs* or not, Rastas share an interest in freeing the sacrament that has inspired and become symbolic of the movement, along with many other activists and (sub)cultural groups. While the medical benefits and relative safety of *Cannabis* and its derivatives have fuelled anti-prohibition movements in North America and Europe, Rastafari brings spirituality into debates about the legality of *Herbs* and other sacred medicines.

From the Rasta point of view, *Herbs* is more than recreational pleasure or even a medicinal plant, though its roles in leisure and medicine have wide recognition and appeal. *Herbs* is a way to connect the higher Self/The Source, in order to make wise decisions

and realise our full potential.[3] Rastafari offers a method of max-
imising the healing powers of *Herbs* while mitigating potential
harms. Meditation with *Herbs* is not the only way to connect with
the divine. However when people are free to cultivate and use
Herbs wisely, this path to *InI* consciousness has both spiritual and
earthly healing effects.

1. Pretorius SP. *The significance of the use of ganja as a religious ritual in the Rastafari movement.* Verbum Et Ecclesia. 2009;27(3):1012–30.
2. Benard AA. *The material roots of Rastafarian marijuana symbolism. History and Anthropology.* 2007;18(1):89–99.
3. Gibson M. 'Rastafari and cannabis: Framing a criminal law exemption.' *Ecclesiastical Law Journal.* 2010;12(03):324–44.
4. Hansing K. *Rasta, race and revolution: The emergence and development of the Rastafari movement in socialist Cuba.* Berlin: LIT Verlag Münster; 2006.
5. Homiak J. *The mystic revelation of Rasta far-eye; visionary communication in a prophetic movement.* In: Tedlock B, editor. *Dreaming: Anthropological and psychological interpretations.* SAR Press; 1987. p. 220–45.
6. Nichter M. 'Coming to our senses: Appreciating the sensorial in medical anthropology.' *Transcultural Psychiatry.* 2008;45(2):163–97.
7. See the Rastafari Council of Britain page on the Lions Den Fam website (http://www .lionsdenfam.org/The_Lions_Den_Fam/About_Us.html) for formal codes of Rastafari. Accessed 2 May 2012.
8. Kebede A, Knottnerus JD. 'Beyond the pales of babylon: The ideational components and social psychological foundations of Rastafari.' *Sociological Perspectives.* 1998;41(3)499–517.
9. Price CR. 'Social change and the development and co-optation of a black antisystemic identity: The case of Rastafarians in Jamaica.' *Identity: An International Journal of Theory and Research.* 2003;3(1):9–27.
10. Touw M. 'The religious and medicinal uses of cannabis in India, China and Tibet.' *Journal of Psychoactive Drugs.* 1981;13(1):23–34.
11. Chen ALC, Chen TJH, Braverman ER, Acuri V, Kerner M, Varshavskiy M, et al. Hypothesizing that marijuana smokers are at a significantly lower risk of carcinogenicity relative to tobacco-non-marijuana smokers: Evidenced based on statistical reevaluation of current literature. *Journal of Psychoactive Drugs.* 2008;40(3):263–72.
12. Available from: www.oneworldarchives.org/Metu%20Neter/Metu%20Neter.htm. Accessed 8 February 2012.
13. Rubin VD, Comitas L. *Ganja in Jamaica: A medical anthropological study of chronic marihuana use.* The Hague: Mouton; 1975.
14. Politi M, Peschel W, Wilson N, Zloh M, Prieto JM, Heinrich M. 'Cannabis water extracts and tinctures analysed by NMR spectroscopy: Different strategies to reduce the content of D9-THC.' *Phytochemistry.* 2008;69:562–70.
15. Dreher M. 'Schoolchildren and ganja: Youthful marijuana consumption in rural Jamaica.' *Anthropology and Education Quarterly.* 1984;15:131–50.
16. Dreher MC, Nugent K, Hudgins R. 'Prenatal marijuana exposure and neonatal

outcomes in Jamaica: An ethnographic study.' *Pediatrics*. 1994;93(2):254–60.

17. Grinspoon L, Bakalar JB. *Marihuana, the forbidden medicine*. Yale University Press; 1997.

18. Waldstein A. 'Menace or medicine? Anthropological perspectives on the self-administration of high potency cannabis in the UK.' *Drugs and Alcohol Today*. 2010;10(3):37–43.

19. Available from: http://www.portadosol.org.br/index.php?lang=en. Accessed 10 April 2012.

A BOLD VISION
(EDITED TRANSCRIPT),
UNIVERSITY OF KENT,
CANTERBURY, UK. 3 APRIL 2011

RICK DOBLIN

When I heard that the theme was "bold visions" I decided to really be bold. So this is going to be about how integrating psychedelics into our culture can play a major role in helping save and sustain the world for future generations. I'm going to be talking about psychedelics and the future united religions, building a global spirituality. I've heard many concerns about how MAPS' vision to medicalise psychedelics is, on the one hand, narrow and, on the other hand, maybe like endorsing a medical priesthood. I'd like to show you that that's really part of a much larger vision that we have to bring about a much better world. There are strategic reasons to be working on medicalising psychedelics, but it is not the biggest part of the picture, but it is a necessary stepping stone towards what we'll be talking about. So what I'm going to focus on is the political implications of the mystical experience and the mainstreaming of psychedelics. We can have our own individual experiences, and many of us have had them, but I think there is something deeper to be gained by trying to mainstream them.

When I was growing up I had this intimation that there was something connected between psychedelics and this movement toward a more peaceful world. The whole psychedelic 60s illustrates how there was this major link between the psychedelic community and these larger social movements, which unfortunately helped lead to the backlash from which we're just now emerging.

The idea that mental changes are necessary for a more peaceful world is not new. Right after World War II, the preamble to the UNESCO Constitution says, "Since wars begin in the minds of men, it is in the minds of men that the defences of peace must be constructed." And Albert Einstein said, "The splitting of the atom has changed everything save our mode of thinking, and thus we drift towards unparalleled catastrophe." We need to ask ourselves, what does he mean by our mode of thinking? What sort of a shift is he trying to point us to? It's a shift towards a more universalistic understanding, a more unitive experience, very much contained in the mystical experience. As long as we think of ourselves as separate individuals identified by our culture, religion, country, race, gender, or any number of different ways that we think of ourselves, we will still find ourselves in conflict. We have to understand something much deeper about our unity.

It has become appallingly obvious that our technology has exceeded our humanity. When I first started to do LSD, I felt like I was overdeveloped intellectually, and underdeveloped emotionally and spiritually. I felt the same about the culture. This is what Einstein was talking about. Among the worst examples are Auschwitz and Vietnam. Yet now we have Dr. Stan Grof saying, "LSD is to the study of the mind what the telescope is to astronomy and the microscope is to biology." So this is a further hint that there is something in psychedelics that will be key to understanding how to make these changes in the minds of mankind.

This connection between spirituality, psychedelics and science was pioneered by Walter Pahnke. The Good Friday Experiment, conducted in 1962 at Harvard, was one of the best things that Timothy Leary ever did; he was the faculty sponsor for this. To give you an idea of how it's possible for psychedelics to be integrated into the mainstream, we should just look back; the Good

Friday Experiment took place in Marsh Chapel, on Good Friday, and the minister was Reverend Howard Thurman—the mentor for Martin Luther King who was getting his PhD at the same time at Boston University.

The key criteria of a mystical experience are the sense of unity (internal and external), transcendence of time and space, sense of sacredness, sense of objective reality, noetic quality, deeply felt positive mood, ineffability and paradoxicality. This is the core. How does this have political implications? The first part is that the Good Friday Experiment did six-month follow-ups to assess peoples' changes in attitudes and behaviour: changes toward self, others, life and the experience. They found that people felt there was something that was persisting from that experiment, something that was positive and helped them lead, in some ways, a better life.

Now, flash forward to 1982. I came across the book *New Genesis: Shaping a Global Spirituality*. Robert Muller was the Assistant Secretary General of the United Nations. In a sense he was the mystic at the UN and wrote this book. His basic idea was that we have the United Nations to help us mediate conflicts between nations, but so many of the conflicts go deeper, into religion. He wrote that we really needed a "United Religions," and he's starting to talk about global spirituality. It was a very persuasive book, but there wasn't a single word in it about psychedelics.

So I decided that, as a young undergraduate, I would write him a letter, mentioning the Good Friday Experiment and basically saying that he made a terrific point. Since every new method of killing people gets unlimited money, practically, from the war establishments around the world, would he be willing to use his political situation, his context, to help start psychedelic research? We had evidence from the Good Friday Experiment and thousands of years of religious use of psychedelics; there was some connection here. Certainly, for the importance that he put on developing this global spirituality, he should be willing to help start psychedelic research. I also mentioned that MDMA was a legal substance and that it would be possible to do research with it.

To my utter surprise he actually wrote me back. He said that he agreed that I understood what he was saying and he agreed with my argument. He would help try to bring back psychedelic research. He gave me a list of religious professionals in a range of different religions he wanted me to consult with. I read between the lines that he wanted me to send them MDMA. So I proceeded to do so. And they reported back to him about their experiences. One of them was Wayne Teasdale, a very politically active Roman Catholic monk, who later wrote *A Monk in the World*. Again I felt this thesis that somehow the mystical experience, psychedelics and people working on political change was being validated.

I worked with Robert Muller and in 1984 I wrote a dream protocol that I would one day still like to conduct. Basically, get 50 people who are from five different religions, ten in each religion, who are studying to be religious professionals. We would take half of these people and they would go through their normal training process and then the other half would be supplemented with psychedelic experiences. At the end of the process we would do a lot of personality and other tests to compare the people who were trained with psychedelics with those trained without psychedelics in the usual way.

A second study would look at the visions that people have, the content of their psychedelic experience, and compare the content that they had with the symbol systems of their own religion. We would predict that people will have a range of experiences that may not be limited to the symbol systems of their own particular religion. One of my more meaningful experiences with ibogaine was much involved with a lot of images of Jesus on the cross; it was difficult. The third level of analysis would be to look at the visions and the experiences of the people in the different religions for evidence of a common mystical core. It's often been said that the mystics of the different religions have more in common with each other than they do with the fundamentalists in their own religion. What we're saying is that we need to help people move from the fundamentalist perspective to more of a mystical perspective. If we can do that, we will avoid a lot of the conflicts that come from fundamentalists, each saying that they've got the one right way.

I went to the UN and tried to figure out where on the property, since it's technically not in the United States, we could actually conduct this experiment. I identified a place, but it was too ambitious for the time; there was no way to do it as psychedelic research was being blocked in the United States and elsewhere. So I wasn't able to do it, but I was able to do a long-term follow up to the Good Friday Experiment as it didn't involve administering drugs, just asking questions of people who had been administered drugs.

In the mystical literature, we can evaluate peoples' experiences on many dimensions, but the real test is the fruits test. What are the implications of the experience to people's lives? You judge by the fruits. After 25 years of reflection, I was asking them—in the midst of an escalation of the War on Drugs, the Nancy Reagan "Just Say No" era—if they had any incentive to turn their back or deny that what they had had was genuine. It was a time when they would be more likely to do that. But, what I found was that the people who had had the mystical experience from psilocybin felt that it was still genuine. Many of them had non-drug mystical experiences with which to compare. They generally preferred the non-drug mystical experiences because they were more uniformly positive, whereas the drug experiences oscillated between moments of fear, terror and challenges of letting go. But they considered them to be the doorway to their future mystical life, increased tolerance of other religious systems, deepened equanimity in the face of difficult life crises, and greater solidarity and identification with foreign peoples, minorities, women and nature. This was the confirmation, for me, that this was the right area for me to focus my energies on and there was something to this idea that blossomed in the 60s.

Now, in 1988 Wayne Teasdale and others who had been inspired by their mystical practices, and also by their psychedelic experiences, began working to establish what they called the Council for the Parliament of the World's Religions to commemorate the 100ᵗʰ anniversary of the 1893 Parliament of the World's Religions at the Chicago World's Fair. It was the largest ecumenical gathering to have taken place in the world at that time.

It is a small organisation, relatively, but it's the seed that will grow over time to really help us navigate through this globalisation process where religions, peoples and nations are all bumping up against each other. We have to learn how to live together and see our common nature. And here's what they say: "The Council for the Parliament of the World's Religions seeks to promote inter-religious harmony rather than unity...The wellbeing of the earth, and all life, depends on this collaboration." There is that sense that we have to all come together, the challenges have become so great for the human species that it's going to take all of us to find our way out.

One of the ways to achieve this goal, of course, is to expand the freedom of religions so that those people who use psychedelics within their religious practise are able to do so. There have been some promising moves in that direction. The US Supreme Court protects peyote use by the 500,000-member Native American church. The Supreme Court has also protected ayahuasca use by the Uniao de Vegetal with cases pending the Santo Daime's use. Brazil and Peru protect religious use of ayahuasca. There are legal cases that are coming up in England. And in Gabon, they protect the religious use of iboga in the Bwiti religion.

From our Western culture we have the Eleusinian Mysteries. For 2,000 years, they were the foundation ceremony of Greek culture. They were ended in 396 by the Catholic Church who saw them as competition. This was about individuals' direct relationship and the church wanted to be the mediator between people and their spirituality. For what we know about it, it seemed to work for most everybody who participated in it. But now, many of the rites of passage that we have in our religions don't seem to work or have lost their potency. So for me, my Bar Mitzvah did not turn me into a man though I anticipated that it would.

We also need freedom from religion. And by that I mean that each individual has a fundamental human right to explore and express their personal spirituality outside of religious contexts. Religions are groups and we need to protect individual, direct spirituality. Individual spiritual use is not protected by freedom of religion; we need some sort for access to psychedelics outside of organised religious, medical and scientific contexts. I'm trying to say that the medicalisation of psychedelics, even religious freedom, is only going to get us part of the way towards having individual rights for spiritual expression through the use of psychedelics.

In some senses, I think Roland Griffiths' research is more revolutionary than what MAPS is doing. His research makes the best case for drug legalisation than any of our other studies because what he has shown is that individuals, not in a religious setting or community, and not in the midst of a religious practice, can have one of the most profound spiritual experiences of their lives. What are the implications of that? It really suggests that we have to go beyond freedom of religion to some sort of legalisation for adults.

The theory of social change to mainstream psychedelics is about shifting the balance from fear to hope. Most of the drug education programmes, drug abuse prevention programmes, focus on increasing perceived risk not actual risk. They also practice harm maximisation in that the policies make it worse for people who decide to use drugs. It's an intentional approach to increase the perceived risk. One of the key findings of surveys conducted in the US by the National Institute on Drug Abuse over the last 30 years or so is that an increase in perceived risk is related to reduction in drug use. To them, use is the same as abuse. This analysis is muddy. Use equals abuse so the more we can do to increase perceived risk, from their perspective, the better. And that's why psychedelic research is such a threat; we are trying to get balanced information about both risks *and* benefits. This runs up against drug education efforts, which are unbalanced and biased, exaggerating risks and denying benefits.

So how can we shift the balance from fear to hope? Medicalisation of psychedelics plays a major part. But not just medicalisation. We need to do the whole range of drug development: preclinical toxicity studies, Phase I safety studies, mechanism of action studies, using psychedelics to probe consciousness. Eventually we hope to start psychedelic research into creativity and problem solving, in businesses and scientific areas; there was great research like this in the 60s and 50s.

End-of-life work is, in some ways, the most important because we will all die. There was an article in *The Boston Globe* about the underground psychedelic treatment of a woman who died in her early thirties of cancer, and it was reported as a good death. To the extent that we can help people get over their fear of death and help them realise that there are ways to have a good death, and this is basically what the hospice movement is doing, we can overcome a lot of people's fears of, and open their hearts to, psychedelic research. The end of life is broad, it reaches all of us.

We've been making progress through medicalisation and working on therapeutic applications, particularly with MDMA for post traumatic stress disorder. In 2001, Oprah did a show on ecstasy. I was working with her staff who said it's so complex that they would do two shows, one on the risks and one on the benefits. The first show was about the risks and, as it turned out, there was no show on the benefits. They showed an image of a graphically manipulated SPEC scan where every area that had activation below a certain level was shown in black, as a hole. The image was a brain with holes in it. This image has made it around the world. I just encountered people in Australia and Israel who were telling me they were scared about ecstasy, MDMA, causing holes in their brains.

MAPS works with highly sympathetic patient populations, with veterans. There is an image from an Israeli newspaper, a soldier in a blood red sea and a happy face ecstasy pill is his lifesaver. This is one of the best images we ever had at the time. In working with the military our message is going to trace through society. I gave an exclusive to military.com and because we are talking about working with MDMA with veterans, they were willing to write it up and put it on their homepage. Then it went to Fox News, owned by Murdoch. Because it came from the military they reported it in a positive way. Then it was on the Navy Seals website, in a newsletter that went to the medical profession, then in *TIME* Magazine. Now in this month's issue of *ELLE* magazine there is an article about the psychedelic renaissance and the potential of MDMA for couples therapy. Of course they say at the bottom, "fighting all the time? There is a new drug that can help you and it's not Viagra." But it is a really positive article.

The fear parents have for their children is what's primarily driving the drug war now. It's no longer psychedelics as symbol of cultural rebellion, although that is there as well. We have that sense from the 60s but it's fading. We have been trying to reach out to mothers, fathers and families. One of the headlines in the May issue of Oprah's magazine, *O* is "Can a single pill heal your pain?" Remember the holes in the brain? Instead, this article has an image of a magic pill. Look where we have come to. This is, of course, propaganda in the positive direction. We don't say that a single pill will do it or that it will work for everybody, but for this kind of imagery to be put out by Oprah's magazine ten years after the biased and graphically manipulated brain scans is really remarkable.

We are moving towards medicalisation. The vision is that eventually there will be psychedelic clinics throughout the world. In 1974, the first hospice centre was opened and 30 years later there were 3,500. Once we get MDMA as a medicine, psychedelics as a medicine, we can expect a generation or so of roll out into society.

The clinics will have highly trained and licensed professionals who treat patients in specialised facilities. Eventually they will expand as culture gets more and more comfortable, and they will expand to the family members of people who are being treated. If you have a spouse who is dying, you might not have clinical anxiety or depression, but you have a lot of things to work though.

The vision is that not just anybody can buy it. Clinics would become a site of initiation. This is like when you go get your driver's license; you have to actually drive under supervision of somebody who prevents you from endangering yourself or others until you have a certain skill level. People will go to these clinics and have an experience, and if they don't have some sort of catastrophic outcome, they will get a license to permit them to purchase it on their own and use it wherever they so choose.

This is my vision of moving from medicalisation to broader legalisation, and then eventually we can get parental override. Many people start the use of psychedelics younger than 18 or 21. Most cultures that have successfully integrated psychedelics have opportunities for young people to be exposed, and that's done in a family context, in a spiritual context. I think that we will be giving parents the right, instead of the government, to permit their own children to have access to psychedelics if they want to. The model is not so strange; in the United States right now 23 states permit parents to introduce alcohol to their children. We already have the idea that parents should be the place, so this is a family values strategy saying that families should be more in charge than the government, which just says no.

Once we implement this vision, people will be using psychedelics in all different contexts. Some will be religious, some will be therapeutic, some will be private homes, but some will also be large-scale festivals. We have to implement, and are already, harm reduction, or here we call it Kosmicare. This is the best example in the world. At Boom festival in 2010, the organisers spent 30,000 euros to create a place for people who were having difficult psychedelic experiences to come to for assistance. We had a team of about 40 people, worked 24 hours a day in different shifts. It was just extraordinary. We are going to have to keep in mind harm reduction as there are risks. But I think that once we roll this out into society in these ways, in maybe 20–30 years from now, then we will have the Council for the Parliament of World Religions and we will have peace next.

FIGURES

5: Abstract geometric incisions made on one side of a red ochre piece around 75,000 years ago found in Blombos Cave, South Africa.

18: (Left) Diagnostic entoptics; (Right) Undiagnostic entoptics.

20: Location map of Newgrange and Knowth passage tombs, Co. Meath, Ireland.

22: The passage tomb at Newgrange after restoration.

23: Entoptic shapes at Newgrange: (1) meander on kerbstone K52; (2) fortification on orthostat R18; (3) arc-spiral on K52; (4) filigree on East recess roof stone; (5) multiple spiral on kerbstone K1.

24: The passage tomb of Knowth.

25: Entoptic shapes at Knowth: (1) meander on kerbstone K83; (2) arc-spiral on kerbstone K56; (3) loop arc on kerbstone K68; (4) multiple spiral on kerbstone K13.

26: (Left) Newgrange kerbstones K1, K52 and K67. (Right) Drawing of imagery of early stages of hallucinogen intoxication.

36: Pre-Columbian gold work.

37: Pre-Columbian gold work.

41: Paraphernalia from San Pedro de Atacama.

42: The Ponce monolith in the Kalasasaya yard of Tiwanaku.

44: Therianthrope with feline characteristics holding a stalk of San Pedro cactus. Circular Plaza of the Old Temple, Chavin de Huántar.

74: Bertrand Russell speaking at a Committee of 100 rally at Trafalgar Square, London on 25 February 1962.

76: "Now we've got a chance to try the new Gas of Peace on somebody!"

81: A Royal Marine struggles to contain his 'inappropriate hilarity' while conducting an exercise under the influence of 200 μg of LSD.

279: Coconut shell chalice.

280: The Throne Position.

282: The seal mudra.

CONTRIBUTORS

CAMERON ADAMS is a research associate in the School of Anthropology and Conservation at the University of Kent, Canterbury. He is a co-organiser of Breaking Convention: A Multidisciplinary Conference on Psychedelic Consciousness.

JOSEPH BICKNELL is a philosopher and psychonautical explorer who graduated from King's college London with a BA in philosophy and an MSc in philosophy of mental disorder. He has hosted and produced the 'Psychonautica' online podcast, and has given presentations on psychedelic phenomenology at the university of Kent, and the university of Amsterdam.

JON COLE is Head of the Department of Applied Psychology in the Institute of Psychology, Health and Society of the University of Liverpool.

HON. BINGHI CONGO-NYAH is the International Ombudsman for The Rastafari Way of Life, director of two small companies (Lions Den Fam and Zion Networks), a musical performer and founding member of the Rastafari Global Council and the Rastafari Council of Britain. He has spoken on Rastafari and *Herbs* for various local community events and national/international conferences.

VAL CURRAN is a member of the Department of Clinical, Educational and Health Psychology, Institute of Cognitive Neuroscience, University College London.

NEŞE DEVENOT is a doctoral graduate student of the Program in Comparative Literature and Literary Theory at the University of Pennsylvania and a contributing editor for Reality Sandwich and Evolver.net. She received her bachelor's degree in philosophy and literature from Bard College in Annandale-on-Hudson, NY. Specialising in visionary art, psychedelic philosophy, futures studies, media studies and performance, she taught an undergraduate course titled "Poetic Vision and the Psychedelic Experience" during the Fall 2011 and Spring 2012 semesters. She has presented on DMT and hyperspace philosophy at the American Comparative Literature Association annual conference in Vancouver, BC, and on psychedelics in academia at Breaking Convention: A Multidisciplinary Conference on Psychedelic Consciousness in Canterbury, UK and Entheogenesis Australis in Victoria, AU.

ROBERT DICKINS is currently undertaking postgraduate research in English literature with the University of Exeter, having already received a BA Hons in journalism from University College Falmouth. The topic of his current thesis is psychedelic literature, examining the way in which texts are formulated through psychiatric and psychotherapeutic practise. Aside from academia, Rob has been a freelance journalist for six years and is currently the editor of the Psychedelic Press UK (psypressuk.com), a web magazine dedicated to drug writing and psychedelic culture.

RICK DOBLIN is the Founder and Executive Director of the Multidisciplinary Association for Psychedelic Studies (MAPS). He received his doctorate in public policy from Harvard's Kennedy School of Government for his dissertation on the regulation of the medical uses of psychedelics and marijuana. His undergraduate thesis at New College of Florida was a 25-year follow-up to the classic Good Friday Experiment, evaluating the potential of psychedelic drugs to catalyse religious experiences. He also conducted a 34-year follow-up study to Leary's Concord Prison Experiment. Rick studied with Stanislav Grof and was among the first to be certified as a Holotropic Breathwork practitioner. His professional goal is to help develop legal contexts for the beneficial uses of psychedelics and marijuana, primarily as prescription medicines but also for personal growth for otherwise healthy people. He founded MAPS in 1986, and currently resides in Boston with his wife and three children.

KEVIN FEENEY, JD, MA is currently a PhD student in cultural anthropology at Washington State University (USA). He is co-author, with Richard Glen Boire, of *Medical Marijuana Law* (2007).

AMANDA FEILDING is a British artist and drug policy reformer. She is scientific director and founder of the Beckley Foundation, a charitable trust that promotes health-orientated, cost-effective, harm-reductive drug policy reform.

TOM FROESE is investigating the intertwining of conscious experience and the dynamics of life, mind and sociality. Froese received a MEng in Computer Science and Cybernetics from the University of Reading, UK, in 2004. In 2010 he obtained a DPhil in Cognitive Science from the University of Sussex, UK. Also in 2010 he was a Postdoctoral Research Fellow at the Sackler Centre for Consciousness Science, UK. From 2010 to 2012 he was a JSPS Postdoctoral Research Fellow at the Department of General Systems Studies of the University of Tokyo, Japan. Currently he is a Postdoctoral Research Fellow at UNAM, Mexico, working on the emergence of symbolic material cultures and civilizations.

JONATHAN HOBBS read Natural Sciences at Cambridge and wrote his dissertation on the medical history of psychedelics. He went on to investigate recently-declassified papers documenting the UK's use of psychedelics during the Cold War for his MSc thesis at Imperial College, UCL and the Wellcome Trust in London.

MIKE JAY is an author and historian who has written widely on the history of science, medicine and drugs. His books include *Emperors of Dreams: Drugs in the Nineteenth Century*, *The Atmosphere of Heaven* (on the discovery of nitrous oxide), and *High Society:*

Mind-altering Drugs in History and Culture, which accompanied the exhibition he curated at Wellcome Collection, London in 2010–11.

AXEL KLEIN, PHD is a social anthropologist at the University of Kent with a special interest in drug use and drug policy. His publications include *Drugs and the World, The Khat Controversy and Caribbean Drugs—from Criminalization to Harm Reduction.*

REKA KOMAROMI is a freelance ethnobotanist with an MSc in ethnobotany from the University of Kent. She is currently documenting Rastafari ethnobotanical and cultural knowledge in partnership with Black Faces Media Production/Big Lips Video Clips and the Rastafari Councils.

BEATRIZ CAIUBY LABATE, PHD is a Visiting Professor at the Drug Policy Program of the Center for Economic Research and Education (Centro de Investigación y Docencia Económicas, CIDE) in Aguascalientes, Mexico. http://bialabate.net.

ANDY LETCHER is an Associate Lecturer in religion and culture at Oxford Brookes University and the author of *Shroom: A Cultural History of the Magic Mushroom*. A folk musician, he fronts weird-lore band Telling the Bees.

DAVID LUKE, PHD is a Senior Lecturer in Psychology at the University of Greenwich, London, where he teaches an undergraduate course on the Psychology of Exceptional Human Experience. He is Director of the Ecology, Cosmos and Consciousness lecture series at the October Gallery, Bloomsbury, London. He recently served as President of the Parapsychological Association (2009–2011), the professional international organisation for the scientific study of parapsychology. As a writer and researcher he has a special interest in altered states of consciousness and he has studied ostensibly paranormal phenomena and techniques of consciousness alteration from South America to India, from the perspective of scientists, shamans and Shivaites. drdluke@gmail.com.

CONTRIBUTORS

LUIS EDUARDO LUNA, PHD., DR HC, FLS has a PhD from the Department of Comparative Religion Stockholm University (1989) and an honorary doctoral degree from St. Lawrence, Canton, New York (2002). He retired in 2011 from the Department of Modern Language and Communication at the Hanken School of Economics, Helsinki. He was an Assistant Professor in Anthropology (1994–1998) at the Department of Anthropology of Santa Catarina Federal University (UFSC) in Florianópolis, Brazil. Dr. Luna is the author of *Vegetalismo: Shamanism among the Mestizo Population of the Peruvian Amazon* (1986), a co-author with Pablo Amaringo of *Ayahuasca Visions: The Religious Iconography of a Peruvian Shaman* (1991), and co-author with Slawek Wojtowicz, Rick Strassman and Ede Frecska of *Inner Paths to Outer Space: Journeys Through Psychedelics and Other Spiritual Technologies* (2008). He is also a co-editor with Steven White of *Ayahuasca Reader: Encounters with the Amazon's Sacred Vine* (2000). Dr. Luna is the Director of the Research Center for the Study of Psychointegrator Plants, Visionary Art and Consciousness, Florianópolis, Brazil.

KIRKLAND MURRAY is a Rastafari activist, musical performer/promoter and global agricultural representative. Through his work with Black Faces Media Production/Big Lips Video Clips and as a member of the Rastafari Council of Britain, he has been linking together Rasta groups and individuals in the UK and Jamaica to support ethnobotanical and anthropological research.

PETER OEHEN was born in 1956 and raised in Canada and Switzerland. He went to medical school at the University of Basel/Switzerland, receiving a Specialist degree in psychiatry and psychotherapy in 1988. He has also completed psychotherapeutic training in Guided Affective Imagery Therapy, Systemic Couple and Family Therapy and in Psycholytic Therapy. He has been in private practice since 1988 and has had a special interest in altered states of consciousness and psychedelic substances for more than 20 years. He is a board member of the Swiss Medical Association for Psycholytic Therapy (SAePT) and Principle Investigator of the Swiss phase II MDMA/PTSD pilot study (since 2006).

ANDY PARROTT is a member of the Department of Psychology, College of Human and Health Sciences, Swansea University.

VÍT POKORNÝ was born and lives in the Czech Republic. He graduated from the Philosophical faculty of the Charles University Prague and is currently on a postgraduate anthropology course in its Faculty of Humanities. He also teaches philosophy, anthropology and religion at the University of Jan Evangelista Purkyně (UJEP), Ústí nad Labeb, Czech Republic. He is married and has two daughters.

FFION REYNOLDS completed her PhD on Neolithic worldviews at Cardiff University, having taken inspiration from fieldwork conducted in the Amazon jungle. She has since worked as a Community Archaeologist, and is the Public Engagement and Welsh Language Manager for Cadw, the historic environment service for the Welsh Government. She is currently co-directing fieldwork at the Neolithic sites of Tinkinswood and St Lythan's Neolithic chambered tombs in south Wales. Her main research interests are the Neolithic of the British Isles and Ireland, focusing on themes of worldview including shamanism, animism, totemism and Amerindian perspectivism, funerary practices, material culture and art, as well as working to integrate anthropological and archaeological perspectives.

ANDY ROBERTS is the author of *Albion Dreaming: A popular history of LSD in Britain,* www.lsdbritain.com. Andy writes about a variety of paranormal subjects, including ufology, landscape mysteries and the survival of pagan belief. He is also monthly columnist and feature writer for *Fortean Times* magazine. Andy is interested in hearing from anyone with an interest in British LSD history and can be contacted at meugher@gmail.com.

CONTRIBUTORS

WILLIAM ROWLANDSON is a Senior Lecturer of Hispanic studies, University of Kent. He has recently published the book *Borges, Swedenborg and Mysticism*.

BEN SESSA is a Child and Adolescent Psychiatrist and psychedelic researcher, UK. He is one of the co-founders and chairs of Breaking Convention. He has worked on several medical psychedelic drug trials in the UK and is currently planning the UK's first MDMA clinical study. Ben is the author of the 2012 book *The Psychedelic Renaissance*.

ANGELA VOSS was a lecturer in Religious Studies at the University of Kent for ten years, where she directed an MA programme in the Cultural Study of Cosmology and Divination. She currently teaches for the MA in Western Esotericism at the University of Exeter, Canterbury Christ Church University and the Phoenix Rising Academy. Her research interests centre on the relationship between imagination and spiritual knowledge in the Western esoteric traditions. She also practices as an astrologer. She is the author of *Marsilio Ficino*, a collection of Ficino's writings on astrology, many papers on Ficino, Renaissance astrology and the symbolic imagination, and co-editor of three conference publications. Details can be found at www.angelavoss.org.

ANNA WALDSTEIN is a lecturer in medical anthropology and ethnobotany at the University of Kent who studies self-medication with herbal medicines as a form of empowerment and/or resistance to biomedical hegemony. Her current research interests include the role of *herbs* in Rastafari spirituality, *livity*, and healing.

ACKNOWLEDGEMENTS

This manuscript would not exist if it were not for Breaking Convention: A Multidisciplinary Conference on Psychedelic Consciousness which was held at the University of Kent in Canterbury, England in 2011. The conference itself received much inspiration from the MAPS conference in California (2010) and the Stichting Open conference in Amsterdam (2010). Their excellent conferences helped solidify our resolve to do this crazy thing. Therefore, many thanks must go to everyone who made that happen.

Sponsorship, facilities and promotion were provided by the Beckley Foundation, the Multidisciplinary Association of Psychedelic Studies, the University of Kent (especially the School of Anthropology and Conservation), the University of Greenwich, the UKC Psychedelics Society, The Grow Report, Shroom With a View Podcast, Graham Hancock, Reality Sandwich, Evolver and Erowid. Obviously, the event itself could not have happened if it were not for all of the speakers who made the effort to come and share their time and knowledge, and neither could it have happened without the interest, support and patronage of the international psychedelic community.

Behind the scenes, volunteers kept everything going. In particular we'd like to thank Reka Komaroni, Anna Hope, Georgios Mitropapas, Marios Kittenis, Elvina Gountouna, Agelos Papadakis, Craig Inglis, Claudia Boulton, Harvey Webb and the army of students from UKC and elsewhere; Gabrielle Fenton, Avi Heinemann, Juliet Suzmeyan, Ollie Hall, Emma Metcalf, Aimee Tollen, Duncan Pope, Rachel Baldwin, Matt Hyder, Jay, Sam Scott, Francesca Harris, Priska Komaromi, Vered Weiss, Bernadette Montanari, as well as Karolina Zychowicz, Inna Tjurinna, Olga Ricterova, Jelena Polonnikova, Tom Misselbrook, Dan Campbell, Chris Salway, Amy Fisher, James Sharpe, Kirk Murray, all of whom did more than free labour ever should. Joe and Nancy Waldstein travelled from the United States to babysit Cameron and Anna's daughter Zoë and allow them to participate in this conference; they deserve much thanks, love and hugs beyond what can be given in text. Banana Video filmed the conference and provided the video from which we were able to transcribe the MDMA debate.

In terms of the manuscript itself, we'd like to thank everyone who submitted essays. Many more than we had the space to include were sent, and it is with sincere thanks that we mention Halvard Hårklau, Marianne Kaspersen, David Lee, Isabela Oliveira, Gastone Zanette, Danny Nemu, James Rodger, Leonardo Rodriguez Perez, Andy Parrott, John Cole, Caspar Addyman, Donal Ruane, Jacqualine Kurio and Merijn de Boer. Much of the introduction to this volume is based on materials that were prepared for a session on 'Progress, Spirituality and Psychedelic Thinking,' which we presented at the Third International Conference of the International Society for the Study of Religion in 2009. Many thanks go to Danny Brown, Ivan Casselman, Tony Knight and Piers Locke for their participation in the reasonings and online discussions that led to the ideas and concepts. Blue Firth designed the cover. It was hard work pleasing five individuals with different aesthetic senses, and you have succeeded brilliantly. We love it! We'd also like to thank the University of Arizona School of Anthropology for providing the wonderful adobe house in the desert where the bulk of this manuscript was put together.

CAMERON would like to personally thank my mother and brother who have always supported whatever I do, no matter how crazy or contrary to their own beliefs. Much love and thanks to Anna, for everything. It is because of, and for, my daughter Zoë that I do this work. Irrational fear, hatred and ignorance are a terrible context in which to raise a child. It's time for it to end. Finally I'd like to thank all of my past students who have made me feel like I have something worthwhile to say and that I am not a complete crackpot. Finally to all of the rest of this Breaking Convention organising crew, who I will for evermore hold in my heart with the deepest of friendships.

ANNA gives thanks to the forces that brought us all together to do this work. Special thanks go to my colleagues on the Breaking Convention organising committee: to Dave King for talking me into it; to Dave Luke for guiding us with previous conference organising experience; to Ben for his voice of balance and reason when our hippie spirits got a bit too free; and to Cameron for taking on the role of lead editor for this volume. I would also like to thank Reka Komaromi for supporting us all and keeping everything together. Big thanks to Selecta Scruffy and Iimabrac, who made the initial link between Anthropology and Rastafari and to Blessed Barak my Rasta teacher, friend and colleague. I'd also like to thank Douglas MacMillan for suggesting the idea of (and providing some financial support for) organising a pre-conference workshop on Cannabis and Higher Education, as well as the students who participated and attended. Finally thanks to Zoë and the rest of my family for their love and patience.

BEN gives thanks to all his invited speakers (Peter, Evgeny, Roland, Andy, Val, Rick, Jon and Neal) from near and far who left their clinics and laboratories behind for a long weekend in Kent to share their knowledge and contribute to the re-emergence of UK medical research. One day I hope I too will be running clinics treating British patients with their long-neglected medicines. Undoubted thanks also go to my kids Huxley, Kitty and Jimi and to my darling Sarah for her un-ending patience and tolerance of my idiosyncratic hobby that is psychedelic clinical research.

DAVE LUKE would like to thank his four new amigos whom likewise voluntarily toiled away solidly for months (though not many months it has to be said, it was very much an event birthed urgently); it really was a trip working with all of you. I barely knew any of you beforehand; we only met together in person at most three times before the event, but after many video Skype meetings adorned in strange wigs and even stranger masks we managed to pull a whopping big white rabbit right out of the hole. It was a massive honour and pleasure to work with all of you. Thanks also to my wider crew of friends who all pitched in in their own way, especially Blue Firth for generously creating the great artwork for the event and the book, Mark Pilkington at Strange Attractor for the publication of the UK edition of this book and for the awesome drone music, Georgios Mitropapas who devoted a lot of late-in-the-day solid time to design the programmes so fast, the rest of the Edinburgh Greek posse and the Greenwich-Brazil extra-dimensional minibus riding ex-students for hands-on assistance at the event, Amanda Feilding for administrational support from the Beckley Foundation, the original UK psychedelic 'Exploring Consciousness' conference crew for inspiration, Craig Inglis, Claudia Boulton, Harvey Webb, Jonny Greet, Nisarg and Gyrus for getting stuck in, anyone else I have forgotten who deserves a mention, and finally, and mostly to Anna Hope for ongoing moral (and immoral) support and helping out with the event.

DAVE KING would first and foremost like to thank his colleagues on the organising committee for the fantastic times shared working together on Breaking Convention, and particular thanks to Cameron for taking on the duties of lead editor for this volume. I am also forever indebted to the other co-founders of the UKC Psychedelics Society, Oli Genn-Bash and Jake Brant, without whom the psychedelic community at the University of Kent could not have blossomed as it has. Thanks and love go to all members of that community, especially those who had time to help out at Breaking Convention. Finally, I thank the girl whom all my work on the conference was meant to impress – Em.

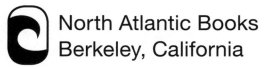 North Atlantic Books
Berkeley, California

Personal, spiritual, and planetary transformation

North Atlantic Books, a nonprofit publisher established in 1974, is dedicated to fostering community, education, and constructive dialogue. NABCommunities.com is a meeting place for an ever-growing membership of readers and authors to engage in the discussion of books and topics from North Atlantic's core publishing categories.

NAB Communities offer interactive social networks in these genres:

NOURISH: Raw Foods, Healthy Eating and Nutrition, All-Natural Recipes

WELLNESS: Holistic Health, Bodywork, Healing Therapies

WISDOM: New Consciousness, Spirituality, Self-Improvement

CULTURE: Literary Arts, Social Sciences, Lifestyle

BLUE SNAKE: Martial Arts History, Fighting Philosophy, Technique

Your free membership gives you access to:

Advance notice about new titles and exclusive giveaways

Podcasts, webinars, and events

Discussion forums

Polls, quizzes, and more!

Go to www.NABCommunities.com and join today.